DUMPING THE MAGIC

A Retired Cynic Revisits Spirituality and Healing

Raphael,
    In celebration of the path we
share. May you always be blessed
with love, abundance and courage.

                    Connie

CONNIE DONALDSON

FOREWORD BY SUZI TUCKER

ISBN: 0983668205
ISBN-13: 9780983668206

Library of Congress Control Number: 2012906088
Hearthstone Rose, Lawrence, Pennsylvania

Cover Art/Cover Design by LES Polinko
www.facebook.com/LesPolinko

HEARTHSTONE ROSE
www.hearthstonerose.com

Manufactured in the United States of America

DEDICATION

This book is dedicated, with love and immense gratitude, to

My Parents
Irene Bordone Shenkel Dunn and John Hartwick Shenkel Jr.

My Grandparents
Alice Francesio Bordone and Peter Ignatius Bordone
Edna Schmitt Shenkel and John Hartwick Shenkel
and to
My Great Grandparents
in all the past generations.

Your courage, love and commitment to life
created and sustained our families.
Your love still lives within us and supports us.

Whatever it was, thank you!

TABLE OF CONTENTS

Foreword   ix

Acknowledgements   xiii

Introduction   xvii

1.   Unimagined Choices   1

2.   The Old Story   9

3.   The Second Appointment   17

4.   What If This is Real?   27

5.   The Birth of Belief   41

6.   My Heroes Have Always Been Canonized   47

7.   The Convent Path   63

8.   New Beginnings   81

9.   Slamming Doors   85

10. Unbelieving   97

11. The Day-to-Day Times   115

12. A Whole New World   123

13. A Sea of Change   129

14. Two Hundred Constellations Later   139

15. The Circle of Generations   145

16. First Prayers   161

17. A Deeper Broader Learning   167

18. The Sword   179

19. November 18th   185

20. The Green Words   191

21. Life Unfolding   201

22. Year's End   207

23. After the Rainbow   215

24. The Middle Garden   229

25. Grandma and Me   241

26. Inner Child Stuff   249

27. Doing the Work   257

28. An End to Jousting   271

29. *A New Kind of Listening*   *279*

30. An Illogical Choice   285

31. The Path of Most Resistance   295

32. The Bible Class   301

33. Making the Break   307

34. My Own Path   317

35. Reflecting and Opening   325

36. A Path Evolving   331

37. In Solitude   339

38. No Mind Can Conceive   359

39. This and Nothing More   365

Suggested Reading   369

Foreword

It seems to me that most of us walk around with two fundamental ideas about the possibility for change: 1. People can change. 2. People cannot change. Perhaps most of us hope that the first is true but suspect that the second is more likely. And, of course, we find plenty of evidence to support that view, as so many of us try to address the same problems again and again, without lasting benefit, sometimes over the course of an entire lifetime. You know how it is: we walk around knocking on doors, buying books, going to workshops, talking to friends, chanting, praying, tapping, listening, singing, stretching, sharing (ad nauseam), all the while trying to manage the whiplash created by our constant companions, *can* and *cannot*.

Dumping the Magic introduces a third possibility, one that holds both *can* and *cannot* while allowing for a different outcome. It is the story of Connie's life, and like all really good stories it reaches beyond the specific narrative of the individual. It is about Connie's search for meaning when beauty and love are difficult to see, to feel, as years of disappointment in others and especially in herself leave her feeling lost, angry, alone and oh so tired. The search is tracked with courage, and self-revelation abounds, thus creating an opening for others to see themselves reflected and in good company. She is clear and honest about herself, but from a distance: she is not a victim showing off her wounds. There are light touches, a pervasive dry humor, poignant recollections, and so many intrinsic lessons.

Along the way, Connie introduces readers to myriad teachers. She never simply accepts their word; rather, she puts their perspectives to the test—and often through the wringer—but ultimately spins them into something greater by virtue of her particular integration. The movement at the most basic level is from lying in wait for the better in life, ready to pounce on it, to living in the most expansive space, the one that includes "better" always, along with everything else that is essential to life. Focused resolutely on *the* answer, a thousand answers may be lost in the rich periphery.

The shift from understanding life as something that can be controlled by us if we just find the right magical combination to understanding that life itself sets the rhythm for us and for all is at the heart of Bert Hellinger's work. The deep acceptance of this simple stance shifts the way one lives every single day. Engagement in each moment with respect and love is a spiritual practice. It begins as we look back toward our first success, the source of our life, to Mother and Father. And, yes, Hellinger's perspective—and the experiential component known as Constellations—sent a major shockwave through Connie's stultified set of interpretations and the convictions that folded out from them, especially her default belief in the *cannot*. And as we read, the reverberations of this work challenge us too. At the same time, with Connie as the guide, they also touch the heart and ignite the intellect. To be right sometimes seals our unhappiness; to be wrong can be a relief.

I imagine Connie writing *Dumping the Magic*. I see her surprise all over again as she exposes some of the dark places in her experience and then steps out into the light with newfound ease. I imagine that she did not set out to "teach" anybody anything, but rather to tell her story because she was filled up and spilling over. I imagine her gratification when the first reader said, Wow, I get that, thank you. I imagine her joy in introducing her mentors, each with something important to contribute to her special mix of greater well-being. As she forgives them their shortcomings, their humanity, she forgives that in herself, and now celebrates each step, each voice along the continuum. I imagine how gratitude moved from a platitude presented by an external belief system to an internal geography of an individual in accord with life.

Connie tells us that this is not the end of the journey. But clearly *can* and *cannot* are no longer in such perfect balance. Held by life, *can* is the largest piece by far; it provides safe shelter for *cannot*. Sometimes it may have to drag *cannot* along or even stop for a moment to rest with it, but now, in ever stronger agreement with the essential movements of life itself, *can* takes the lead. I have had the privilege of witnessing Connie's transition along these lines, allowing a new level of engagement with the world, including a more compassionate view of the past, a more peaceful sense of the present, and a clearly anchored confidence about the future. This book could not have been written without all three of these layers in place.

Who is the perfect audience for *Dumping the* Magic? The grumpy, depressed, discouraged—and yes, the still hopeful and searching. Me. Maybe you.

Suzi Tucker
Co-Founder, The Bert Hellinger Institute, USA

Acknowledgements

Each of us has cause to think with deep gratitude
of those who have lighted the flame within us.
~ Albert Schweitzer

For the book:

This book would never have been possible without those who read drafts and parts and smatterings of the story along the way. To Maureen Carlson, Frank Casorio, Ross Donaldson, Eileen Dougherty, Linda Foltz, Carla Horcick, Debbie Johnson, Kathy Linger, Carol McCracken, Les Polinko, Lisa Slage-Robinson, Flo Roth, Rege Schilken, Greg Smart, Judy Smitley, Beth Soucie, Carmen Stenholm, Carol and Len Teodori-Blahut and Diane Winter, I offer my deepest thanks. First of all, thank you for your friendship and caring support. Second, thank you for your insightful comments and thoughtful suggestions. This book is better and more honest because of you.

Jonas Marry, thank you for challenging me to begin and for supporting me throughout this process.

Les Polinko, thank you for creating cover artwork that truly reflected my highest hopes for this book. You graphically conveyed the book's soul.

Marla Frankenberg, thank you for so painstakingly proofreading this book. I knew it was in good hands from the moment you accepted the job.

Stephania Harden-Martin, only the bravest of souls takes on the challenge of editing an editor. Thank you for your courage in accepting the job and your gentle strength in directing a patchwork of text into a complete story. Your insights were invaluable; your suggestions were spot on. Thanks for insisting I make the changes that made this story stronger.

For the journey told in this book:

The story I tell here would have been impossible without those who stood in their truths and lighted my way.

Bill Cagney, Dorothy McCall, and Carol Hughes, thank you for the compassionate and insightful counseling that kept me afloat during the rough years before this part of the adventure began.

Mark Wolynn, thank you for steadfastly holding your lantern high and challenging me to see a reality I never imagined. You walked me through the darkest part of the forest and gave me hope.

Suzi Tucker, thank you for subtly guiding me toward hidden paths and graciously allowing me to discover them on my own. You were kind when I felt I was undeserving of kindness and shared so discreetly I sometimes didn't comprehend the immensity of your gifts.

Carmen Stenholm, thank you for standing with me, unflinching, like a mother bear, in the midst of my rage and pain. Your gentle strength and wisdom enabled me to enter forbidding paths and emerge stronger than I have ever been. Your caring enabled me to continue on through my deepest fears.

Lisa, Ken, Leslie, Tim, Hannah, Steven and Liam, thank you for the love and delight you always bring into my life. You are the bright rays of sunlight who make every day worthwhile and joyful. I'm so grateful you're my family.

Jonas Marry, thank you for leading me to God. Thank you for your patience—your endless patience—in the face of my cynicism, pain and confusion. Thank you for sharing from the deepest parts of your heart, especially when I didn't understand your words. Your strength enabled me to be strong; your constancy helped me to persevere. Your outstretched hand enabled me to stand again each time I fell.

Ross, thank you for walking with me all these years. Thank you for your faithful and fearless love. You have been the huntsman in the deepest woods who shared my journey and sheltered my heart within your own. You are, my love, my heartsong—always calling me home.

INTRODUCTION

What does a 58-year-old cynic do when, after almost 40 years of decrying God and religion, she stumbles across proof—tangible, verifiable proof—of a world beyond the senses and, ultimately, of a real and loving God?

At five I knew God was real. At nine I had some doubts but was sure they would be resolved when I became smart enough to understand what the grownups were telling me. At 17 I entered the convent, determined to really know God. A year and a half later, disillusioned, I left.

At 21, in college, married and pregnant with my first child, I walked away from God. Believers referred to me as "fallen away." But I didn't fall away. I looked at the real world—senseless wars, starving children, genocide and horrific disasters—and then at the theology of my Church—salvation through crucifixion; principles before people—and stood up straight and tall, turned on my heel, and walked away.

For the next 40 years I alternated between disparaging all spirituality and frantically searching through the texts and practices of every religion and metaphysical belief system I could find, looking for some proof of a spiritual world.

Then, at 58, when I'd pretty much given up the search, I stumbled onto Bert Hellinger's Family Constellation work and came face to face with a spiritual world I couldn't deny. I experienced—in my body, mind, and family—a force that was real. Over a series of years, in one surprising occurrence after another, I looked behind what Joseph Campbell called the *Masks of God* and found there was a real transcendent something—an entity, a being, a force—that could be experienced.

The story I share is not about Amazing Grace swooping down, sweeping me off my feet and carrying me to a Happily-Ever-After Land. It's a story about finding, in the course of everyday life, wondrously kind mentors, understanding friends, and little sparks of God's light in unlikely places.

And it's a story about learning. I learned you don't take spiritual truths and apply them to the world. You take the world—with all of its amazing good and horrific evil—and make it your spiritual journey.

I learned that life is almost always *both and*, rather than *either or*. For instance, I found that sometimes the best spiritual insights came after a lot of meditation *and* some tough sessions with a good therapist.

I learned that the act of excluding—excluding anyone, anything, any part of life—is less spiritually sound than including. In that same vein, I found that doubting, pouting, quitting and being a jerk didn't disqualify me from spiritual gifts, especially when I was willing to dust myself off, come out from under my blankets and begin again.

This has been a journey about choosing to dump the magic of my beliefs and beginning, very tentatively and often with visceral fear, to open my mind to the possibility that I'd gotten it wrong for the first 60 years. It's been about taking down the wall of my personal certainty, stone by stone, and digging a new foundation.

Along the way I've learned that spirituality is as much about people as it is about God. It's also about a lot of things I never thought were spiritual. Much to my surprise, I discovered that spirituality's challenge is the same as life's challenge—finding the courage to open our hearts to love and to full participation in our very own lives.

This is a little story. I didn't leave my home and family. I didn't travel to the ends of the earth to find my path. I didn't get a Ph.D. in theology, read the sacred texts of all the major religions or meditate in silence for years.

It's a story about finding God and life and love in the most unexpected places because I finally gave up looking where I thought God should be. Maybe it's a story of finally getting too tired of doing it the way I thought it should be done—and allowing life to open me up and show me its treasures.

It's also the story of the many mistakes I made after I found a path. Once I thought I'd discovered a hint of enlightenment, I kept trying to make the journey go faster—and the effort always made it slower and more painful. I tried to scale the mountains of Ultimate Truth and kept getting lost on the footpaths. I often looked for the one grand gesture that would grant me The Keys to the Kingdom and learned to settle for small movements that brought me to a wondrous oasis—where I could rest a bit before the journey began again.

I wanted continual thunder from the heavens. I got a lot of silence. Sometimes I had the wisdom to stay with the silence long enough to hear the still, small voice within it. At other times, when I really listened with an open heart, I got the answers I needed—from a friend, or a leaf or a song.

I wanted clear and definitive signs I was on the right path. Instead, I occasionally came across a sea of violets or a lone wild rose bush whose beauty melted my heart. I wanted the Hand of God on my shoulder all the time. What I got—and eventually came to appreciate—was the hand of a fellow traveler helping me over a fallen tree in the road, offering me a cup of tea, holding up his lantern so I could see—or accepting my assistance as he stood again after a major fall.

I wanted to find a reason for life. I wanted to find a purpose for *my* life. What I got—finally, after years of depression, after years of wishing I didn't have to go on—was the desire to live.

This is just my story. It doesn't—as I'd often hoped it would—give any profound answers. It's simply a tale shared as our paths cross along this road to let you know you're not alone and that your path—just like mine—is a precious gift.

~

Help also came to me from the abundance of wondrous books available today. I've listed those I refer to in the text, and others I found helpful, in a *Suggested Reading* chapter at the end of this book.

CHAPTER 1

UNIMAGINED CHOICES

What we choose changes us.
Who we love transforms us.
~ Jan Richardson

March 15th—ten days after my 58th birthday. A dozen different things went through my mind as I headed down the Parkway that Tuesday afternoon. None of them had anything to do with God or my mother. I'd given up on both of them years ago.

My thoughts bounced from the weather—it's March; it shouldn't still be snowing—to my dislike of driving to Squirrel Hill. As a native Pittsburgher, I generally tried to avoid going any place that involved crossing a bridge and going through a tunnel on the same trip. Bottlenecks at these junctions were a fact of life. Plus, once I arrived, I knew I'd have to find a parking space on Murray Avenue, one of the busiest streets in the universe.

Only something as huge as my need to find a way to remove the emotional boulder lodged deep inside me, keeping me from resuming my life, was incentive enough. After almost eight years of debilitating Chronic Fatigue Syndrome and years of therapy before and during the CFS, I ached to get back to real life with a vengeance.

I smiled as I pulled into an extra large parking space in front of Mark Wolynn's office. I loaded the parking meter with gusto. I'd completed the challenging part of the journey. I was ready to face the easy part—the therapy.

I liked Mark's office. The walls were filled with photos and cultural artifacts; the sofa and chairs gave it a casual, friendly feel. Mark seemed genuinely friendly and intelligent. He listened intently. His eyes never left mine and he nodded in all the right places. When I finished the synopsis of my reasons for coming—depression, the need to lose weight, the desire to find a new career—he asked just one question: "And your mother; how are things with your mother?"

He caught me off guard. I hadn't even mentioned her. I smiled. "I've worked with that issue a lot already. I think I'll wait until one of us is dead before I deal with it again."

He didn't smile back. "So she's still living. How's your relationship?"

I was a little angry as well as nonplussed.

"That's not why I'm here."

"Then you might want to find someone else to work with."

For a second, I thought of leaving. Then I thought—and for some strange reason it mattered to me at the time—*"Wait, I have almost an hour and a half left on the parking meter."*

"OK, I'm at least willing to listen. What do you mean?"

"In the kind of work I think would help you most, Family Constellation work, one thing is key. Healing your relationship with your parents is essential to understanding and healing your life. I can explain it to you in detail. I'll be glad to suggest some books and articles to read. But let me just say this: If you give this approach a chance, I can assure you that you'll come back here some day and say to me, 'Mark, I'm grateful we did this work while my mother was still alive. I can't believe what's happened!'"

I forgot about the parking meter; I still felt skeptical but now I was also intrigued. I decided to take a chance with him.

Mark asked me to put my relationship with my mother into a couple words, maybe a sentence. I thought for a while. I wanted to make sure I presented my answer accurately.

"I guess I always felt I wasn't safe with her, that she just might abandon me because I wasn't good enough."

"Did she ever abandon you?"

"No, but you asked me what it felt like. I *felt* like I wasn't safe, like I feared she would."

He asked for more information about my mother. It embarrasses me now to remember how arrogantly nonchalant I was about her life that afternoon—and for so many years before. With a sigh, I gave him the standard story I knew.

"My mother was the middle child of a butcher and a housewife. Although she was born in Pittsburgh, her family sent her and her older sister to live with their maternal grandmother in Italy when she was almost three. Her own mother, my grandmother, was seriously ill and couldn't take care of her children. They returned to the States when my mother was five years old."

Mark stopped my recitation. "What was your grandmother's illness?"

"I don't know. I don't think anyone ever talked about it."

"How odd you don't know. You have children. What kind of illness would make you send your own little children away—to a foreign country—for years?"

Wow, I'd never thought of that, of what could have been going on in my mother's family—during my mother's young life—to make Grandma send Mom and Aunt Norma away. It gave me a moment's pause.

But Mark didn't let it drop there. "How old are your grandchildren?"

"Four and three."

"Can you imagine what it would be like for them to be sent away at this age? Is there anything you could say or do that would make them understand? Is there anything that would make such a thing OK for them?"

"No—and I don't want to imagine it. I don't want to even think about it!"

"But that really did happen to your mother. Talk about abandonment issues. Do you think that, when she had children of her own, these issues might have affected her in some way? Do you think her own fears could have—consciously or unconsciously—affected how she treated you? It's just something to think about."

I was still holding on to my righteous indignation toward my mom, just a little less firmly. Mark was planting some big depth charges to destroy my old belief system.

He asked about my position in the family, how many siblings I had.

"I'm the oldest of five."

"No deaths of siblings? Your mother had no miscarriages?"

"Actually, I had a sister who died at birth and my mother had several miscarriages."

I told him of my mother's appendicitis attack during her fifth month of pregnancy with my younger sister. She carried the baby two more months but went into labor well before her due date.

"So, you're the oldest of six, not five." (In another conversation weeks later, we would amend the number again to include my half-brother Erik, from my dad's second marriage.)

"Yeah, I guess so. I just never thought about it."

"So after all the other trauma and loss in her life, your mom lost her second child? Was it a girl or a boy?"

"A girl. Judith Lynne."

"And the miscarriages, how many?"

"I don't know for sure. My mother tended to exaggerate those kinds of things."

"But she did miscarry several children, right?"

"Yes". Again he made me see my mother in a different light.

We talked a little more about Family Constellation theory. Mark wrote down the titles of some books and then glanced at the clock. We'd gone way over the hour designated for the appointment.

"We'll begin next week with the actual Constellation. Let's see when we can schedule it."

As I got out my checkbook, my mind was racing. I didn't want to wait an entire week. Something in his confidence, something in this new perspective, something in the weight of his promise and the depth of my need clicked.

"Do you have someone scheduled for the next hour?"

He glanced at his appointment book. "No."

"Well, now you do. Let's do it today."

Mark hesitated a moment, perhaps weighing the advisability of it, perhaps just rearranging his afternoon. Then he faced me with a smile. "OK. Let's do it."

Typically, Constellation Work as Bert Hellinger introduced it in the 1980s is done in a group setting with members of the group volunteering to represent parents, siblings and ancestors. However, the method can be amended to one-on-one work where the facilitator acts as the director of a guided visualization. That's what we did that day.

The first part of the process involved my dad, who had died twenty-eight years before. In the visualization exercise, Mark had me imagine myself as a little girl standing in front of my dad. He asked me to get in touch with how it felt being with him. He told me to make the visualization as real as I could, using as many senses as possible.

I pictured how Dad looked when I was little. I remembered the cigarette smell of his soft flannel shirt. If he was wearing flannel, it was the weekend, and he'd be home with me all day. I felt my muscles loosen with that image. I pictured Dad telling me a story—acting out a story—with different voices and the flash of an imaginary sword rousting the bad guys from Sherwood Forest. I felt wonderful.

"In your mind's eye, just bow your head and let your dad know how grateful you are that he's your father."

Bowing my head felt a little hokey, but the words came easily as I imagined myself standing in front of him. "I love you, Daddy. Thank you for being my father. Thank you for being my dad."

Mark brought me out of the visualization and we talked a bit about it. He was satisfied I understood the process. I was a little surprised by how real the experience felt. It seemed to touch more than just my imagination.

"Ready to do something similar with your mom?"

"Sure, but it won't do any good. I wouldn't be sincere and she wouldn't accept it even if I were."

Mark took my hesitation seriously; he led me in another, easier, visualization first. For this one, he put a tall pillow beside me on the couch and asked me to imagine it represented my mother. Then, when I got into the visualization, he asked me to try to just lean into the pillow a little, to see if I could imagine relaxing into my mother's embrace. I tried. I failed. I wasn't being stubborn. I was scared.

When I opened my eyes from this exercise, Mark said we had two choices. We could leave it here and continue next week, or we could try to move forward. I felt apprehensive but also excited. I felt we were on the verge of something big.

"Let's do it."

"What if you're not sincere? What if your mom doesn't accept it?" Mark was throwing my own objections back at me, planting more depth charges.

"I'll do it anyhow."

"OK, if you're sure you feel ready, let's keep going."

At first I had to work hard to get back into a visualizing kind of space. Then, as I continued to breathe deeply, I felt myself get into it. In my imagination, I saw myself standing in front of my mother. I felt the discomfort in both the little girl I used to be and in my adult body doing this exercise. The feel of the visualization with my dad had been like being in a warm spring breeze; this felt like a hot dry desert. My entire body felt tense and brittle.

My attention was immediately drawn to my mother's well-manicured, red fingernails. I saw the disapproval in her raised, perfectly arched eyebrows. Mark tried to get me to relax with this image. It didn't work. But I stayed with it, waiting for more instructions.

Mark continued, "Connie, see if you can find that little-girl place inside you that still longs to be loved and cared for by her. Where do you feel that place?"

My hand went to my stomach. "It feels very deep in my gut."

"Great, now breathe into it. Now, from *that* place, just bow your head and tell her: 'I'm grateful that you're my mom.'"

I started to tense up, but I didn't want to leave the visualization. The little girl in the image stood her ground. I watched her take a deep, determined breath. She bowed her head very stiffly, very slightly, and then said the words: "Thank you. Thank you, Mom, for being my mother."

Mark added more words and little Connie repeated them in my head: "Thank you for giving me life. Thank you for loving me. Thank you for not leaving me."

Then it was over. Mark instructed me to open my eyes. I felt a little disoriented but nothing else. No feeling of relief. No rush of emotion. I remember thinking to myself that the visualization probably hadn't been effective. "*If this had worked,*" I said to myself, "*wouldn't I be crying now?*"

We talked a little more and I wrote him a check. Mark suggested I wait until I felt ready before we made another appointment. This made sense to me. At that moment, I wasn't sure I'd ever come back.

Then I stood up. To this day, I don't know what standing up had to do with it. Maybe my body was on delayed-reaction time. But as I stood, a feeling of—not happiness, not joy, not lightness—of *movement* deep inside me took place. I could feel my face flushing.

I stood there in the office, a little dazed. I knew I should just walk out the door, but I couldn't. I needed to ground myself.

"I need to give you a hug."

Mark chuckled and nodded.

I hugged him hard; then I could speak. "Thank you. I don't know what just happened, but I know it's big." The next words I said surprised me as I heard myself say them. "Whatever just happened, happened on a tectonic level. It's as if continents shifted inside me."

After I left his office, I sat in the car for a while until I felt normal enough to drive home.

CHAPTER 2

THE OLD STORY

We are first moved by pain, and the whole
succeeding course of our lives is but one continued
series of actions with a view to be freed from it.
~ Benjamin Franklin

The ripples of that tectonic shift didn't stop the whole next week. Everything I thought I knew about my life felt challenged, not just by what had happened during our session, but by the underground tsunami that kept shifting in the deepest part of my being. I knew and understood my old story, but I couldn't seem to imbue it with the old emotions anymore.

For as long as I could remember, I'd known two things: First, I really wasn't naturally good enough to please my mom but, if I really worked hard, I could almost prove my worth. Second, I needed to compete with everyone else in her life for my mother's love.

I knew instinctively I was a disappointment to my mother, that I wasn't quite who she wanted. My mother was extremely beautiful and charming. When she entered a room, heads turned, strangers smiled. She seemed at home in every situation and was usually the center of attention in a crowd. People always told us kids how lucky we were to have her as a mother. Some of my friends had told me how they wished she were their mother.

I'd always felt that, just being me, I let her down. I wasn't pretty, agile or popular. I was too serious and far too sensitive. And, I was a girl. The qualities I had didn't match her requirements for an acceptable child. Did she come right out and tell me this? No, not directly. Few things were said directly in our family. However, she made enough jokes, sighed enough disappointed sighs and made enough comparisons with other children for me to know how she felt.

Probably the best thing about me was that I was aware of my shortcomings and tried to correct them. If the best I could be was a good child—nice, hardworking, dependable—I learned to be very good. I pleaded with her to teach me to iron and cook and be just like her. I took an active role in helping with my younger brother and sisters. When I went to a friend's house, I'd always pop one of my younger sisters in the stroller and take her with me to give Mom a break. I became Mom's right arm. (I knew it was true because I overheard her tell other people I was.) I got good grades and shared her faith in God and the Church. Granted, I always fell a little short. I couldn't become totally acceptable but, when I really worked hard, I sometimes got close.

As an adult, however, I had a very different view of our relationship. Years of therapy aimed at helping me see my own worth made me aware of how her treatment had undermined my self-acceptance. At some point in my thirties, while I never stopped trying to please my mother when I was around her, I got my revenge when we were apart.

If *her* rejection of me was the cause of *my* problems when I was too young to know better, as an adult I made sure I spoke up for myself loud and clear. If there was going to be a competition now, it was going to be one I could win. I turned those childhood hurts and insecurities into the best damn stories in a hundred-mile radius.

You put me in any conversation—with a friend over lunch or a group at a party—and I could dazzle my audience with tales of how she "done me wrong." I could slide in a one-liner that would make seasoned therapists' jaws drop. I could do twenty minutes on a theme—Christmas, weight, adolescence—or build from inconsequential incidents to a crescendo of unbearable devastation, and do it in way that was both entertaining and amusing. "Connie, tell the one about. . . . Connie, you have to tell my friend the one about the time your mother. . . . Hey, you think that's something, listen to what happened to Connie when. . . .

Some of those stories tied my siblings and me together. We chuckled about them as we watched our own children behave with so much more spirit than we ever dared to have. They were our own form of "Mom Olympics." Which one of us could claim the most horrific put-down or neglect in a particular category? Which one of us could get the most laughs in telling about it?

Other stories were the beginnings of friendships—the common ground I shared with new acquaintances. We recognized each other through our childhood stories. Our battle scars matched. We felt safe with our own.

My stories gave me the power in my life I'd never had when I was young. They were my revenge for the lack of love I still felt from her.

After that first experience with Mark, when I chose to stop talking about my mom in the old way, I was shocked at how little I had to say when I chatted with friends at lunch or met new people at a party. More than once, right after I chose to delete the *Mom Stories* from my repertoire, a friend asked if I was feeling OK because I seemed so quiet.

I'm now uncomfortable and embarrassed to remember how much of my life was taken up in this pursuit. I'm hesitant here to retell even one, but I also think the depth of the change in my life can only be understood by seeing the kind of stories that dominated my life before my first Constellation.

A Typical Old Story

When I went into the convent right out of high school, I opted out of the normal stream of scholarships and grants offered to high school seniors. A year and a half later, when I came home and prepared to go to college, the traditional doors for financial aid were closed. I had only one shot for a scholarship. A friend of the family had some connections at Mount Mercy College. He pulled some strings and got me a temporary scholarship designated for someone who had dropped out during her first semester. If I did well, the staff in the Financial Aid Office would consider finding me further help. But, if I didn't at least make Dean's List, the deal was off and college was out of the question.

I really worked hard that winter. I knew I'd done well in four of the six courses, but the last two were up for grabs. Both could have been Cs. If they were, I was probably done with college.

The day my grades arrived at the house, Mom quickly opened the letter. She was anxious too. Then she smiled. As she handed me the papers, she just said two words, "Dean's List." We were both ecstatic. I'd done it. I'd earned the right to renegotiate the scholarship. I was bouncing around the dining room table holding that paper to my chest. I had hope.

"I just can't wait to show this to Daddy! He's gonna be so proud of me!"

As the words came out of my mouth, I knew I'd made a huge mistake. I could feel the air in the room change. Somehow, I'd taken it from *our* celebration to one that included my dad too. I don't remember how I knew. Was there one flash of something in Mom's eyes? A tiny shift in her body language? I can't recall. All I can remember was thinking, "Damn, I've ruined everything. I'm really going to pay for this!"

We continued talking for a few minutes and then went into the kitchen to start supper. I started peeling potatoes while Mom went to the basement to shift a load of laundry from the washer to the dryer. Seconds later, I heard a horrific scream and the thud of someone falling down the steps. I flew down the stairs. "Don't move, don't move. I'll call an ambulance." I remember the little kids crying. I was crying.

Mom claimed she would be OK. She kept insisting she had to cook dinner. I slowly got her to her feet and, with her arm around me for support, we made it up the stairs and into the living room. When she was on the couch, I knew what to do—ice for her knees, heating pad for her back and TV for the little kids to keep them distracted. But just when everything was settled, she started to get up.

"Look at the time."

I looked at the clock. My dad would be home in less than 20 minutes. He worked two jobs and had only an hour between the first and second one to change out of his suit, eat something and go to the other job.

"I can take care of it, Mom. Please, please, just sit."

When Dad came home, I brought his dinner into the living room so he could sit by Mom while he ate. After that, I fed her and the little kids, did the dishes, got the youngest ones ready for bed and picked up the toys. I knew the drill. I'd been here many times before.

When Dad returned around 9:30 that night, we planned out the next few days, juggling our schedules to ensure that all the responsibilities for the household were covered while Mom was laid up. Then he helped Mom off the couch and up to their bedroom.

I'm sure that, at a point when it felt appropriate, I mentioned my grades to my dad—or maybe he simply saw the letter from school. He probably said something nice to me. But I have no memory of it.

Recreating this story on paper now brings back my feelings of self-pity—my righteous indignation. I can feel my victimhood. I find myself empathizing all over again with the poor soul I was. But after that Constellation experience, as I continued to work with Mark, an odd thing happened. As I recalled this story, I just couldn't get back to my comfortable state of martyrdom. Now different thoughts kept getting in the way.

When I replayed the tape of that day in my head, I saw the same scenario but, along with my own pain, I also saw the terrible pain my mom had to be in to feel so threatened by my inclusion of Dad. I wondered if this was how she had survived as a little girl. Did she constantly have to be the center of everything to feel safe? Now the look in her eyes I'd identified as disdain became something else—fear, desperation or just profound sadness. Where before I saw only the effects of her actions on me, now I also saw in them the painfully harsh way she treated herself. She paid such an immense price to stay at the center of every situation. Now, seeing it from that vantage point, I started to lose my anger about my own childhood.

After the Constellation, every time I tried to conjure up my rage, the face of that three-year-old girl my mother had been filled the space. I couldn't let go of the image of her being ripped away from her family to go to a country where she didn't speak the language, where she knew no one, for reasons she didn't understand. I thought of my grandchildren. I imagined Hannah, Steven or Liam on a boat to a foreign country, never to see home for years. My heart ached at the thought. For the first time in my life, my heart actually ached for my mom.

When the indignant thoughts of how she was so indifferent to me came up, so did fresh thoughts. *"Maybe someone with that much childhood trauma might have some abandonment issues. Might those memories have left her anxious about the bond between parents and children when she became a parent? Maybe everything really wasn't about Mom disapproving of me."*

Now the stories of her life became as real to me as the stories of my own life. Now the death of my sister Judith became real to me. I imagined how I would have reacted if one of my children had died at birth, how it would have felt to have never held the child I brought into the world. (That was how they handled things in those days. They knocked my mother out when they sensed a problem with the delivery. When she awoke, her baby was gone. The only comfort she had was the assurance that Judith had been baptized immediately.)

Now the story she told of how she made my dad stop and buy a baby doll for me on the way home from the hospital wasn't just the same old guilt-provoking story she always told. Now, I could see the love behind it. In the midst of her own grief over her dead baby, she had the strength, the love, to think of her two-year old anxiously awaiting a new brother or sister.

When I recalled her short temper over the smallest infractions when we were little kids, I also wondered what she had been living through during the early years of her own childhood in Italy. Was it possible that her grandmother, suddenly forced to raise two pre-school children, might have been a bit ill-tempered too?

I also reflected on what was going on in Mom's life when I was little. In the first seven years of her marriage, she'd had three children, buried one of them, moved out of her own house and back to her childhood home to care for her dying mother and then lost her mother. It really became hard to keep my anger alive. Try as I might to return to my old way of thinking—and I tried, I'd been damned comfortable being a victim—I couldn't.

CHAPTER 3

THE SECOND APPOINTMENT

Each one of us has that capacity to move from a limited and confining
sense of identification to an expanded sense of awareness.
That is what we mean by transformation.
~ James O'Dea

When I returned for my second appointment with Mark a week later, I felt lighter than air. I couldn't wait to tell him about my new insights and feelings. He listened and smiled—and then assured me we had just begun our real work.

"Now," he said, "let's discuss your notion of forgiveness. When you think of forgiveness, who is the better person, the one who forgives or the one who is forgiven?"

"I'm not sure."

"OK. Close your eyes and imagine a set of scales—like the one the blindfolded Lady Justice uses. On one side, put the person who forgives. On the other, put the one who is forgiven. Which side is lighter, which person is higher in your mental picture?"

"Obviously, the one who forgives is in the higher position."

"Exactly. And that's just the problem with forgiveness. In most instances, when we forgive, we put ourselves above the person we're forgiving. We're the virtuous ones. We're the heroes and the other

17

ones are the villains. But Bert Hellinger saw things differently. He believed two people have to be on equal footing to create real healing in a relationship. One can't be above the other.

"Now close your eyes again. Imagine you and your mom on the scales and imagine saying to her, 'I take you just as you are.' No forgiveness, no judgment. No hero or villain. Just 'I take you just as you are.' How does that feel?"

As I pictured the scene, something again happened in my body that went far beyond the simple understanding in my brain. These weren't just words. They weren't another philosophical theory. My body felt the threat of accepting such a statement. Part of me wanted to embrace this new premise, but another part of me wasn't willing to give up years of being the righteous one. I became nauseous and dizzy. This was big. I couldn't say the words.

I opened my eyes, ready to defend my stance. Mark met my gaze with a smile. "Connie, we could debate this forever or you could just try it. Let your spirit have a voice in this decision too."

I agreed because, right then, I just didn't have the mental acuity to fight. And, quite honestly, because I figured there would be time later to rehash my childhood wounds and my ability to forgive. This was, after all, therapy, wasn't it?

"OK, now let's do it for real, Connie. With the insight you have from our last session, instead of forgiving your mom, take her into your heart—just as she is. Close your eyes. Imagine yourself standing in front of your mom. Picture it clearly.

"Now, say these words to her: 'Mom, I take you into my heart, just as you are. Mom, even with the distance and all the hurt between us, I got enough. The rest I will give to myself. And when I do, I will do it in honor of you, knowing that this is what you would have given me if you could have, if more had come to you from your mother.'"

As I did this exercise, I sensed the gravity of what I was doing. I felt myself saying the words slowly—with respect, with reverence—in a tone I usually didn't use when I thought about my mother.

I felt blood rushing to my head. It made a *whooshing* sound in my ears. Whatever was happening felt monumental. I had a sense that if I really meant what I was saying, everything would have to change. I don't think I hesitated. (I'm a sucker for change, for jumping off emotional cliffs.) But I also didn't *fully* understand the depths of this action.

Slowly, over the next weeks and months, those words would grow inside me. As I continued to take my mom into my heart, I had to give up my one-sided view of our relationship. This simple action put my mother and me on a level playing field. No good guys; no bad guys. No victims; no perpetrators. I started to see both of us as hurting—and being hurt. Now if I blamed her for what she had done to me, I had to blame myself for all I had done to her—and to my children, my husband and my friends and family. As I stood with my mom without labeling her, if I saw both of us as just human, I started to see my own shortcomings as surely as I'd seen hers. If I condemned her, I condemned myself.

But on that March day, when I really didn't fully comprehend the consequences, I did it. I said those words and, to the best of my ability, I meant them. On some level—on the level of spirit or brain chemistry or something else—it was done. Another shift had occurred.

When I opened my eyes, Mark's eyes were there to greet me and to challenge me further.

"Now you have to put this into action. I want you to invite your mom to lunch."

I winced. I was much more comfortable in the world of visualizations and thoughts than in the real world of actually facing my mother. Mark caught the wince and chuckled.

"I want you to invite your mom to lunch and I want you to tell her some things. First, let her know you're OK.

I started to protest, "She doesn't care…"

Mark interrupted. "Mothers care. It's their biggest concern. They need to know their children are OK."

He began again, "I want you to tell her you're OK and your life is good. And I want you to thank her for being your mom."

"What! No way! I can accept her, I can give her a place in my heart, but I can't lie. Don't you…."

He interrupted again. He wouldn't let me go down my all too familiar road.

"Connie, I didn't say you had to tell her she won some Mother of the Year Award; I just said you should tell her you're grateful she's your mother."

"But what if I'm not?"

"OK, let's put this in logical terms."

I calmed down. I knew I could win this argument on logical terms.

"If she didn't give birth to you, who would you be? Would the Connie who is sitting in front of me exist? "

"No."

"You know enough genetics to know that only one set of parents, at one particular point in time, could have created exactly who you are. True?"

"True."

"So if she didn't bring you into this world, would you be the you who is sitting here?

"No."

"Are you glad you're alive right now?"

"Yes."

"Are you glad to be you?"

"Yes."

"Are you grateful your mother gave birth to you?"

Now it was my turn to chuckle. I nodded. He'd outwitted me.

"All right, I'll do it. I'll tell her I'm OK. I'll tell her I'm glad she's my mother."

Oddly, this new way of thinking intrigued me. Despite my skepticism, I couldn't deny what had happened in the first session—and how good I still felt. I was interested in seeing whether these new concepts would continue to keep the good feelings coming.

"And there's more, Con. Can you handle more right now?"

"Sure. Definitely."

"I also want you to write your mom a letter. It's not going to be one you send her, but one you write—and then reread—to help anchor the changes in your own feelings. It will be part of a ritual I'd like you to consider. We'll work on it in our next session."

Surprised, I looked at his clock. We'd gone way over the hour again, but I couldn't quit. I smiled sheepishly.

"Do you have someone scheduled next? If not, can we do a double session again?"

Mark smiled in disbelief but agreed.

"Sure, grab your notebook. I'll get you started on the letter and you can amend it later as you see fit. You may find that, as you continue to read it every day, the words will change as you do."

He dictated. I wrote. Reading that letter now, I realize how very little I understood about what it said and what a gift Mark and the Constellation work were giving me. Just like the first

Constellation work we did, the power of this letter grew with the passing months.

> Dear Mom,
>
> By cutting myself off from you, I cut myself off from my own body, my own soul.
>
> I've been afraid that if I get close to you, I'll become like you. I'll be cut off from being myself. But the truth is I've already been cut off from myself. I was wrong, and it didn't work the way I thought it would.
>
> Now I understand that by getting close to you and seeing what we share, I have a chance to leave you with the parts that don't belong to me.
>
> I'm learning to honor you for how you had to cut off your feelings of sadness and manipulate what was happening around you—because you were afraid to cry—because you didn't feel safe. (Like me, Mom, just like me.)
>
> Mom, I respect you and how you feel you have had to defend yourself. I honor it as part of your fate.
>
> Mom, you were abandoned, not me. It was your fate, which I have to respect as part of you. It was not mine, because you had the strength **not** to leave me.
>
> But Mom, I'm too small to do it like you did. I'm just your daughter.
>
> If I do it like you, it serves no purpose.
>
> Please give me your blessing, Mom, as I get in touch with my body, with myself. Please bless me the way you couldn't when I was younger.
>
> Now I'm coming to love you without the fear that I'll be like you.

Now I'm coming to love you and respect you, Mom, for the courage and strength with which you've lived your life.

Love,

Connie

"Do you have candles at home? Or tea lights?"

"Yes."

"All right. Every morning, I want you to make this a ritual. Light a candle. Center yourself and read this letter. Picture yourself as your mother's child, with her big and you small. I know this is hard. You have so many years of thinking of yourself as the adult in the relationship. Just do the best you can. One way to make it easier is to do it from a place that has no arrogance, no anger.

"That's it. OK, you've got your homework. Call me if you want another appointment."

I'm a good beginner. Blundering full force into something new excites me. I was ready to lurch forth, even if I had some doubts it would really make a difference. Still, I found it difficult to make the call.

The relationship between my mom and me had become so strained that, while I called often to see how she was—there was a certain shame in being the last kid in the family to know if she were ill or in the hospital again—my mother and I never made plans to meet outside of holidays and birthdays.

I feared she wouldn't accept my invitation or would insist on bringing Ed, her new husband. She did neither. She graciously accepted. We made plans for the next day.

We small-talked as I drove her to the restaurant. Once inside, we caught up on family and church news. Then, over the salad, I said the fateful words I rehearsed a hundred times since I'd left Mark's office.

"Mom, I just want to let you know that I'm OK, that my life is really good. And I want you to know I'm really glad you're my mom."

To my surprise, I meant those words as they came out of my mouth.

To my further surprise, my mom reacted in a way I hadn't imagined.

First she smiled; then she cried. It wasn't anything dramatic. Her eyes just welled up and spilled over. It seemed like a cry of relief or understanding or gratitude.

We were both crying as I repeated how I was glad that she was my mother. I reached across the table and squeezed her hand, hard. She squeezed back, hard. We both laughed a little through our tears. The air in the room changed. It got clearer—not brighter or lighter—just clearer.

A few moments later, we dried our tears, picked up our forks and continued to eat lunch.

For a while, I was aware of things happening on different levels inside me. One part of me continued to be involved in our conversation. Another part saw an image of a sponge—dried up so completely that it seemed impossible to restore—suddenly filling with water and coming back to life. Still another part, the kid who had been so scared to take this step, was shouting in my ears, "Holy crap! I can't believe this is happening."

Through it all, the change in the air in the room remained. I think we both sensed it. Mom was different. I was different. And we both recognized the difference.

That was it. No hosts of angels or chariots swooping down from the heavens. No clouds opening. As we had lunch, despite all I'd feared, we came together in a new way and the old way disappeared. I sensed my mom wanted this as much as I did. She didn't question it, didn't ask why I hadn't said something sooner, or if this was for

24

real. She saw the shift and made it with me. It was that simple. And it lasted the rest of her life, and beyond.

The lunch crowd was gone by the time we left the restaurant. For the first time in my adult life, I didn't rush to take her home after our visit.

If my Constellation experience had ended there, with new insights and the potential for changing some relationships, it would have been wondrous and miraculous. But it wouldn't have been earth shattering. I would have grown up a bit. My mom and I would have had a much better connection and both of our lives would have been enriched. It would have been a great therapeutic experience but not what I considered a spiritual one.

My next experience as a participant in a Constellation workshop moved things onto a different plane.

CHAPTER 4

WHAT IF THIS IS REAL?

The eye sees only what the mind is prepared to comprehend.
~ Henri Bergson

From the beginning, Family Constellation work and its philosophical base were a conundrum for me. The theory behind Hellinger's work, in the simplest terms, is that we are all influenced by the fates and entanglements of family members who lived before us. He believes that trauma in a family's past causes an imbalance that blocks love from flowing freely among the family members in future generations. The purpose of a Constellation is to bring these entanglements to light, acknowledge them with respect for the people involved in them, and to find a resolution in the present, which balances the family energy. The healing process involves acceptance of what was and gratitude to those who came before us and the creation of a new way to resolve the entanglements. I'd never learned anything like this as a psychology major, nor had I read anything comparable in the last forty years.

Further, Constellation work involves receiving this generational information from the family's energy field, on an experiential basis, in real time. If I'd heard this premise before I experienced the work, I wouldn't have considered having a Constellation. But since

I experienced the results of my Constellation before I heard the theory—and I couldn't deny the results—I was left with the challenge of trying to balance the profound and joyful changes in my life with a philosophical approach I didn't comprehend or accept.

For a while, I just suspended my normal skepticism. I couldn't deny the power of my Constellation. It was one of those walking-from-the-darkness-into-the-light kinds of experiences. I also couldn't deny its continuing effects in my life.

When I started my days with the morning ritual Mark suggested, each became an experiment and an adventure. Every day, as I reread my letter to my mom, I really tried to get back to that feeling of taking her into my heart, just as she was. When I succeeded, I could feel my heart softening around her and around other people and situations in my life. In those first weeks, I often felt like a shore that was washed by gentle waves. The more I accepted the changes, the more they came. With each layer of mistrust and hardness that fell away, I felt cleansed and refreshed.

Gradually, things I'd thought were important weren't. Little things I'd ignored before took on a new significance. Each nuance, every little change in my attitude felt like a thunder clap in my chest. Questions about philosophy had to keep taking a back seat to the tangible results of the work.

Constellation work was one of the most important things I'd ever discovered. It picked me up and turned me around 180 degrees. I wasn't sure where the new road was taking me, but I couldn't help but follow it.

As I struggled to get a better intellectual understanding, I read everything I could get my hands on. I burned through *Acknowledging What Is* by Gabriele ten Hovel, a book-long interview with Hellinger by a very bright woman who was both open and skeptical. A lot of her questions were also mine.

I diligently slogged through Hellinger's own books, *Love's Hidden Symmetry* and *Love's Own Truths* with highlighters, notes in the margin and frequent rereading. (I finally quit highlighting when I realized I was marking more than half of every page.) Although his books are prose, Hellinger is a poet. He packed so much into each paragraph, into each sentence, that a future reading would sometimes give me an insight I'd completely missed the first three or four—or ten—times through. The readings also made me yearn to experience Constellations as Hellinger usually presented them—as part of a group workshop.

Ross couldn't help but notice the changes in me. Granted, it had only been a few weeks, but after years of battling CFS and depression, we both recognized that weeks of steady energy and a positive attitude were a big deal. He was curious about the work too. So when I suggested that Ross have a Constellation at Mark's next workshop, he agreed.

~

The morning of the workshop was overcast, with sporadic rain. But I was darn close to manic as I bounced out of the car at Mark's office. I remember thinking I should tone myself down so Ross wouldn't feel uncomfortable, but I couldn't do it. I was bringing Ross to the place that had changed my life. I was sharing something wonderful with the man I loved. And he'd agreed to take part in it!

As we walked toward Mark's building, a preppy young couple approached from the opposite direction, looking a bit unsure of where they were going. When they hesitated at the steps leading to his office, I asked if they were looking for the Family Constellation workshop. When they said yes, I assured them they were in the right place. I punched Ross in the shoulder. "Serendipity!

We arrived just when they needed us," I said. "It's a sign we're all exactly where we should be." Ross and the other guy just shared sympathetic glances.

The workshop met in the conference room adjoining Mark's office. A dozen chairs formed a circle in the middle of the room. As Ross filled out pre-Constellation paperwork, more people arrived. Some were also having a Constellation. Others were former workshop participants who returned to assist by acting as representatives. By the appointed time for the workshop, all of the seats, except the one to the right of Mark, were filled.

Mark gave a brief introduction to the basic concepts and explained the protocol for participating. And then we began.

Group Constellation work was like nothing I'd ever seen before. Although we sat in a circle, it was not group therapy. Although some people represented others as they would in a Virginia Satir group, it was not her Family Systems therapy.

It's probably best if I just describe the process as I saw it unfold.

Mark asked who would like to begin working. Alan (a pseudonym), the young man we'd met in front of the building, offered to go first.

He sat next to Mark in the empty chair and stated his issue. He was having difficulties with depression and making decisions on his life's work. After Mark understood the problem, he asked the typical Constellation questions: Do you have siblings? What's your place in the family? How is your relationship with your parents? Are there major traumas in the family history—violent deaths, deaths of children, hidden relationships? This part took just a few minutes.

Mark then asked Alan to select representatives for himself, his mother and his father. Alan chose two experienced representatives for himself and his father and chose me to represent his mother. I hesitated. I waited for Mark to tell Alan to choose someone else to represent his mother because I was new and didn't know what to do. But Mark just nodded OK.

He asked Alan to center himself and slowly, without speaking or explaining, place us somewhere within the circle of chairs in a way that represented Alan's understanding of the relationship between himself, his mother and his father.

After a moment's hesitation, Alan placed his representative in the center of the room and placed me close by, facing him. He placed his father's representative at the edge of the circle.

When he was done, Alan sat down again. Mark then spoke to us. "Representatives, your job is simply to be in service to Alan and his family. Center yourselves. Just be willing to be an instrument for their family's energy. You don't have to do anything special. Simply stay open to the energy you feel."

Mark walked into the circle and stood by each of us in turn. Sometimes he just stood. Sometimes he asked how the person we were representing was feeling. For instance, instead of saying, "Connie, how are you feeling?" he said to me, "Mother, how are you feeling?"

When Mark stood beside me the first time, I remember saying something. It wasn't much. I was trying to be centered, but also afraid I'd make a mistake and mess everything up. When Mark moved to the next person, I felt relieved. I guessed I'd given an appropriate response.

After he'd stood beside each of us, he suggested we move around the room if we felt so inclined. His exact phrase was, "Go with your movements. If you feel inclined to move, go with that feeling. If you don't, stay where you are."

Damn. I wasn't sure. So I just stood there. Then, suddenly, I was a bit more sure. I felt the need to walk away from the center of the room and turn from Alan and his father. I turned around, took a few steps and stopped. How did I determine when to stop? The best I can say is that where I was when I stopped felt more right than where I'd been standing a few seconds before.

The main action of the Constellation now took place behind me. There was a lot of interaction between Alan's representative and his dad's. Mark brought in another person to represent Alan's grandfather, his father's father. Because the activity didn't involve me, I just relaxed and listened. I learned that both his father and grandfather were physicians. I wondered if Alan's mother was intimidated by marrying into a family of doctors.

About ten minutes later, Mark asked me, "Mother, what are you feeling?" I was honestly surprised at my response.

I stood up quite tall, still facing away from the other representatives, and said the only word that came to mind, "Haughty."

"What do you mean by haughty?"

I felt myself stand even taller. I felt something in my body that was different from what I thought I should be feeling. I didn't know how to answer. My brain started to analyze...

Mark reacted to my hesitation. "Remember, you are in service to Alan's family."

This brought me out of my internal argument. I decided to go with my feelings instead of my thoughts. Referring to the representatives for Alan's father and grandfather, I said:

"I hate listening to those two prattle on and on. I feel they're beneath me. They think they know what's best for my son. But they don't. They don't understand him the way I do."

I didn't know where the words came from. But as I said them, they came out strong, with more than a hint of arrogance.

Mark asked Alan, "Was that the way you mother felt about your father and grandfather?"

Much to my astonishment, Alan said yes. He said she always felt her family was better than her husband's. I exhaled in relief. I hadn't messed things up. But I was also thinking, *"What the hell? How did I know...?"*

I didn't have much time to worry about it. Mark soon had me turn around and come back into the middle of the circle. At that point, Mark asked Alan if he were ready to do the rest of the Constellation himself, without using someone to represent him. When Alan agreed, his representative sat down and Alan and I faced each other.

It's hard to explain, but at that moment, I wasn't just me. I was also Alan's mom. Mark gave us both the words to say. In the interaction I, as Alan's mother, gave Alan permission to love and respect his father. I repeated Mark's words as I looked into this young man's gentle blue eyes and could see something shift. I didn't fully understand what was happening, but it felt very real and very meaningful.

As we finished, my self-consciousness had left me. I was totally involved in what was happening with Alan.

Mark then directed Alan to face his father's representative. The final moments of the Constellation were heartbreakingly exquisite. Alan stood before his father and, using the words Mark gave him, asked his forgiveness and blessing. Again, the interaction felt real and powerful. Although Alan spoke the words Mark supplied, the emotions were his own. As Alan repeated them, tears streamed down his face.

The Constellation ended with Alan's father, again using Mark's words, giving his son his blessing. When the two of them embraced, the emotions didn't belong to Alan and some guy who represented his dad. The emotions were between Alan and his father.

When it was over, Alan looked like a different person. Yes, his face was red and his eyes filled with tears, but there was also an expression on his face that hadn't been there when he arrived. Peace? Relief? Joy? I didn't know. But I could sense in Alan what I'd experienced weeks before. Somewhere deep inside him, I suspected the tectonic plates were shifting.

Mark ended the Constellation by thanking all of us who had served as representatives and directing everyone not to talk with Alan for a while. "It's important for Alan to just sit with this experience, just allow it to sink in without talking about it, without thinking about it."

I had a million questions, a million feelings, but there was no time to think about them. Within a few minutes, we were into the next Constellation.

The third Constellation that day was Ross'. It was powerful and highly personal. Ross is a private person, so I won't say much. However, I can say that Ross went into the Constellation wholeheartedly, with honesty and vulnerability. His work deeply touched everyone in the room. When it was over, everyone—Ross, the representatives who worked with him and Mark—was in tears. But more important, it changed Ross' life.

In the months to come, when I became frustrated and angry with the work and thought I wouldn't continue studying it, Ross was always the one who brought me back to it.

"Con, you may not understand what's happening. You may disagree with some of it. But you know this work is real. You have to hang in there. You know this stuff changed our lives."

Those words, coming from the man who had shared my disbelief and cynicism for almost 40 years, kept me working with these concepts when nothing else could have.

We left the workshop exhausted and light-headed. We probably talked about it more than we should have. It was so new and strange and wondrous we couldn't help ourselves. Luckily it was also so strong we didn't dissipate its effectiveness with all our chatter. Now, if I were to give someone advice after a Constellation, it would be to really respect the time afterwards. Give yourself the gift of quiet acceptance. Give your spirit time to integrate it. Allow the seeds of the work a chance to take root in your soul.

I was ecstatic about Ross' work. In the days that followed, I could feel the shift in him. He became more settled, more at peace with himself. That's where my heart was—in seeing and appreciating the change in Ross.

My brain, however, was elsewhere. What I kept coming back to—what baffled me and kept me both excited and confused—was what happened when I represented Alan's mother. How in the world had I known what to say? Where had the words come from? They weren't the logical words that fit the discussion I'd heard between Mark and Alan. They weren't from some nonverbal cue I picked up from Mark or the other representatives. My back had been to all of them.

It's one thing to see or read about other people having inexplicable experiences. It's another to have one yourself. I was totally intrigued. I couldn't understand it and I couldn't wait to experience—and to test it—again.

I was back at Mark's office for the next workshop two weeks later. This time I brought my friend Eileen. She and I had shared almost thirty years of searching for a meaning and purpose to life. I wanted her to experience Constellations with me.

The format was the same. In the first Constellation of the workshop, a young woman named Doreen (a pseudonym) chose Eileen to represent her mother. Eileen was far braver, far more open, than I. Even though I'd experienced profound changes as a result of my Constellation, my movements as a representative had been small and hesitant; my words were guarded and uncertain. I'd fought my need not to embarrass myself. Eileen had no such hesitations. She was sure and deliberate from the start. She didn't seem concerned about whether she would make a mistake. She was there, in the moment, ready to be of service to someone and something else.

Doreen placed all three representatives—herself, her mother and her father—close together in the center of the room. As soon as Mark said, "go with your movements," Eileen walked swiftly to the edge of the room, out of the circle of chairs, right up to the wall. When Mark asked her how she felt, she answered without a moment's hesitation and with tons of emotion, "I've got to get out of here. If I could, I'd walk right through this wall. I need to get as far away from those people as I can."

I remember thinking, "*Oh man, what if she's wrong? How will this mess things up? Why would Eileen take such a huge risk, make such a flamboyant gesture? How will Mark be able to incorporate a movement this strong if it isn't right?*" But my worries were in vain.

Mark asked Doreen how things had gone with her mother. Doreen, in tears, said her mother abandoned her when she was nine months old and had never returned. I was dumbfounded. I could feel something like electricity coursing through me. Eileen had unselfconsciously taken a huge leap into this work—and she had been correct!

In an odd way, Eileen's representation had just as strong an effect on me as my own Constellation had. Seeing Eileen, who had never experienced the work before, step out so far on a limb—and be accurate—knocked my socks off. Even with all that had happened with my mom, Ross and me, witnessing Eileen doing the work blew me away. It was hard to cling to my cynicism in the face of something like that. Just like Ross and me, Eileen had tapped into something inexplicable.

I had no choice but to reevaluate my beliefs.

If Constellations were real, if past family energy could reach into present time, then some sort of communication between the everyday world and the spiritual world was possible. And for the last 40 years, I'd been wrestling with just that possibility.

At 58, I was a jaded and exhausted agnostic. Before this Constellation work, I thought I had finally acclimated to a world in which spirituality was an illusion. For decades I'd gone down tons of traditional and non-traditional roads looking for something spiritual—and was always disappointed.

Now, when I felt I was just too old and exhausted to care, when I had simply stopped looking, I found evidence of something I assumed was impossible.

If Constellations were true, I'd have to question the conclusions I'd reached in decades of searching. If Constellations were real, what else in the spiritual world was real?

I needed to look back at who I'd been and how I'd gotten to this place in my life.

Section Two

Where it All Began

Chapter 5

The Birth of Belief

Give me a child for his first seven years and I'll give you the man.
~ Ignatius Loyola

I was born into what my mom called a proper Catholic family. Not only were both of my parents Catholic, so were all four of my grandparents—and everyone went to Mass every Sunday.

On the outside, our house didn't scream Catholic, with statues of the Blessed Mother and St. Francis in the yard and the flames of red and blue vigil lights visible through the living room window. Rather, it stated our Catholicism firmly and irrefutably the moment you walked in the door. With the exception of the bathroom, a crucifix hung in every room. On the wall of the landing between the first and second floor was a painting of Christ whose eyes did, indeed, seem to follow you as you walked by.

For at least the first ten years of my life, we had a small holy water font hanging by the front door. Every morning each of us kids dipped two fingers into the water and, with the sign of the cross, blessed ourselves before we began the long walk up the hill to St. Justin's Elementary School. I can still feel my pride when, as an eight-year old, I was asked by Mom to go to church and refill our supply of holy water from the dispenser in the back of the vestibule.

I can still feel my nervousness as I walked home—very carefully, very deliberately—clutching the freshly scrubbed mayonnaise jar filled with holy water, which Mom had instructed me to wrap in two brown bags to ensure that nothing would spill or break.

Our parish calendar, supplied by the neighborhood Catholic funeral home, hung in the kitchen. Each month had a different picture of Christ or one of the saints. Dried palms leaves, distributed at the church each Palm Sunday, hung behind the calendar and all of the crucifixes. Palm leaves, because they were blessed, couldn't just be thrown away each year when we got new ones; they had to be burned or buried. So they tended to accumulate on any surface that could accommodate them. We had palms clipped to mirrors, above archways and even behind family photos.

There was a small statue of the Blessed Mother on the upright piano in the dining room. During May, the Month of Mary, we would set up a May Altar, a little shrine with doilies and fresh flowers to honor Jesus' mother.

We subscribed to *The Pittsburgh Catholic*, a weekly newspaper listing diocesan events as well as the movies approved or condemned by the Church.

In those days, good Catholics also subscribed to one of two magazines—either the *St. Anthony Messenger* or *Liguorian*. The *St. Anthony Messenger* was down-homey. Along with the articles it had drawings of families at prayer, pictures of saints, and photos of church groups visiting the Holy Land or Lourdes. Sometimes it even included recipes for Lenten meals. The Liguorian's format, on the other hand, was strictly theological. No pictures. No recipes. No sweet poems about children's faith. Just the facts. We were a *Liguorian* family.

The Church set the rhythm of our lives. Everyone over the age of seven (the age of reason, when we were old enough to understand evil and commit sins) went to Confession on Saturday and Mass on Sunday. This required planning and juggling schedules. In the 1950s the slogan "The family that prays together, stays together" meant praying at home. No one wanted crying babies or fidgety preschoolers interfering with the sanctity of the Mass, so we never attended as a family.

The canonical year—feast days, Advent, Lent, Holy Days of Obligation—further impacted our lives. We offered our throats to be blessed on St. Blaise Day and our foreheads to be marked with ashes on Ash Wednesday. We knew we'd have to give up our favorite things for Lent. Most of my memories of Lent include my mother warning me, "Connie, you can do all the fake coughing you want. Wild cherry cough drops are candy, not medicine— and there will be none in this house until after Easter!"

Feast days weren't just extra days off school. We knew their meanings and honored them by attending Mass, even in the summer when the nuns weren't around to remind us. And although it wasn't mandatory, some of us (usually Mom and me) attended all of the Holy Week services. If there were special days of Eucharistic Adoration or parish novenas, representatives of our family were there. My dad, who was active in the Holy Name Society, organized the yearly weekend retreat at the Passionist Fathers' retreat house for the men in our parish.

Only the tradition of the daily family rosary never took root. Each May, Mom would try to corral us kids into the house to recite the rosary with the priest on the radio at 7:00 PM. Thankfully, our recalcitrance usually wore her down in about a week. After a few frustrating evenings trying to get us to kneel reverently around the kitchen table, she would "forget" to call us in and we continued enjoying springtime kickball games with the public school kids.

Those were just the outward manifestations of our Catholicism. The spirit of being Catholic was even stronger. Especially when I was young, that atmosphere permeated the walls of our home—like the odor of Dad's cigarettes or Mom's *Wind Song* cologne. We were a Catholic-Catholic family, first tier, no holds barred. Grace was mandatory before supper and encouraged before lunch. Night prayers were said kneeling beside the bed. Dinner discussions, before Dad had a second job, often took a theological bent. We talked about how many angels could dance on the head of a pin and why the practice of selling indulgences in the Middle Ages was responsible, at least in part, for the Protestant Reformation. We were drilled on the Ten Commandments and the names of the apostles just as rigorously as we were drilled on the multiplication tables.

No part of our lives was unaffected, even our humor. My dad's favorite joke involved God's sly admission that He liked Jesuits better than other religious orders (Dad's brother was a Jesuit seminarian); my mom's involved a priest, a confessional and a little boy selling a chicken.

We were also aware of everyone else's level of Catholicism. We knew which Catholic neighbors and relatives sent their children to Catholic schools and which risked their immortal souls by sending them to public schools. We knew who the true Catholics were and who allowed their boys to attend Cub Scout meetings in the basement of the local Lutheran church or who—much worse—allowed them to join the local YMCA basketball team. We feared for the soul of the woman in our parish who attended her daughter's wedding to a Presbyterian—in a Presbyterian church. And, while we hoped her daughter had the common sense to get her fiancé to sign a promise to raise the children Catholic, we knew, in our heart of hearts, that nothing good could ever come of a mixed marriage.

We often had priests dropping in. Dad liked to think it was because they could count on a spirited theological discussion—and a second glass of scotch with no judgment. Mom assumed it was her home cooking. Some of the priests were stuffy and unapproachable. Some actually learned our names and spoke to us, kindly and informally, when they ran into us at parish functions.

Sadly for us kids, the most mean-spirited, alcoholic, manic-depressive priest of the bunch eventually became a fixture in our house for almost 20 years. Father Tokay (a pseudonym) was tall and handsome and something more. I guess worldly would best describe him. He'd come to the priesthood later in life. After a stint in the Air Force, he was a salesman and had traveled extensively in Europe. He knew things about style and good taste the other men in my life, including Dad, didn't.

He brought the dark side of the Church with him. Almost from the beginning I could sense the wrongness in him. Several things bothered me.

One was his feeling of ownership in *our* house. We had a red leather wingback chair in our living room and, on days when he visited, it became his chair. He often arrived right in the middle of the most chaotic part of the day, as Mom and I were in the kitchen cooking and the little kids were playing games or watching TV. Immediately, the living room became his territory so he could read his breviary. Everyone would have to leave the room so he could sit—cigar in one hand, breviary in the other, with a glass of white wine on the end table beside him—and read the psalms and prayers he was required to read before six o'clock.

Another thing that bothered me was the backrubs. When I was ten or eleven, he would occasionally claim his old war injury was acting up and ask me to give him a backrub. He'd lie on the couch, with his shirt off, and give me explicit directions on how to rub his shoulders and back to ease the pain.

It always felt a little odd but he was a priest, and priests were to be respected and obeyed. Besides, Mom didn't object and Father Tokay said I was very good at it. The backrubs continued for almost a year. Then one day Dad came home from work during one of these sessions. I could tell from his eyes, from the way he looked surprised and then a little angry, that my instincts had been right. No one ever said anything and I surely didn't ask anyone about it. But after that day, there were no more backrubs, no matter how bad the war injuries hurt poor Father.

Some people thought we were lucky to have a priest for a family friend. My siblings and I considered him a curse—more like the drunken uncle who ruined holidays and special occasions year after year.

Once I asked my sister Mary, who has a spot-on wicked sense of humor, if she ever thought about Father Tokay. "Yeah, sometimes I do," she said, "And I've decided that, if I ever run into him someday, I'll just back up the car and run into him again."

CHAPTER 6

MY HEROES HAVE ALWAYS BEEN CANONIZED

The books one reads in childhood create in one's mind
a sort of false map of the world.
~ George Orwell

Just as thoroughly as my family provided the soil for our early beliefs, the nuns at St. Justin's planted the seeds—bushels of them.
The 1950s was the last decade of Catholic education taught almost
entirely by nuns. The Second Vatican Council that brought so many
changes to the Church also ushered in a massive exodus of nuns.
Some orders faced a defection rate as high as 50 to 60%. More significantly, the 1960s and 1970s saw the number of women choosing
to enter the convent plummet. When I was in school, there were
about 180,000 nuns in the US. Today there are fewer than 70,000—
and their average age is 70.

Our nuns, swathed in yards of floor-length black fabric and
starched headpieces, lived communally and meagerly, with little access to the real world in which they taught. Their clearly defined
spiritual world offered little room for things that were not "of God."
They invited us into that magical realm daily, and I was often first
in line.

I was a quirky kid. Not an outlandishly, get-beaten-up-in-the-playground kind of quirky, but I was quietly—and definitely—different. I always had good friends at school and on our street; I played nightly neighborhood games and participated in a number of extra-curricular activities. But I also knew my drummer's beat was a bit out of sync with the crowd's.

I was serious because, to me, life was serious. As I understood what the Sisters taught us, earth was our testing ground. It was our one shot to prove we were worthy of spending eternity with God, and I wanted to get it right. It often surprised me when my classmates weren't as concerned as I was.

It wasn't as though they didn't have enough information. At St. Justin's grade school, everything was about being Catholic and getting to heaven. In our first readers, the public-school characters Dick, Jane and Sally were replaced by John, Jean and Judy—children properly named after saints. And our dynamic trio didn't just advise their dog to "Run, Spot, Run," they also reminded us that Catholic families were prayerful families. In math class, our word problems often began with the phrase, "If Father Tom baptized six children and Father Joe baptized eight children..." In geography class, we learned what percentage of the population of each country was Catholic. I don't remember a lot of history but I surely remember that John Carroll was the first Catholic to sign the Declaration of Independence.

We were reminded every day to be grateful for the gift of Catholicism and of our responsibility to support the church's outreach to the unsaved world. We understood the importance of sponsoring our missionaries by contributing to the Society for the Propagation of the Faith. If Catholics were the only people who could get into heaven—and they were—we knew it was part of our job to support the Church in spreading our Good News of Salvation to everyone.

We learned the difference between mortal sins, which could lead directly to hell, and venial sins, which would prolong our time in purgatory but wouldn't keep us from eventually sharing eternity with God. We understood how the sacrament of Penance, if done with the proper attitude of contrition, absolved us of our sins and gave us a fresh start toward salvation.

These facts were important to me. If earth was the testing ground, I wanted to make sure I made it through the tests. I liked knowing the rules.

We also learned the bonuses, the special ways to guarantee salvation even if we sometimes went astray. For example, we learned that wearing the brown scapular of Our Lady of Mount Carmel (two small pieces of wool cloth connected by string that is worn over the neck, under one's clothing, so one piece of cloth hangs over the chest, and the second piece hangs over the back) guaranteed us instant entrance into heaven if we were hit by a bus on the way home from school. Making First Fridays—attending Mass and receiving communion on the first Friday of the month for nine months in a row—guaranteed us the grace of final repentance. And final repentance was important. It meant that, no matter how bad a life we'd led, in the end we would see the error of our ways and have the common sense to either receive final absolution from a priest or make a perfect act of contrition. All of the Sisters seemed to know someone personally who, after years of depraved living, was saved from eternal damnation because in third grade they had made the commitment to the First Fridays.

In the early years of the Cold War in the '50s, many of us kids feared that the end of the world—or the overthrow of our country by Godless Communists—was imminent. The air-raid sirens that had us scrambling under our desks, the Civil Defense shelters with emergency supplies in the basements of the school and church, and rumors of people building fallout shelters in their backyards made it obvious that a Communist attack was always possible—and potentially just moments away.

It must have also been on the minds of the nuns. I remember quite a few warnings from them about how we must all be ready to die for the faith when the Communists came. No story of martyrs—and they told us lots of stories of martyrs—ever ended without the reminder that we, like them, must also be ready to make the same courageous choice for Christ, the Holy Father and the Church.

We learned how to pray and to whom to pray. It was an interesting hierarchy. We said the "Our Father," but—on an emotional level—we rarely directed our prayers to God the Father, the First Person of the Trinity. He was too frightening. He was the Old Testament God who banished Adam and Eve from Paradise and demanded Jesus die for our sins.

We could pray to Jesus, (although we never called Him by name; He was always Lord or Our Lord). But we often didn't. I remember assuming He must have often been busy with other things because He seemed to have established an elaborate system of intermediaries.

The Blessed Mother was the intermediary the Sisters liked best. She was Our Lord's mother and had been taken up to heaven bodily, so she was the closest human to God. As I understood the scenario, when you really needed something or had been behaving badly, it was best to ask the Blessed Mother for help. The theory was that, just as she did at the Wedding Feast at Cana, she would ask Jesus to break the rules a little and answer your prayers.

Her status was highly evident at school. Every classroom had a large statue of her, dressed in blue and white robes, holding out her arms to us on earth. October was the month of the rosary, one of the best forms of prayer after the Mass. The rosary is a series of 67 prayers—53 of them *Hail Mary's*. In May, the month dedicated to the Blessed Mother, just as all the spring flowers were coming into bloom, we'd set up a special May altar and take turns bringing in bouquets to decorate it.

After the Blessed Mother came the other saints. Some had special jobs and some were prayed to because they had something in common with you. For example, St. Anthony was the patron saint of lost articles. If you lost something important, like homework or a library book, a quick prayer to him often helped.

St. Francis was the patron saint of people who loved animals. If you had a sick pet, St. Francis was your saint. When I was about six or seven, I tried to do as St. Francis did and speak to the animals about the love of God. A tiny gray mouse lived in the wall in front of our house. One summer, I brought little pieces of bread or crackers to the wall and tried to coax him out. But he seemed unimpressed with my intentions, and I was certainly impatient with his lack of understanding, so I quit after a few days.

Other saints had specific jobs. St. Monica, for instance, was the patron saint of mothers who prayed for wayward or troubled children. As the mother of St. Augustine, she had prayed continually for him during his reckless and sinful youth. Finally, when he matured and dedicated his life to God and the Church, he freely admitted he owed it all to his mother's prayers. Other saints were connected to certain countries or groups—St. Patrick for the Irish, St. Christopher for travelers.

Then there were guardian angels—spiritual creatures created before mankind to do God's bidding. We each had one to look over us, to protect us from harm and to talk us out of committing sins. They would walk with us on the way to and from school, sit beside us during school and watch over us at night as we slept. Some of the nuns took their presence very seriously. Sister Cabrini, my first grade teacher, certainly did. She insisted we each sit on just half of our wooden desk seats and leave the other half free for our guardian angels. I remember my angel liked sitting on the left side of the seat, even though the left side was supposed to be the devil's side.

This worked well on most days, but I recall being a little worried the first time both first-grade classes doubled up for a special talk from the pastor. When the other 40 children came into our classroom, some girl I didn't know sat down on my angel's part of my seat. I waited for Sister Cabrini to scold her. When Sister didn't, I figured that, in crowded situations, both angels probably stood beside the desks.

Finally, there were the unofficial saints—family members who had died and gone to heaven. For example, my younger sister, Judith Lynne, who died immediately after she was baptized, went directly to heaven. So she was a personal—although not officially sanctioned—saint for everyone in our family. I also felt Grandma Bordone, who died when I was almost five, went to heaven pretty quickly. Her life here on earth had been hard, and she was a really kind and good person. I just couldn't imagine she needed to spend much time in purgatory. Besides, I knew that one of the reasons she died was because God missed her and wanted her in heaven with Him. So it didn't make much sense for her not to be there. Asking for help from Grandma and Judith, while it wasn't something the Church *formally* approved of, felt more comfortable to me than asking the Blessed Mother or the official saints.

But I did admire the saints. My favorites were the martyrs. Death in one blow, or even in a frighteningly painful way—being shot to death with arrows like St. Stephen or burnt at the stake like St. Joan of Arc—seemed much better than staying alive in this valley of tears we called life. I loved the guarantee! No time in purgatory, no questions about past sins, just instant acceptance into heaven.

Heaven was my goal. I understood this earth was a place of exile—something we had to endure to prove our worthiness for heaven. That made sense. I just had to look around—at my neighbors, my relatives, my friends' families, or the nightly news—to see this world was only the secondhand reality. There was pain and suffering and injustice everywhere. If martyrdom was the fastest way out, I was more than ready to accept it.

My favorite martyr was Blessed Miguel Pro. His dying words, as he stood with arms outstretched before a Mexican firing squad in 1927, were "Long live Christ the King." His crime? He continued to say Mass and minister to his people in a country that had banned the Catholic Church. I read the story of his life in seventh grade, in a book called *Dawn Brings Glory*, and was immediately head over heels in love. Father Pro was everything I wanted in a man. He was funny, smart, and charming—and he loved God with all his heart. In the seminary, he was a gifted athlete and practical joker; but he also knew what was really important. He could be a four-star cut-up on the soccer field, but the moment the bell rang calling the young men to prayer, his demeanor immediately changed. Nothing came between him and his commitment to living for God.

My attitude put me a bit at odds with most kids of my generation. I was often genuinely surprised by what my peers were interested in. I didn't understand how someone like Elvis Presley could even begin to compare to Father Pro. When the other girls gushed as they heard Elvis' songs on the radio or saw his picture on the cover of a magazine, I couldn't relate. Yeah, his songs were cool. Yeah, there was something dangerously appealing about that deep voice and pouty mouth. But Father Pro had so much more going for him. He was brave and funny and wonderfully creative, sneaking into his parishioners' homes to say Mass or distribute communion without getting caught. One of the reasons the Mexican government chose

to execute him publicly was because he made the government offi-
cials look like fools. In the moments before his death, after refusing
a blindfold, he looked his captors straight in the eyes and said, "May
God bless you! Lord, You know that I am innocent! With all my
heart I forgive my enemies!" Wow. He took my breath away.

~

My childhood understanding of the Church's message also created an odd lack of commitment to this world. As far back as I
can remember I'd seldom felt a strong connection to life or a strong
will to live. Earth was the testing ground. Heaven was home. Why
bother getting too comfortable in the test zone?

As a kid, I used to dream of the day when I could go to heaven
and be happy for all eternity. Heaven—where there was peace and
fairness and God and my grandma and Judith—seemed so much
better to me than this world. There I would never be lonely. There no
one would ever make fun of me for being sad—because I wouldn't be
sad. Grandma and Judith and I would be together every day.

My images didn't go much further. I didn't imagine us doing
things together. The Sisters told us we would have the Beatific Vision—we would see God face to face—and that would be enough. It
was frivolous, maybe even sinful, to imagine activities such as picnics
or pets or even scenery in heaven. Anyway, what did it matter how
the place looked as long as we got to be with God? But even then, I
knew I wouldn't be cherishing *only* God's presence. I knew heaven,
for me, would be about sharing it with the people I loved and who
loved me.

I was surprised to see that not everyone held this belief. Others, even good Catholics, seemed pretty darned attached to this life.
I remember reading a book by Giovanni Guareschi, the author of

The Little World of Don Camillo. Generally, his books humorously described the lives of a parish priest and a communist mayor in a little town in Italy. There was a chuckle on every page. So I was caught off guard by Guareschi's, *My Secret Diary*, the story of his life in a concentration camp during World War II. What struck me the hardest—what I couldn't understand—was his description of how he survived those horrible years. He said his one thought was, "*I won't die. I won't die. Even if they kill me, I won't die.*"

This made no sense to me. I couldn't imagine fighting to stay alive in a concentration camp. Why would I? Why work to stay alive in a horrible place when heaven was just on the other side?

Guareschi also described those who gave up hope and turned their faces to the wall and just let themselves die. "*Wow,*" I thought, "*that would have been me! If I had been alone in some hellish prison camp, I would have been the first in line to check out! There would have been no scrambling for food, no trying to escape. I would have planted myself firmly on the floor close to a wall, turned my head to it and willed myself dead. Why stay alive for no good reason at all?*"

I believed everyone in the Church should think that way. Our real challenge wasn't to cling to life; it was to maintain a proper distance from life. The nuns were quite clear: "We, as followers of Christ must be *in* the world, but not *of* the world." The world—the flesh and blood world of people and pleasure—was the place where Satan had his kingdom firmly established. It was the place of temptation where he would do anything in his power to keep us from getting to our heavenly reward.

Satan's reasons made sense to me. In pridefully rejecting God's will by refusing to honor His creation of mankind, he had been condemned to eternal damnation. Therefore, in Satan's mind, he had been condemned to eternal punishment because of man. It was logical to believe he wanted to bring as many of mankind with him into hell as he could.

So we had to be constantly on guard. The world harbored all kinds of temptations. Some—like money—were easy to spot. I learned to distrust money because it could lead to greed and, eventually, to hell. Besides, being poor was far better than facing the judgment implied in the words the nuns quoted so often: "It is easier for a camel to go through the eye of a needle than for a rich man to enter the kingdom of heaven." I also remember Mom telling us how not having a lot of money was a good thing. It not only kept us from being tempted by greed and pride, it was a sign God loved us in a special way. Wasn't one of the main tenets of Christ's Sermon on the Mount "Blessed are the poor, for theirs is the kingdom of heaven"? Our struggles with finances—the used cars, hand-me-down clothes and no money for bikes—were sure signs we were on God's list of favorite people.

Other temptations weren't that easy to spot. This world was tricky. Even love had the potential to be a problem. Yes, it was good to love our families, our friends and homes, but not too much! Too much love of anything left us vulnerable to temptation. The nuns even had a phrase for it—*inordinate love*. It meant loving something, or someone, so much you might choose them above God or the Church.

Luckily, the attachment to things wasn't a big one for me. Stuff just didn't seem worth it. I wasn't willing to give up my shot at a secure place on *God's Favorites* list for something that trivial.

Other attachments, however, were very difficult to release. These usually involved feelings. The seven deadly sins—pride, anger, covetousness, sloth, greed, lust and gluttony—were all about feelings. And the worst—the one that got Satan condemned to eternal damnation—was pride.

Pride was the one I fought with the hardest. I knew I felt proud when I did something good, when I got a good report card, when I helped a friend or gave my allowance to the missions. I also knew, in those moments of feeling good, I was just on the edge of feeling something that could, in the long run, condemn me forever.

Pride was cunning. It seemed to pop up everywhere, especially when I was trying my best to do things right. I still remember my mixed feelings when I ransomed my very own pagan baby. (*Ransoming a Pagan Baby* was part of the Holy Childhood Society's program for encouraging Catholic school children to support the missionary efforts of the Church in the 1950s. For a contribution of five dollars, a student could partner with a missionary in some foreign country and ensure that a baby would be properly baptized. In return for the contribution, the donor chose the child's baptismal name.)

When I was in fifth grade, I'd saved enough to ransom a pagan baby. On the day the Holy Childhood certificates arrived at school, Sister showed the class two adoption certificates—one acquired by donations from the whole class and one just for me. I remember how I felt when, in front of the entire class, Sister handed me the certificate stating that Cynthia Anne was now a Catholic. Part of me was beaming—exuberant beyond belief. I was part of the team! I helped to ensure another child the chance to go to heaven! Someday Cynthia and I would meet in heaven and she would know I was her spiritual mother—that I had given her that beautiful baptismal name and a chance at salvation! But another part was sure this exuberance, this delight, was also a sin. Was I happy because of the soul I'd helped to save or because I was the only one in class to adopt a pagan baby all by myself? I remember how my stomach hurt as I walked back to my desk, holding my certificate, trying to look both happy and humble. Boy, this spiritual stuff was really hard.

I eventually decided I needed a logical, mind-based spirituality. The mind could read, listen to teachers and priests, understand doctrine and make rational decisions. The mind was always clear and clean. It knew right from wrong and, unless messed up by the body and feelings, chose correctly. OK, I could sometimes think incorrect thoughts, make mistakes in logic. But when I did, I could also count on a grownup pointing out my errors. If I had an incorrect thought, someone older and wiser could show me my mistake. All I needed was the common sense to ask and the humility to change my perspective in the light of the truth.

My body, on the other hand, was almost always a source of trouble. It couldn't be trusted. My body wanted chocolate during Lent and, when no one was watching, it escaped piano practice early every chance it had. It wanted to skip rosary and play on warm spring evenings or to sleep in on cold winter mornings instead of going to Mass for First Fridays. My mind knew what was right, but my body only knew what *felt* good. That was the other problem—feelings.

Feelings were totally illogical and undependable. Tears popped up when things weren't really all that bad. Uncharitable feelings of jealousy sprung up when someone else got something I wanted. Anger boiled inside me when forgiveness was the appropriate response. Emotions were unpredictable and uncontrollable. They were *of* the world, and because I was too damned sensitive to begin with, they brought me far more trouble than they were worth.

When my emotions were wrong, there was no recourse. I could think the right thoughts, but I couldn't count on my emotions following my logic. My feelings still were hurt when, logically, they had no right to be. For instance, I can still remember the day when I was nine or ten and my younger sister, Sue, was explaining to my dad that she needed an allowance. I didn't join Susie in the argument. I knew from Mom that finances were pretty tight. And in all honesty, I was feeling pretty self-righteous about not making any demands.

Eventually, my dad, who didn't like talking about finances with us kids, ended the discussion with a joke. "You want to get paid for being good, Susie," he said with a smile, "But look at Connie. She isn't asking for anything. Yeah, that's Connie. She's good for nothing!" Sue caught the double entendre immediately and laughed with him. I burst into tears and remained hurt for days. Logic told me Dad was just joking, but my emotions wouldn't let go of the pain. They couldn't be trusted.

My soul was on the other end of the spectrum—the spiritual side. It was both a conscience and a score card—the ultimate Permanent Record. It advised me on the correct choices and displayed how well or poorly I was doing. It was the part of me that needed continual vigilance and care and also the part that offered me the best chance of getting what I wanted—a guarantee that I was always moving closer to God and to the promise of heaven with Him.

For me, it was a simple equation: Trust your mind, don't trust your body and be careful not to harm your soul.

I even had a visual to accompany these thoughts. I pictured my journey through life as a walk down the street. I could choose to walk in the gutter (in the real world of temptations and emotions) or on the sidewalk (in the spiritual world). While I often had to walk in both—that's what having a body *and* a soul was all about—it was surely safer to walk on the sidewalk. As often as I could, I chose the sidewalk.

But even these concepts didn't remain clear cut for long. By the time I was nine or ten years old, I'd discovered I couldn't trust my mind completely either. My earnest desire to believe exactly what the Church taught ran into some difficulties. Sometimes I had thoughts I couldn't reconcile with Church teachings. Two experiences formed fault lines in my beliefs even as I was trying to be the best Catholic I could be.

The first was the story my dad told us about his time in India during World War II. Because there was no fighting in India, he had the opportunity to spend a lot of time exploring the country and getting to know the people. One of his favorite people was an Indian guru who lived in a small hut a short distance from Dad's barracks. Dad would often go to his hut and discuss the meaning of life with this man. The guru, who spoke English quite well, both inspired my dad and got him through some tough personal times.

On his last visit before being shipped back to the States, Dad meant to give the holy man some money to thank him for all his help, but he got so involved in their conversation he forgot. However, not more than ten steps outside the hut, he remembered and turned around and went back into the hut. When he entered, no one was there. The hut was sparsely furnished. If the guru had been in it, Dad would have seen him. Dad then went outside and scoured the area. The hut stood alone in a clearing—with no trees, no bushes, no other buildings. Again, if the man had just left, Dad would have seen him. Bewildered, Dad went back to his barracks. But his encounter with the disappearing yogi always stayed with him. It led both to his life-long interest in Eastern religions and his belief the Catholic Church didn't have a monopoly on spiritual truth.

The other doubt came from viewing Oral Roberts on TV. Whenever I could, which wasn't often because Mom didn't approve of it, I watched Roberts' crusades. His emotional preaching style was a bit off-putting, but his healing services totally intrigued me. At the end of each program, he asked those who wanted to be healed to come to the stage and, in Christ's name, he healed them.

I knew healings occasionally happened in the Catholic Church. The nuns all seemed to personally know someone who knew someone who had been healed by a visit to Lourdes or Fatima. But this was different. Oral Roberts healed people week after week, on TV, in front of my own eyes. And he wasn't Catholic!

I knew Protestants were in error and would pay the price for their heresy when they died and were barred from heaven. But if this were true, why was Our Lord working through this Protestant to heal people? And why didn't anyone else seem to notice this contradiction?

The official answer—this question was so big I had to ask my parents and the nuns about it—was that the healings weren't real. They said Roberts paid people to pretend to be healed. But this didn't seem logical. Even if he paid some people, there must have been others in those huge revival tents who eventually made their way to the stage and were truly healed. If not—if no one in the vast audience was ever cured or knew someone who was—his ministry would have eventually withered away. However, it seemed to be growing all the time.

So even when I was young and totally committed to the Church, there were seeds of doubt growing alongside the seeds of faith. I couldn't help but wonder if Catholics really did have the only true connection to Christ and, if they did not, how I could find the *real* belief system that guaranteed me this access? I knew The Ultimate Truth was out there somewhere; I just needed to find it.

CHAPTER 7

THE CONVENT PATH

Our hearts are restless until they rest in Thee.
~ Saint Augustine

As much as I embraced it, logic alone didn't rule my quest for the spiritual. There was also something irrational, something achingly emotional at the root of my search for a connection to the Divine.

I don't know how old I was when I heard the quote from St. Augustine, "Our hearts are restless until they rest in Thee" but as soon as I heard it, I felt its truth.

The older I got, the more keenly I was in touch with this emotional aspect of my search. Kneeling in prayer—whether in the dim after-school light coming through the stained glass windows in church or beside my bed in the dark—felt right and safe to me. I knew getting close to the Creator and Savior of the whole world had to be magnificently wondrous. Something in the fervor of the saints who truly knew God, something in the passion with which my dad kept searching, something in the mental pictures I had of Christ—dying for us, getting angry at the apostles for shooing the children away, thoughtfully feeding the 5,000 people who wandered into the desert to hear him preach—kindled a thirst in me to truly love and be loved by God.

In the sixth grade, when I heard Sister give the "vocation talk," stating some of us might be called to a life dedicated to God, I felt sure I was one. In the convent I could learn whatever it took to make the connection. I could learn to really pray, to open myself with such humility and honesty that God would see I would be a good vessel for His love and grace.

If some people could experience this love before they died and went to heaven, I wanted to be among them. I wanted to know God and understand Him and bring that understanding to the rest of the world. Even more, I needed to fill the corner deep inside me that, no matter how many people loved me, no matter how much I loved my family and friends, felt empty and yearned for something more. There was an ache inside me that couldn't be soothed by anything I knew.

Finding this level of understanding God would probably not be easy. If it were, I'd have known at least some people—in real life, not just in books and stories—who had done it. My dad, who was always searching, would have done it. I knew it would take dedication and humility and single-minded focus, but I also knew it would be worth the struggle.

After that grade-school realization, the decision to become a nun was a done deal for me. I was going to choose the high road— the sidewalk instead of the gutter. I was going to be neither *in* the world nor *of* the world. For the next six years, until I graduated from high school and had my parents' permission to enter the convent, my decision never wavered. My only question was which order.

I didn't want to enter a regular teaching order. That felt like a horrific waste of a calling. Why would I dedicate myself to God and then spend the rest of my life teaching history or chemistry? If I were going to be a nun, I wanted to do something meaningful—to bring God to the world and people to God.

I also didn't consider going into the order that staffed the school I'd attended for twelve years. I didn't want to become the kind of nun they were. Don't get me wrong. They were dedicated; they worked hard and they gave us a fantastic education. Yet, I felt so little human kindness or joy—so little humanity—in their relationships with us. I couldn't imagine living in community with them for the rest of my life. Several experiences created this viewpoint.

During my first years in high school, my youngest sister, Duffy, was quite ill and required frequent trips to the hospital for blood transfusions. More than once, Mom had to call the school to have me come home and watch Mary, my other pre-school sister, as she raced Duff to the hospital. So the nuns knew about Duff's health problems. However, not once did any of the nuns ask about her—or about how my family was coping. If this was their idea of detachment from the world, I wanted no part of it.

Another experience occurred when we returned to school after John Kennedy's assassination. The nun who moderated the Mission Club, of which I was president, called me to her classroom to reprimand me for going straight home after our early dismissal that tragic day. She reminded me we had a club meeting scheduled for that afternoon and didn't understand why I had assumed I could forgo it simply because we were dismissed early. I was shocked. Even as I apologized, I knew she was being unreasonable. It hadn't even occurred to me that anyone would think of a club meeting when we just received word that the President of the United States had been killed. No one kept their normal schedules that day. Offices closed. Stores were empty. People cried in the streets. Even Walter Cronkite teared up. To have no emotional reaction, to simply go about your day and assume everyone would be present for an after-school club meeting—that was a level of detachment I wanted no part of.

~

I don't remember how I found the Mission Helpers of the Sacred Heart, but once I did, I knew I wanted to be one of them. The Mission Helpers didn't teach in schools; they ministered. They taught religion, trained lay missionaries to teach religion, led campus ministries and worked with the poor. Their mission statement convinced me they were the kind of nuns I wanted to be: "You shall be witnesses unto Me to the uttermost parts of the earth. ~ Acts 1:8."

In the fall of my senior year I took a streetcar to town and walked to their convent on Duquesne University's campus. The Sister I met, Sister Marietta, was cordial and kind and answered all my questions. She introduced me to the other two or three nuns who shared the convent with her. She gave me the address of the Mission Helpers' motherhouse so that I could make my request to be an applicant to the order. It was just as simple as that.

After I was accepted, the Sisters invited all the applicants from Pittsburgh and our families to their tiny convent for the afternoon. Over cookies and lemonade, they graciously answered countless questions from our parents. Then Sister Marietta led everyone in storytelling games. The little kids were astonished to meet a nun who played with them. After that visit, my parents relaxed about my choosing to enter an order based in Maryland rather than somewhere close to home. It certainly made me eager to join this band of very kind and special women.

A month or so after that, the Mother Superior sent each applicant a list of things to bring on Entrance Day—things like two pairs of sturdy black oxford shoes, twelve handkerchiefs, eight pairs of old lady underwear—as well as some packets of readings and spiritual exercises we could do to prepare ourselves intellectually and spiritually for our arrival. Shopping for the shoes and underwear was a surreal experience, but I loved doing the readings and saying the prayers. I felt like part of the community even before I got to the motherhouse.

I continued working full-time at Murphy's Five and Ten until the end of August. I really wanted to be able to pay for everything I needed to enter and, quite frankly, I knew the days would pass faster if I were busy.

A couple of days before I left, our friends threw a wonderful farewell party for my best friend, Sandy, and me at the parish hall. Sandy was entering the Franciscans. I said my goodbyes to everyone without shedding a tear.

On my last evening at home we discovered something on the convent list we'd neglected to buy, so my mom and aunt herded me and a couple of the younger kids into the car to get it. They were all in a giddy mood. I was somber. While everyone else in the car joked around, I sat staring out the window, saying goodbye to Pittsburgh and promising—ah, the arrogance of youth—I'd return one day and bring the peace of Christ with me. Good grief! I have to be in an especially compassionate mood not to be embarrassed by this memory.

Entrance Day was September 8th, the Feast of the Birthday of the Blessed Mother. Ten of us came to the motherhouse with our families. At the appointed hour we were whisked off to changing rooms to don the attire of postulants—black chapel veils, white blouses, long-sleeved beige jackets, ankle-length beige skirts over black cotton stockings and those amazing black nun shoes. One moment we were *of the world*; the next moment we weren't. After we had a quick round of picture-taking in our new clothes, a short ceremony in the chapel and one last hug-a-thon with families (again, no tears from me), we were ushered into the novitiate. The doors closed and we were on the inside.

Sister Beata, the novice mistress responsible for our spiritual formation, was both kind and no-nonsense. As we sat talking at dinner that first night, she assured us this wouldn't be the case at breakfast the next morning. For the three years we'd spend in the novitiate learning the basics of our vocation, breakfasts and the first half of every lunch and dinner would be in silence. After dinner, we were shown our cells—small private rooms with cinder-block walls, freshly painted in welcoming pastel colors, with a bed, closet and sink. At the end of the tour, we went to the recreation room. Of everything I encountered that day, the rec room was the most surprising. It was a large room with linoleum floors, curtain-less windows and 30 rocking chairs in a circle. "Recreation" on most days meant sitting in a circle and talking as a group.

Before we knew it, it was time for evening prayers in the chapel, silence and bed. Once in my room—the first time I hadn't shared a bedroom since Susie was born when I was three—sitting on the bed in my floor-length, long-sleeved white cotton nightgown, I finally burst into tears.

Convent life was an odd blend of the very easy and the very hard. The day-to-day duties were easy. We cleaned the whole novitiate, top to bottom every day, so nothing ever got really dirty. We took college courses and courses on spirituality. We learned what I came to the convent to learn: theology, how to foster a spiritual life, how to meditate and some basic philosophy. We always had more than enough time to study. We also spent a half hour each day reading from spiritual texts unrelated to our classes. Mass, meditation, Stations of the Cross, the rosary, and morning and evening prayers made up the rest of the day.

Every minute was structured around prayer, chores, classes—and silence. We did our appointed duties in silence; we studied in silence. Unless a specific time for recreation was scheduled, all conversations were kept to the minimal needed to get a specific job done. There were no TVs, radios, newspapers or non-spiritual books in the novitiate.

To ensure our focus remained on our spiritual formation, notes and letters from friends back home were forbidden. In addition, the novice mistress censored all mail from our families. If she considered something inappropriate, she simply didn't give it to us. She also read all outgoing mail. There were no phone calls—we had no phone in the novitiate. And, during the first year, there were just three visiting days. These things felt different and odd but not overwhelming.

The hard parts were much more subtle. I missed sharing a room, talking to someone as I drifted off to sleep. I missed normal family interactions. I missed joking with Sue and John and reading to my little sisters—who were just six and eight years old. I missed the sweet smell of their freshly shampooed little heads and tucking them into bed at night. My biggest fantasy the whole time I was in the novitiate was that an orphanage would catch fire and the kids, *who all escaped unharmed*, would have to come and live with us. I wistfully imagined bunk beds filled with toddlers in my cell.

I also pined for the turmoil of family life—and the feeling of being indispensible. If someone got sick at our house—and they often did—we all had to band together, rearrange schedules, get up at odd times, make special meals, and take care of at least one person—sometimes several—in the family. It was often dramatic and heroic. If someone got sick in the convent—and they seldom did—nothing much changed. Someone else took over their job that day (or not); another person (not me) brought them some soup, and life went on.

It was the ban on friendships inside the convent, however, that really challenged me. I'd never lived without friends. Heck, my sister Sue was my live-in best friend. My friends at school were an essential part of my life. One of my mom's serious problems with me was my need to be on the phone every evening talking with the very people I'd just spent the day with at school. One of the reasons I'd entered the Mission Helpers was because I thought this order had people in it I'd like as friends.

The young women in the novitiate were some of the most interesting and kind people I'd ever known. They were smart, funny, idealistic women who wanted to dedicate their lives to something beyond themselves. I watched them work very hard to love God and bend their wills to fit the mold of what they thought would make them worthy of their callings. We were all a little scared and in awe of the life we'd chosen. We had the same hopes and fears. We were kindred spirits. It felt insane not to have these women as my friends.

But a ban on friendships was the rule. On paper, the reason was twofold. First, it fostered detachment from everything but God. Second, forming friendships went against the rule of charity. If we formed friendships, some people might feel left out. But there was also a third reason. Friendships could lead to the dreaded *particular friendship*, the convent code phrase for lesbianism.

In cases where a postulant couldn't get with the program and continued to favor talking with some postulants more than others, she would one day open her desk and find a book with a brown paper wrapper on it and instructions to read it in private. In it the fear of the dreaded concept was discussed. I know because one day I found "the book" in my desk. I got the message. From then on I tried to talk with everyone equally.

Although I felt ashamed and confused by the book so many years ago, I now look back at that incident and smile a bit. In the typical style of the Catholic Church in those days, the text was unusually circumspect when dealing with anything sexual. In addition, as a product of the times, I was unusually naïve and uninformed about anything sexual. After reading it, I still wasn't sure what either a particular friendship or a lesbian was or what sort of a threat this was to spiritual growth. The only things I knew for sure were that friendships in the convent were wrong and I couldn't be a good nun if I had friends. After that day I tried to become a person who didn't care about friends.

One of my hardest days in the convent was that first Christmas. Christmas Eve had been beautiful. Sister Beata had planned a surprise for us. We were awakened just two hours after we'd gone to bed by the novices singing Christmas carols in the halls and told to get dressed for midnight Mass.

The only light in the motherhouse chapel came from the candles interspersed among the myriad poinsettias and pine trees. When the organ played *Adeste Fideles* and the whole chapel filled with the voices of every nun in our community who had returned for Christmas, there were few dry eyes among us postulants. Then, as we returned to the novitiate, we were silently directed to the dining room where Christmas cookies and milk awaited us. It was a heartwarming surprise, made even more special by the giddy novices who couldn't stop smiling as they enjoyed our disbelief at this radical departure from our very structured lives.

Christmas morning brought visits from some of the professed nuns to the novitiate, or we may have gone over to the motherhouse and visited them. I don't remember which. I only remember that we hugged total strangers—when I wanted to give a big Christmas hug to the people I'd lived with for the last four months.

We then had visitation with our families. It was the first time I'd seen my parents since I entered. Naturally, they brought gifts. Most unnaturally, I had nothing for them in return. I hated that. Even more, I hated feeling like I was becoming a stranger in my own family.

I remember my parents catching me up on what was happening with relatives and friends at home. Naturally, they were eager to hear about my new life. I recall sharing, in great detail, with sincere enthusiasm, my misadventures in the novitiate bakery as I tried to learn to bake communion wafers. The punch line was that I was so totally inept as a baker, I was finally transferred to the laundry room. That was my BIG story—and I could sense that they didn't quite get the same emotional bang from it that I did.

The Sisters prepared a beautiful mid-afternoon meal for our families, but we were not permitted to eat with them. (Such strange rules.) Our awkwardness was palpable as we tried to make conversation while not calling attention to the fact that we just sat with everyone as they ate. By the time visiting hours ended, I was uncomfortable enough with the oddness of the whole encounter to be quite ready to go back to the novitiate. (Maybe that was the point of those rules.)

That evening, at recreation, Sister Beata broke tradition—a second time in two days—and opened one of the many boxes of chocolates our families brought and just left it out on a table. This was a big deal—unregulated snacking. I remember hating that gesture too. This was, to me, the worst part of the vow of poverty we were preparing to take. Our poverty was backwards. We had everything we needed. We had more than we needed. What we didn't have was the opportunity to give anything to the people we cared about. The inability to give, to show something beyond generic, detached caring, was really the hardest part of all.

Christmas night, alone in my room, I questioned my vocation for the first time. I'd adapted to the outward changes of convent life. Now I wondered if I could ever adapt to the inner detachment this life demanded.

The next morning, however, sanity returned. Religious formation was supposed to be hard. I knew I couldn't say goodbye to the ways of the world without some suffering. And, in balance, so much of this life was also beautiful. I was learning something new almost every day. I finally had the time to really think and pray and get close to God. I was living the sacred life I believed I was called to. I was on the spiritual sidewalk every minute of every day. I knew, if I hung in long enough, I'd be changed into a person who really understood—and could share—the secret of a life connected to God. I redoubled my efforts to embrace my calling.

Most of the time the rhythm of the novitiate carried me along. I began to enjoy the silence. I wrote some poetry. For the first time in my life I really appreciated nature and the changing of the seasons. I studied hard. I kept a spiritual journal. I felt I was truly learning to live in service to God. There were only two things that still confounded me. On Wednesday afternoons and Sunday after Mass we had unscheduled free time. During those times I felt terribly, hopelessly lonely. I just couldn't get the hang of interacting with people without being their friends.

The other thing that kept nagging at me was, despite my growing feelings of loving God, something was still missing. On the cover of my prayer journal, I'd written the words, *God is Love*. I truly believed it. I worked as hard as I could to earn His love. I felt good—not prideful, just honest—about my efforts. Yet the love I sought still eluded me.

When we got out of bed each morning, we began our days by kneeling and kissing the floor as we said this prayer: "Take and receive, Oh Lord, my entire liberty. All that I have and all that I am, You have given me. I surrender it all to be disposed of according to Your will. Give me only Your love and Your grace. With these I am rich enough and desire nothing more." It looked like others, professed nuns and those in the novitiate with me, were sensing that love. I was willing to do anything to experience it. But my life still remained laced with a deep emptiness. In a world of so much spiritual abundance, I still craved the connection that remained just out of my reach. I started to wonder if a truly spiritual life really meant a life of unrelenting loneliness.

Winter turned into spring, and with spring came thoughts of receiving the habit and choosing a new name symbolizing my re-birth into religious life. I was still struggling with loneliness but felt receiving the habit and deepening my commitment would probably be the answer. In June, on the Feast Day of the Sacred Heart of Jesus—after a nine-day, total silence retreat—we postulants knelt at the communion rail in the motherhouse chapel, received our habits and became novices.

As the youngest, I received my name last. I remember trying to remain focused and reverent while cheering inwardly as each of my sisters got their first choices from the list of names they'd submitted. I became Sister Mary Josetta. Forty-five years later, I can still feel the excitement, anticipation and fear in taking that step. As I picture the sun shining through the stained glass windows onto the white marble floor of the motherhouse chapel, I remember my sense of commitment, my sense of the rightness of this passage. I felt sure I was moving closer to the life I sought.

I also remember how good it felt to be with my family—with both families. On that day, although I was really eager to spend time with my parents and the other folks who had come for the ceremony, I felt I belonged to the Mission Helpers family, too.

My heart pounded with excitement as I changed out of my pos-tulant clothes into the habit—floor length beige skirt, long-sleeved beige blouse, long beige scapular that covered the front and back of the outfit, and the squared-off bonnet with a white veil. I couldn't wait to go to lunch to see how everyone else looked. We were like little kids when we gathered in the novitiate dining room. We all oohed and ahhed at each other, at how different we looked, at how different we felt. We hugged (finally!); we laughed. After nine days of silence we couldn't stop talking. Sister Beata had to gently remind us this was lunch time and, perhaps, we should put some food on our plates and sit down to eat.

After lunch, the excitement erupted again as we went back to the motherhouse to greet our families. They were just finishing their lunch as we arrived. I hugged people non-stop for the longest time—my mom and dad, my sisters and brother, Grandma and Grandpa, friends from high school, aunts and uncles and cousins. I was so happy to see them, so surprised they'd driven all the way to Baltimore just to share this day with me. I tried to talk with each of them, but never finished any conversation. Every time I turned around there was someone new to see, someone to pose with for pictures. More hugging, more laughter, more pictures. It was the first time I'd seen my sisters and brother since I'd entered nine months ago. I needed time to talk to Sue and John, to snuggle with Mary and Duff. They'd grown so much. It felt so good to see them. I expected the easy give and take we'd always had, but each of them—especially the little kids—was a bit distant. It hurt to see they weren't quite sure how to be themselves with me.

The whirlwind of talking and laughing came to an end much too soon. In almost no time at all the bells called us back to our real lives. This time I cried as I hugged everyone goodbye. Now, in a way I couldn't see on Entrance Day, I sensed clearly that everything with my family would change. I would always be a member of the family, but I'd also be on the outside—*in* the family, but not *of* the family.

~

Summer was interminable. With the exception of a trip to see the Dead Sea Scrolls exhibit when it came to a Baltimore museum, we hadn't left the convent grounds since we entered the previous September. In the fall and winter we'd taken some college courses taught by our own Sisters in the novitiate classrooms. Now we didn't even have college classes to keep our minds occupied. We were simply to work on our spiritual development. It also felt like we had more free time than before.

Some days I began crying at morning prayers and continued right through morning chores. Several times Sister Beata and I talked about what was going on with me. Did I want to go home? Did I want to consider medication? (This was long before anti-depressants, so I'm guessing she meant some sort of tranquilizer like valium.) When I assured her I wanted to stay, she assured me I wasn't alone. This was a tough year for many prospective nuns. She'd then suggest a special novena to St. Joseph, in whose honor I'd taken my convent name, to help me find my balance. And time and again, after nine days of special prayers for clarity on my vocation, I felt a little stronger and recommitted myself to this life.

Fall eventually arrived. September 8th came again. Now we were on the inside waiting for the postulants to arrive. I felt pleased when Sister Beata assigned some of them to work in the laundry room with me. It meant she trusted me to be a good role model, not just a good keeper of the rules. She was correct in her assessment. In my laundry room we did our jobs in silence, for the greater honor and glory of God. Despite my really strong desire to talk with the new members of our community—find out why they'd entered the Mission Helpers, give them a pep talk when they were down, or joke around a little when I could sense they felt overwhelmed—I didn't. Sister trusted me to keep the rules, and I lived up to her trust.

And, quite frankly, that was the beginning of the end for me. One day in late October I realized I didn't know any of these new members of the community on more than a cursory level. I was astonished. With this group, because I'd followed the rules and talked only at recreation times—in one big circle—I knew almost nothing about them as individuals. Had they left big families behind or small ones? Were they challenged by the convent life or exhilarated by it? What made them choose this life? What were their dreams for it? I knew none of this, and I couldn't figure out how I ever would.

In addition, a few Sundays before, I'd been outside the motherhouse kitchen when I passed two professed Sisters planning to take a walk and enjoy the fall weather. They were stopping all of the other nuns who came out the door, looking for a third person to join them. That was the rule. You either walked alone or with at least two other nuns. Even after ten or twenty years in the convent, they were still worried about anything that smacked of the possibility of *particular friendship*. I shuddered as I imagined spending the rest of my life living like that—in community but without friends.

From that day, I began to seriously question my vocation. After more than a year of trying to mold myself into a person worthy of God's love, I still didn't feel His love. I felt I loved God; I felt God loved all of mankind. But the hole inside me, that deep place I knew only God could fill, was still almost as empty as before. For months I'd treated the emptiness as a temptation and immediately dismissed it. By November I started to see it as a fact I'd have to deal with. I started to think about going home.

But leaving the convent was tricky. I had entered because I thought I'd heard God's call. If this was true, did I have the right to say "no thanks" to God? Could I just walk away from my vocation? On the other hand, if I wasn't suited to this kind of life, was I some sort of prideful jerk, pretending to be called when I wasn't? Was a relationship between God and me sufficient to build a life on? Did I really want to live the rest of my life without deep connections to other people? Could I really serve people without getting close to them, involved with them? And, if not, should I leave?

There were also practical matters to consider. When I left home for the convent right after high school, I'd turned down a number of scholarships. I doubted I could get them back and knew I couldn't go to college without them. And what would it matter anyhow? I now had no idea what I wanted to do with my life if I left. Since I'd been eleven years old, I'd known this was what I wanted to be. If not a nun, what in the world, *who* in the world, would I be for the rest of my life?

Two interesting events happened then to give me a different perspective. The first was so minor I'm surprised I've remembered it after all these years. As I sat in the yard one day, I looked up from my spiritual reading just as a gust of wind blew. As I watched the grass in front of me react to the wind, I noticed that—unlike a tree where all the branches seem to bend in the same direction—each of the blades moved independently. Immediately I thought, *"The same is true of people—each of us moves differently to the same gust of God's will. Maybe there's more than one way to live a life dedicated to God."*

The second happened as I was walking alone on a Wednesday in mid-November, taking advantage of a burst of Indian Summer weather. As usual, I was trying to figure out if I should stay or leave. On this day, however, I had a new thought.

Whether or not I originally had a vocation, I now knew one thing was true: I was a person who needed to connect deeply with other people. I loved little kids. I loved having friends. I truly loved talking with just one person at a time, sharing stories and jokes, hopes and fears. Maybe I didn't have the temperament, the personality, to walk through life without those connections.

Then another thought occurred to me: "*Maybe this is the real decision: I can either be a good nun or I can be myself.*" And at that very moment, after months of bouncing back and forth, praying and thinking, rethinking and praying, my answer became clear. I stopped dead in my tracks. Yes, this was my choice: I could either be a good nun or I could be myself.

I was pretty certain I had it in me to become a good nun. I thought I could probably persevere long enough to become a holy nun. But now I realized that, if I did, I could never be myself. And, surprisingly, once I understood this, I saw there really was no choice. I had to be myself. How could I be anyone else?

As I made that decision—as I simply chose to be myself—I felt a huge gong, deep and low, like something you would find in an ancient shrine, sound inside me. It was just one low tone, with ripples that vibrated a very long time. It felt like a direct gift from God, a way of His saying it was OK for me to leave. Being myself—the unique person He created—was even more important than being a nun.

The doubts and confusion left. I could leave the convent with a clear conscience. I wasn't deserting God; I was just allowing myself to be who I was. I'd tried this path and found it wasn't right for me. And that was OK.

When I went to Sister Beata's office later that afternoon, she sensed the difference in me right away. She didn't offer to pray a novena with me or suggest other prayers I should say before I made a final decision. She reminded me that, if I left, my decision was irreversible; I could never come back. But once I assured her I understood, she simply gave me directions to an office in the motherhouse where I'd find a phone to call home.

The walk through the motherhouse seemed to take hours. It was close to dinner time, and the Professed Sisters passed me on the way to their dining room. I kept my head down.

The office was tiny. It contained only a desk, a chair and a phone. My hands shook as I picked up the receiver. This was the first phone call I'd made in over a year.

My mom answered on the second ring.

"Mom, it's me. Connie."

"Connie, what's wrong. Is something wrong?"

"No," but I started to cry. "Mom, I want to come home."

"Oh, no. Why, why would you want to do that? You're not coming home for our sake, are you?"

My dad had been listening in the background. After a few seconds of muffled conversation, I heard his voice.

"Con, is that you?"

"Yes, it is. Daddy, I want to come home."

"Then we'll come right down and get you, honey," was all he said.

I stopped holding my breath. Tears of gratitude and relief kicked in. I was sobbing as my mom got on the extension in another room and the three of us discussed our plans. After a few minutes they decided, since it would be a 10-hour round-trip drive and they had to make arrangements for someone to watch the kids, they would wait two more days and come down to Baltimore on Saturday.

That was fine with me. I didn't care when. All I knew was, despite my fears that they would be terribly disappointed in me, all my dad said was, "We'll come down and get you, honey."

It was OK with God. It was OK with Dad. Nothing else mattered.

CHAPTER 8

NEW BEGINNINGS

We must let go of the life we have planned,
so as to accept the one that is waiting for us.
~ Joseph Campbell

What a sight I must have been the day my parents came to take me home. I'd lost a lot of weight in the novitiate, so the dress I'd worn when I entered just hung on me. And, since I hadn't shaved my legs for almost a year and a half—hadn't worn clothes that showed my legs in all that time—the only sensible thing to do was wear my black cotton nun stockings with the dress. I'd spent a lot of time outdoors, so my face looked tan and healthy. But my arms—which seemed to go on for miles in my short-sleeved dress—were pasty white.

The worst was my hair. We didn't have to keep our hair particularly short under the veil, but one fine summer Wednesday, on a lark, several of us decided to cut each other's hair really, really short. It was a hot day; we were all a little silly. When we were done, our heads looked like a cross between a monk's and a marine's. My hair had grown out a little by November, but it was still far too short to be acceptable, let alone fashionable. Sister Beata found a piece of fabric she cut to resemble a headscarf, but it was so stiff it only accentuated the problem. There were no mirrors in the changing room, but I imagined I looked a little like a refugee at Ellis Island who had been seasick the entire trip across the ocean. My mom's expression when she first saw me indicated I looked a bit worse.

I said a quick farewell to Sister Beata who, much to my surprise, cried as we hugged goodbye. Then we were on our way. We weren't even a mile from the convent when Mom reached into her purse and pulled out her lipstick. She handed it to me in the back seat saying, "Maybe this will help." It didn't.

Mom called her beautician as soon as we got home. The next morning I went to the earliest Mass possible in the hopes of running into no one I knew until I could look somewhat normal. Our first trip on Monday morning was to have me fitted for a wig.

It took surprisingly little effort to adapt to home life. Once I assured Sue I wouldn't reclaim the *Peter, Paul & Mary* albums I'd given her when I left for the Mission Helpers, she was pretty glad to have me back as a roommate. The people at Murphy's were happy to rehire me for the Christmas season. By the end of the year, I was enrolled for the spring semester at Mount Mercy College (now Carlow University).

The hardest part of the first weeks at home was having no contact with the women I'd left behind in the convent. In the 1960s those were the rules. Before you left, you could tell no one you were leaving. Once you left, there was no further contact between you and those who remained. I may not have gotten to know the new group, but I sure missed the people who had entered with me.

(A lot has changed since then, not just with the Mission Helpers, but with most orders. Now nuns can have friends both inside and outside the convent. Now people who leave are welcome to stay in touch with those inside. Just recently, in fact, I was invited to a reunion of both ex- and current Mission Helpers.)

Going to Mt. Mercy, a women's Catholic college, was probably the easiest transition possible from the convent. Although it was the late '60s and a lot of college students were tuning in, turning on and dropping out, that wasn't the case at Mt. Mercy. At the height of the campus war protests, when people were holding buildings hostage and being tear gassed and shot at, our biggest demonstration involved the dorm students marching to protest having to wear skirts to the cafeteria after school hours.

School was still a challenge, however. I knew I had to do well or lose my makeshift scholarship. I also knew I needed to start doing normal things—like dating.

Boy, I was so ill-prepared and naïve. I met Don at the first mixer I attended. He was an architecture student at Carnegie-Mellon and a non-Catholic. He played the guitar and wrote me poetry. I fell hard. Things were good when we went for walks through Oakland together or when he came to my house for the evening. Things were horrible and confusing when we went to frat parties. For starters, beer was the only thing they served, and I couldn't handle more than half a beer before the floor started to move too much for me to dance. And I didn't dare NOT dance. Sitting in the afternoon and talking was great. Sitting together at a frat party, when the lights were low and the music was so loud you couldn't think, meant French kissing—which I was pretty damn sure made you pregnant! Our relationship lasted barely two months.

The next guy I dated was Catholic and didn't belong to a fraternity. Our morals were a better match and we dated for a few months. But I was pretty sure I wasn't in love with him.

Then, not even a year after I'd left the convent, Ross came into my life. He had the most beautiful green eyes, and the way he looked in a pale blue shirt sent shivers down my spine. After our second date, I broke up with the other guy because I knew he'd never be as right for me as Ross.

I liked Ross right away but wasn't sure how he felt about me. He was different from other guys; he was old fashioned and gentlemanly, almost a little formal. I remember telling my mom I wasn't sure if he really cared for me. He didn't kiss me on our first date, and all I got on our second was a peck on the cheek. She laughed and said, "He doesn't have a car. He takes a bus and a streetcar to pick you up. He likes you."

She was right. Soon we were a couple. Thankfully, blissfully, big chunks of the hole in my heart were filled by this wonderful man and his love. We dated through his senior year at Duquesne. He proposed right after graduation. Six months later—because he had a job as a city school teacher, because we thought we were old and mature and couldn't wait another minute to spend the rest of our lives together, and because we wanted to have sex—we married over the semester break of my junior year.

CHAPTER 9

SLAMMING DOORS

The uncompromising attitude is more indicative of
an inner uncertainty than a deep conviction.
The implacable stand is directed more against
the doubt within than the assailant without.
~ Eric Hoffer

Ross and I settled into a tiny apartment in Squirrel Hill, halfway between college and Peabody High School, where he taught. We talked of postponing a family until one or both of us had obtained our Master's Degrees. We used the rhythm method of birth control, but without a lot of dedication. Four months later I had to quit my summer job as a waitress because of morning sickness. We were both delighted by the thought of starting a family. The following September, I took 21 credits, trying to finish as many courses as I could before our baby arrived.

Our lives were busy and fun. Ross taught during the day and went to grad school a few evenings a week, so most of our evenings were spent studying. Weekends were filled with entertaining friends or visiting our families. Still, the question of spirituality was never far from my mind. Although we'd enrolled in the parish in our new neighborhood, we didn't attend Mass regularly. I think Ross felt we were just taking a break from what had been mandatory attendance while we'd lived at home. But for me, non-attendance marked the beginning of a big shift in my thinking.

My break with the Church had been coming for some time. When I'd entered the Mission Helpers, I chose to accept the magic of convent thinking completely—to subjugate my brain for the sake of my spirit. I made a conscious decision to accept, unquestioningly, everything I was taught as divinely inspired. In the long run, my convent experience actually weakened my ties to God.

As a Psychology major, I soon learned that some things we were taught in the convent were unhealthy or at odds with human nature. Blind obedience, I now learned, was more a sign of emotional immaturity than virtue. Most people didn't go astray by loving too much but by loving unwisely. And healthy relationships with other people were the cornerstone of a healthy spirituality, not a roadblock to it. In the convent I'd swung on the pendulum toward true believing as far as I could go. If the Church or my superiors said it, I believed it. Now I swung full force to the side of cynicism and disbelief. If some of what the Church taught was not right, how could I know which part was correct and which wasn't? If some of it was wrong, perhaps all of it was.

I remember—vividly—the day I walked away from God and the Church. I was 21 years old, in the first semester of my senior year and six months pregnant. It was between three and four o'clock on a November afternoon. I sat on the second floor of Antonian Hall, facing the huge wall of windows overlooking Fifth Avenue. It had snowed the day before and the snow was covered with soot and dirt.

I'd just finished classes for the day and was waiting for Ross to pick me up on his way home from work. I had about an hour to kill and thought I'd do some easy reading. For me, easy reading meant

Theology. I'd learned a ton of post-Vatican-II theology in the convent. And because I usually carried a class or two over a full schedule, I'd generally enroll in a Theology course to pad my schedule. Even though I didn't agree with a lot of what the Church taught, I was pretty knowledgeable. In a semester that included Statistics and Biology, three credits in Theology meant I could keep my QPA high enough to keep my scholarships.

I'd stacked my coat, purse and books beside me on the floor and reached for this semester's text. The course was Christology. The textbook was small with a red cover. It was an effortless read, perfect for the end of the day.

I was chugging along, delighted to be in familiar territory instead of the world of probability theory and chi-square tests, when I read the author's passage on redemption. It went something like this: God, the Father, knew the expiation for the sins of mankind would have to be great. No sacrifice from a mere man would suffice. So, in His love for mankind, knowing redemption for our sins would have to be a perfect sacrifice, He made the only perfect sacrifice— He chose to send his Son to earth to be crucified for our sins.

This was pretty standard Catholic teaching. The Church was built around John 3:16: "For God so loved the world that He gave His only begotten Son, that whoever believes in Him shall not perish but have eternal life." I'd read and heard these words hundreds of times. But that day—maybe because I was pregnant with my own child, maybe because I'd been slowly walking away from the Church anyway—I heard them with new ears. And they made me furious!

"What kind of God makes up rules like this?" I thought. *"What kind of God sees the sins of His children—the children He's created—as unforgivable? What kind of God says, 'Well, the only way they can make it up to Me is perfectly? And for Me, perfection means the suffering and crucifixion of my Son.'"*

I pictured an egotistical deity saying, "Well, *I'm* not happy about this sacrifice thing, certainly *My Son* isn't happy about it, but you know how I am! Anything less just won't be good enough for Me."

I remember thinking, *"Wait a minute! Whose rules are these? If God is who the Church says He is, He is the one who makes the rules and He is the one who can change them!! The creator of the world is accountable to no one but Himself! Don't talk to me about God so loving the world that the only thing that satisfies Him is to have His Son crucified!! That's not love. It's brutal, selfish, arrogant, immature cruelty—or insanity!"*

Then, from a place deep inside me, this thought followed, *"And if this is the God of the Catholic Church, they can have him! I would rather spend eternity in hell than one moment in the presence of this deity!"*

Immediately, I felt something in my chest—something like a thick metallic cello string—simply snap. It shook my body. I felt scared and wobbly, as if my backbone had been severed. I also felt very self-righteous. At that moment I decided I'd never be able to continue being a Catholic. I slammed the book shut, grabbed my things, and went downstairs to wait for Ross. I didn't even want to be in that part of the building for another second.

Later, when I calmed down, I rethought my reaction and was equally sure I was wrong.

"I know I'm overly emotional these days. I've probably missed something important. I'm sure my Theology professor will be able to show me my error in the next class. After all, I can't be the first person to think these thoughts. Surely there's a logical explanation I'm missing. It doesn't seem realistic to think I can walk away from God and the Church so easily—so completely."

However, in the days that followed, when neither the professor nor I could explain this concept to my satisfaction, I just kept walking. Years later, when I met someone who said that they'd left the

Church because of the rules on birth control or because they'd had a bad experience with an untrustworthy priest, I was kind of jealous. If only my leaving had been on those terms, I think I could have found a way to return. I had already worked my way around the problem of man-made laws and corrupt clergymen. But, try as I might, I couldn't figure out how to accept the Catholic God—a God of such monumental and fierce sadism.

I chose to give up trying to walk with one foot on each path, one spiritual and one worldly. If disbelieving meant I walked in the gutter of life, then that's what I'd do. I decided, from then on, I would be *in* the world and *of* the world. The Catholic Church had shown me the flaws in other religions. Now I'd gone and found the flaws in the Church. I had no religion I could believe. I wasn't particularly happy about it, but I honestly couldn't see my way clear to envision life any other way.

It was late November, 1968. Three years after I'd left the convent I'd become an agnostic. My path had taken a very unexpected turn. Now, rather than simply finding out what kind of Catholic I would be outside the convent, I realized I'd become a person with no religion at all.

~

Ross thought my departure from the Church was far too abrupt and final. He'd become less diligent in his attendance at church but continued to believe. When Lisa was born a few months later, he insisted she be baptized. I, however, didn't recant.

Nonetheless, it took several more months and an odd encounter with Ross' good friend for me to concretize my departure from all religion. To tell this part of the story, we have to go back a few years to 1966, when Ross and I first began dating.

I not only loved Ross, I loved his friends. They were, like Ross and me, the complete opposite of the hippie stereotypes of our generation. Many of us were the first in our families to go to college. I think all of us were on some sort of scholarship or work-study program. We didn't drink or smoke—let alone do drugs. Of the three guys who were Ross' attendants at our wedding, two also married ex-nuns.

The friends we hung out with most were a couple I'll call Phil and Toni (pseudonyms). We often attended parties and picnics together. One of my favorite memories is of the four of us at the Highland Games in Ligonier, Pennsylvania. In the morning we watched bagpipers and Scottish folk dancers compete. In the afternoon the guys rowed us around the lake in a funky old rowboat, serenading us as they rowed. It was unsophisticated and corny to the extreme—and it really touched my heart.

Our relationship with these friends changed, however, around February of the next year. Phil and Toni had gone on a university-related retreat that, although consisting of only a handful of students and professors, was to become the genesis of the Catholic Pentecostal movement (later renamed the Catholic Charismatic Renewal).

As I understood it, the movement had its roots in the ecumenical freedom following Vatican II. As Catholics looked for a personal relationship with Christ, they were open to learning from their Christian counterparts—including fundamentalist Protestants. One of the people whose message really touched these first seekers was an Assembly of God minister named David Wilkerson. Wilkerson wrote *The Cross and the Switchblade*, a story of the workings of the Holy Spirit in his life and his calling to change the lives of gang members in New York City. Phil lent us his copy. I read it in one sitting. Wilkerson, a country preacher from a small town in Pennsylvania, wrote well and from the heart.

Phil's life was profoundly changed that weekend. During that time, he felt that he'd come into direct contact with God. His experience of what he called "being baptized in the Holy Spirit" touched him deeply. He and Toni remained close to the other attendees. They met and prayed together often, and sought to bring others into the same deeply rewarding experience.

Phil certainly wanted to share his newfound spirituality with Ross, and they began attending prayer meetings together. The idea of prayer meetings fascinated me—probably more than Ross—but most of them occurred in the eastern suburbs, close to Phil and Ross but 45 minutes from my house. So Ross, rather than both of us, attended the first few meetings. When, on an occasional weekend, the guys had time to pick me up and I joined them, I had such mixed feelings about the meetings. There was definitely something happening there. When these people gathered in prayer together, I could feel the air in the room change. Often, when someone spoke in the group about his conversion experience, I was touched by his sincerity. Many of them seemed to exude a joyfulness and peace I'd never experienced.

At first I thought I would continue to attend until I eventually saw the light and was drawn back to some sort of spirituality. One of the group members, Ted (a pseudonym), taught at Mt. Mercy and we occasionally met for lunch. I liked Ted. He was brilliant and funny. He joked about everything but his relationship with God. He was, in a way, a lot like Father Pro—the Mexican martyr who had stolen my heart when I was 12. I really wanted to believe as Phil and Ted did. I wanted those feelings in my life. I wanted their sense of community and friendship.

But something in their beliefs also made me cringe. It was their certainty—their belief they were 100% right and everyone who didn't see things their way was wrong, evil or misguided. The depth of their certainty kept me both intrigued and repulsed for months. The tipping point came when we went to a prayer meeting at a young couple's house in early fall. I enjoyed meeting our hosts. They were bright and welcoming, with a nice sense of community about them and—I have no idea why I remember this—they had just redone their bathroom in such a way that their old claw-footed bathtub looked like a piece of art rather than a relic in a room they couldn't afford to totally renovate. The getting-acquainted part of the evening was easy.

Then the meeting began in earnest. After a song or two (several people played guitars) they moved to Bible readings and prayers to the Holy Spirit to make His presence felt in the room. This led to speaking in tongues—glossolalia.

The speaking in tongues definitely unnerved me. Hearing people who, just minutes before, sounded perfectly normal as they talked about finding a babysitter or getting tied up in rush-hour traffic suddenly go into guttural soliloquies was unsettling. I remember feeling very much out of my depth, very uncomfortable. I kept thinking that whatever was happening was both important and way beyond me. I sat very still, unable to move, finding I had to remind myself to breathe. I didn't understand it, but it affected me deeply.

The meeting then shifted to a new phase—interpretation of the gift of tongues—where one of the group leaders began to translate what someone else had said while speaking glossolalia. Almost immediately my wonder and fear turned to skepticism.

"*Hold on,*" I thought, "*if this is coming from the Holy Spirit to an individual, how come the individual who's speaking doesn't know what's being said? Why does he have to wait until someone else interprets it for him? And why are the same people always doing the interpreting?*"

They were also discussing whether or not some of the glossolalia might actually be a foreign language—perhaps a biblical one, perhaps pre-fourteenth century French. This also seemed strange to me. *"If it is the word of God, why would the language matter?"* My awe of the meeting's sanctity disappeared, replaced by a very definite sense of cynicism.

By the time a break came in the meeting, I needed to go outside. I didn't want to interfere with Ross' experience and my thoughts were too disjointed to talk with anyone. It was a nice evening, so I walked down the street a bit. Soon, Ross was beside me. He understood my mixed feelings and didn't attempt to convince me of anything. I insisted he go back in for the rest of the meeting. He insisted on staying out on the porch with me while we waited for Phil. I don't think we talked much as we waited, but I do remember feeling grateful he stayed outside with me.

Ross continued his involvement with the group without me. He and Phil volunteered to teach CCD (religion classes for public school kids) on Sunday mornings. He attended more prayer meetings. I occasionally joined them for non-religious get-togethers. Eventually, however, Ross had some experiences with the group that left him uncomfortable too. By the time we were married in January of 1968, although Phil and Ross remained close friends, our involvement with the group was pretty minimal. Phil's, on the other hand, was all-consuming. He'd found both a belief system and community in which he felt very comfortable.

I often felt jealous of Phil. I disliked my half cynical/half true-believer mind. I yearned to have the rock-solid faith in something spiritual but couldn't accept Philip's rigid and exclusive beliefs. It was a frustrating quandary. Phil had the solid ground on which to build his life; I was still out in the middle of the river, not quite sure I'd ever find dry land.

I think the four of us would have continued our friendship for a while until, as we had less and less in common, we drifted apart. However, that's not what happened.

Two years after I walked out of that first prayer meeting, several months after Lisa was born, we'd invited Phil and Toni for dinner. I know it was right after Easter because one of Ross' students had given him two little Easter chicks, and we hadn't yet figured out where to take them so they wouldn't die in our apartment.

After dinner Ross and I were in the kitchen getting dessert while Phil and Toni sat in the dining room. As I poured the coffee, Ross bent down to check on the chicks and I tripped over him, pouring the steaming contents of the electric pot right on Ross. When he ripped off his shirt, he had a burn mark at least a foot long on his back. Phil and Toni rushed into the kitchen and helped me apply cold towels to Ross' back. But Ross is pretty stoic and hates to be fussed over. Within a few minutes he was in a clean shirt and we were all back in the dining room.

As we settled in for dessert, the cynical part of me wondered why Phil and Toni—such believers in the power of the Spirit to heal—hadn't offered to pray over Ross and his burned back. In my head, I debated the social propriety of mentioning this to them. I didn't want to offend them; they were guests in our home.

Before I could pose the question, however, Phil announced he had something important to say to us. He cleared his throat, said it was hard and he'd prayed over it a lot, but he had to tell us that—knowing full well we'd never spend eternity with them because of our lack of faith—he'd decided it was probably best we didn't spend any more time together on earth either. This was the last evening he'd spend with us.

I looked at Ross' face, at the hurt and astonishment in his eyes. I wanted to hit Phil with something very big—perhaps a 20-ton truck. I was dumbstruck—at both Phil's arrogance and his insensitivity. He and Ross had been friends for years. And now he was dissolving the friendship because he was sure we were not going to be in heaven with him!

I don't know how we responded or *if* we responded in any way at all. We must have gotten up from the table, said goodbye and shown them to the door. I don't remember. All I can remember about the rest of the evening was the pain in Ross' eyes.

The incident with Phil and Toni was my final straw with religion. I stopped looking for what I was doing wrong that kept me from believing. I came to see religion as contemptible nonsense. With Phil, I watched a basically good guy turn into an arrogant, self-righteous jerk because of his religious beliefs. I remember thinking of the verse from Matthew, "By their fruits shall you know them." Well, I'd checked out their fruits, and I didn't want any part of them. If this was Christianity in action, deal me out. I was done with the game!

At that point, I didn't just walk away from religion, I ran. If the believers shouted their Good News from the rooftops, I'd shout my doubts right back at them from the trenches. If cursing the Church and its representatives would cause me eternal punishment, so be it. If my disbelief caused a lightning bolt to strike me down, I was ready to stand out in the open to receive it. After Phil, I became a very hurt, very bitter, and very verbal advocate for anything and anyone that rejected religion and the God it espoused!

However, the incident with Phil didn't end my fascination with religion and spirituality. Actually, it increased it. I now needed to understand how it was possible for rational people to believe in anything spiritual.

CHAPTER 10

UNBELIEVING

Never knowing if believing is a blessing or a curse,
or if the going up is worth the coming down.
~ Kris Kristofferson

Agnosticism is hard. It offers no refuge—no comforting beliefs on which to rest your head. It gives you nothing to get you through the night. On the other hand, it's clean. If you expect nothing, you're seldom disappointed.

Truth be told, I was a poor agnostic. One part of me always remained skeptical, but the other was like a puppy running to the window every time she heard a car coming down the road. I mistrusted my beliefs, but I didn't know how to live without believing. Every time I encountered the possibility of believing in something spiritual, I checked it out.

Like the pilgrim in Kris Kristofferson's song, I never knew if the risk was worthwhile but I kept taking it. Over and over, for the next 30 years, I'd allow myself to be enticed into some sort of belief in God and take a few steps into the realm of faith. And inevitably, I'd back away, knowing I was wrong—again.

My experience with Lillian (a pseudonym) is a good example of how these forays worked. I met her in a discussion group she led on Edgar Cayce, a 20th century American psychic. She started the meeting with a meditation enhanced by Paul Horn's flute music. I loved the music and the meditation, but once the meeting started, I became pretty uncomfortable. There were a few too many true believers in the group. I enjoyed studying Cayce but sure didn't need him to be put on a pedestal. I'd left the Church because of its insistence on having a lock on truth. I didn't want to trade Catholic dogmatism for a new one.

But I liked Lillian. She was married with several grown children and seemed to have her feet firmly planted in this world. While she respected Cayce's work, she didn't consider it the ultimate, infallible truth. So although I didn't take part in the study group, Lillian and I kept in touch for a while. In the course of several afternoon-long conversations, we both shared a lot about our spiritual search and our struggles with clinical depression.

Eventually we drifted apart. Then about a year after our last conversation, I read in the paper about someone who had committed suicide by jumping off a bridge. It was Lillian. The article stated she'd recently been released from a mental hospital.

Anger raged inside me immediately. I thought, *"No. This is totally unfair. She'd worked so hard. She'd done all the right things. She prayed and studied to get free of the damned depression. She'd gone for help from traditional and non-traditional sources. Still, she didn't make it. How did this happen?"* I understood the level of pain and desperation that would cause someone to jump off a bridge. I knew how much she loved her husband and her children and didn't want to hurt them. I believed she fought her suicidal thoughts with all her strength. She didn't want to let them win. But they did.

I was angry with Edgar Cayce's teachings and the hope Cayce had brought into her life. I was angry with the people in her study group. But mostly I was enraged at God. I was angry at a deity who didn't give her the help she needed. I was sure she'd reached out to God—as she had done all the other times her depression hit—but there was nothing, no one, to help her when she needed it most.

Within minutes I turned my anger against myself. *"You jerk! You did it again. You really thought Lillian's beliefs, her hard work and her sincere prayers were going to help her. You were duped into trusting again. Hey Sweetie, if someone like Lillian couldn't make it, how the hell can you?"* Again I had the proof I needed. All this spiritual stuff was crap. If there was something/someone out there, why was Lillian dead? It was a short and easy road back to cynicism and rage.

After Lillian, I decided I'd look for a path that didn't place me directly in a relationship with God. I looked instead for something involving spiritual tenets, which didn't sucker me into putting my faith in a being who always let me down.

~

Our son, Ken, was born in 1972. For a while the joys and responsibilities of a new baby and a spirited toddler were more than enough to keep my mind and heart occupied. We moved to a bigger apartment with young neighbors close by. Spirituality simmered on the back burner of my mind—until, serendipitously, I discovered Silva Mind Control.

The day before Ross and I planned to go to the mall for nursery-school clothes for Lisa, our car landed in the shop. With Lisa's first day of school looming, we decided the kids and I would meet Ross in downtown Pittsburgh after work to shop. For some reason—a store coupon? a special sale?—we chose to go to the department store that was furthest from our trolley stop.

As we headed to Horne's Department Store, we walked down a pretty seedy looking street. Right in the middle of a block littered with bottles and cigarette butts we saw a guy sweeping. His eyes met mine and he smiled a quick hello. In response, I made a comment about how nice it was to see someone caring about the sidewalk in front of his shop. Again the quick smile as he explained this was a pretty atypical place. He asked if we were familiar with Silva Mind Control and offered to go inside and get us information. Ross gave me the look he gives me when I get too involved with strangers, but I glared back and said we could at least look at the man's brochures. Less than a minute later I'd stuffed them into my purse and we continued on our way. I'm sure Ross never gave the place or the information another thought.

I read the material several times after we got home. The Mind Control program was a multi-weekend-long workshop in just the things I'd been seeking. It offered ways to open to our untapped spiritual potential, proven techniques for expanding ESP, and knowledge of the new scientific findings that made all this possible. Spirituality without religion! It was more tempting than chocolate-covered strawberries.

The next day, while the kids were napping, I called to get more information. Immediately another chunk of coincidence struck. The woman who answered the phone was a volunteer who helped out in the office because the course had changed her life. As we talked, I found out she was also an ex-nun. This was off-the-charts serendipity.

Soon I was back in town to talk with the woman who would be teaching the course. Joann was an exceptional woman—bright, articulate and positive—with that special kind of second-generation Italian warmth that made me immediately comfortable. The more she talked about the workshop, the more I wanted to take it. However, September was a bad month for a teacher's budget. Despite Ross working two jobs, summers left us without discretionary cash.

I'd decided to postpone taking the workshop for a few months—perhaps forever—when Joann mentioned the person who helped her with publicity was leaving town. I asked if I could earn my tuition for a future workshop by doing some writing and PR work for a few months. Joann agreed, graciously insisting I take the very next one.

The workshop had many facets. Some focused on attitude change, positive thoughts and actions, memory devices and ways to relax. The heart of the work, however, centered on techniques to reach an Alpha brain wave level where we could get in touch with our own inner powers of perception and clairvoyance.

On the final afternoon, we broke into teams of two and practiced our newfound skills by doing psychic readings on people in each other's lives. For instance, I would give my practice partner the name, age and location of someone I knew—Bob Jones, 36, of Pittsburgh Pennsylvania. He would then tell me what he saw or felt about the person, and I'd give him feedback on the accuracy of his perceptions. Then I would "do a case" on someone my partner named. It felt both hokey and real at the same time.

As I did the cases, I actually could sense and see different things about the person my partners named. Much to my surprise, my co-hort often verified what I was saying. For example, I once said "I'm feeling a lot of pain in my abdomen. It feels hot." My partner replied, "Well, Uncle Harry has had problems with bleeding ulcers for the last 10 years. So that may be how your intuition records bleeding ulcers."

Sometimes the verification came immediately. Sometimes it seemed my partner and I just kept sharing symptoms and symbols until something jived. It could have been real, but it also could have been our need to find ways to support each other in this new and odd experience. I was guardedly intrigued—until my last partner.

Alicia (a pseudonym) and I hadn't talked much during the two weekends of the course. We knew nothing about each other's lives. The only thing I knew about her from her actions in class was that she was an especially frank person who asked intelligent questions. I couldn't imagine her giving me positive feedback just to make me feel good. I thought she'd be excellent to work with.

I don't remember a lot about what I said when I was doing her case, but she quickly and unemotionally confirmed just about everything I was sensing. As I worked with her, I began feeling a bit more comfortable with the technique

For Alicia's case, I gave her the name of Ross' aunt, who was dying of cancer. Alicia picked up the cancer very quickly. She also sensed Aunt Molly was in a lot of pain. Then she said something pretty odd. She told me that, as she mentally scanned Molly's body, she seemed to come to a place in her back where there was no pain—where the feelings just came to a dead end. I couldn't explain this but thought she'd done a really great job on everything else. So when Alicia asked if we could possibly get together and practice sometime, I agreed and gave her my phone number.

That evening, after the kids were in bed, I explained to Ross what had happened at the end of class.

"I gave this woman Aunt Molly as a case, Hon. She got some things right, but others I couldn't confirm. For instance, she talked about this place on Aunt Molly's back," I touched his back to show him, "where she thought feelings, especially pain, just came to an end."

The color drained from his face.

"Con, right there, right where you touched me? Did she really say there was no feeling there?"

"Yeah, I think she said something like, 'Things just stopped right there, like it was the end of the road.' Why do you ask? Why are you looking at me like that?"

"Con, I never told you this. Remember when they operated on Aunt Molly several months ago? By that time, the cancer had spread to just about every part of her body. The doctors decided there was nothing they could do for her, but before they sewed her back up, they cut some nerves in her back, right where you showed me, hoping to give her some relief from the pain."

We both sat and stared for the longest time. Then I cried. Maybe, just maybe, I'd found something to believe in. When Joann offered her next workshop, we scraped together the money for Ross to take it.

Our involvement with Silva Mind Control led to other interesting excursions into the psychic field. Alicia and I became friends and remained case-study partners for several years. She would come over one night a week after the kids were in bed and we'd give each other cases to improve our psychic abilities. And over time, we did. We became more accurate and it took less time to see problem areas. Once, when Ross gave us the names of several little known historic figures, we were quite accurate in describing both their physical ailments and how they died. It was pretty amazing. It was also an odd skill to have.

Despite its lack of practical value, it had great emotional value for both of us. It gave us a way to tap into something we'd always suspected was there. For me it was a way to enter the spiritual world without contact with the Christology God. Yes, there was something out there—and I could reach it without prayer or believing in a particular religion. I could do it scientifically. That felt safe.

Safe was not, however, how I felt with a lot of people on this road with me. The Silva people were cool. We enjoyed the company of Joann and her husband and some of Joann's other students. Most of them seemed to have their feet planted firmly on the ground; they had jobs and other interests. We could go to dinner with them and also discuss politics, sports or art. However, a lot of the people in the metaphysical world seemed a little off to me. Too many of them spent too much time meditating, hanging out on Ouija Boards or checking things out with their spirit guides to bother with day-to-day life. And they certainly didn't have the inclination to check their guides' opinions against something as mundane as reality. It often seemed like I'd run into a different version of nuns or Pentecostal Phil. They had their Ultimate Truth and, once they got it, they stopped thinking.

On the other hand, I was ready to believe in something again. True Believers' stories tempted me. My years in the non-believing desert were lonely. The true-believing years in the Church caused a lot of pain and weren't always psychologically healthy. But they were also a land of community—a place to share with kindred spirits. I genuinely missed them. Most of all, despite my intense desire to be strong enough and smart enough not to, I missed the idea of a loving God. Maybe this group of believers had discovered a truth that kept evading me.

I was soon hip deep in the world of psychic spirituality. I attended lectures on astral projection and paranormal phenomena. I sat and talked for hours with folks who had out-of-body experiences or encounters with wise spiritual entities. Sadly, I usually came away disillusioned. When I got to know these folks, their lives were often just as screwed up as mine. What good did it do to have paranormal experiences if they didn't bring any clarity to normal life?

For example, Nina (a pseudonym) told me she was considering having an affair with Curtis—someone she'd been involved with "incarnations ago." She seemed ecstatic. She'd checked with her spirit guides and they assured her this was where her karma had been leading her—despite the fact she and Curtis were both married and Curtis was not much older than her children. When I ran into her again a year or so later, she was pregnant with Curtis' child, getting a divorce, estranged from her other children—and Curtis had gone back to his wife. Perhaps, ultimately, all of this was good for her. I don't know. But it sure wasn't where I wanted to put my faith. This kind of personal spirituality had the potential to be even less trustworthy than Church spirituality. At least the Church had rules and guilt to keep a person from wandering too far from the path.

It was then I made up my One Big Rule. If I were going to believe what I learned from these sojourns into the psychic world—whether it came from a well-known psychic source or my own intuitive feeling—it had to pass the reality test. If I could bounce the concepts I'd learned from the psychic world against the stark reality of daily life, I'd take them into account. If the precepts made life better, not just for me, but for my world in general, I'd think seriously about them. If they didn't meet these criteria, no matter how appealing the source or how sure my gut feelings were, I wouldn't accept them. And if the answers were so ambiguous I couldn't be sure of a direction, I'd just ignore them. I couldn't waste my time or energy on *possible* answers. I surely couldn't risk putting my faith in a message that didn't have the decency to be understandable.

I think my One Big Rule served me well. It definitely kept me out of a lot of groups and from going down some shaky paths. It also showed me I was pretty bad at making practical decisions using solely psychic abilities.

Eventually Alicia made what I thought was a great decision. She went to grad school and got her Master's Degree in Counseling. She'd come up with a practical way to use the real, if somewhat odd, talent we'd developed. After grad school and a divorce, she moved out of state and we lost contact. But I was always grateful for the years we spent exploring the psychic world together.

A few months before Alicia left town, she introduced me to Eileen. Eileen and I had a lot in common. We were full-time moms with young children, ex-Catholics and were both dealing with weight issues. As our friendship grew, we discovered we were both looking for something more in life, for a spiritual path that was logical and practical. We talked non-stop for hours every time we got together. We found in each other a kindred spirit. We've been friends ever since.

Eileen introduced me to the writings of Jane Roberts, a woman who claimed to channel for an entity known as Seth. Her book, *Seth Speaks*, profoundly affected our lives. The entity who spoke through Jane—or what I thought of as Jane's creative subconscious—was an odd combination of the practical and the esoteric. Even now, more than 40 years later, these theories still have a presence in the metaphysical field—and some have found verification in the neuroscience of beliefs.

The idea of creating your reality with your thoughts attracted Eileen and me. We decided to form a study group to discuss and experiment with ESP, hypnosis and creating reality. We had only one major criterion for admission to the group: people had to either hold nine-to-five jobs or be stay-at-home moms. We'd both had our fill of professional seekers.

This led to the Monday Night Group, a loosely-structured weekly meeting of like-minded folks—a couple of teachers, an engineer, a lawyer, a technician and some moms—that met at our house for more than three years. After meeting some of the participants, Ross joined us too.

It was a pretty egalitarian and laid-back group. Everyone contributed in their areas of expertise and came to the experiments with a nice balance of openness and skepticism. One member, John, who had traveled the world studying meditation and metaphysical subjects, set the tone by graciously sharing his knowledge and never seeking the spotlight.

We discovered and shared a lot in the group. We definitely became aware of the reality and power of the psychic world. We learned that serendipitous discoveries, as well as mistakes and misjudgments in that arena, echoed in our everyday lives. Our experiences left us with no doubt that the psychic world was real—and far from predictable.

The Monday Night Group disbanded soon after I started a full-time job. On the surface, it was a logical decision. Everyone in the family was adjusting to my working outside the house for the first time. Juggling meals, chores, homework and the children's activities made it impossible for us to continue to give our time to weekly meetings—and the housecleaning that needed to precede them.

But that was only part of the truth. Dipping into the psychic world created its own set of problems. My foray into it was not without emotional bruises and mistakes. I made some big ones and our marriage suffered because of them. Ironically, considering my condemnation of people who followed their intuition when it felt good, I fell in love with one of the men in the group. The emotional intimacy we felt on a psychic level dwarfed what we were both feeling toward our spouses. Despite my lack of respect for those who talked of finding soul mates, I felt this man was the love of my life. In the end, common sense and a realization of the harm we would do to both of our families outweighed our psychic sense of righteousness and passion and it never went beyond an emotional relationship. But that was enough. I hurt Ross. He hurt his wife. We put our families in jeopardy. It would take years for Ross and me to get on solid ground again.

I came away from this experience knowing the psychic world was real but seemed to have no moral boundaries. And if I didn't always have the common sense to follow my own One Big Rule, it just felt better to abandon this world completely. At least for a while. It was always *for a while*. In reality, just about everything I was interested in led me back into the spiritual realm.

By the same token, my inability to just plunk myself down on the side of unreservedly believing in anything always kept me on the outskirts of every spiritually-based group I discovered. For example, one of the ways Ross and I worked to heal our marriage was through Marriage Encounter—and in Pittsburgh in the 1980s, this meant *Catholic* Marriage Encounter. Our first Encounter weekend was life-changing. It brought us to a place of honesty and forgiveness that enabled us to rebuild our relationship. It added a whole new level of intimacy to our 15-year marriage, and gave us the tools and support to continue to reach out to each other.

In addition, after the weekend, we were invited to join a ME community that lovingly welcomed and accepted us even after we made it very clear we were unrepentant ex-Catholics. We had some beautiful times of serious sharing and wonderfully enjoyable weekends and dinners together. We made some lasting friendships and remained active members of the group for years.

However, the belief issue was always there too. It was odd. Ross and I were always silent during the personal prayers at the end of the meetings. We were the couple who didn't go to communion at ME masses. We constantly had that little uncomfortable pause in the conversation when we met new Marriage Encounter folks who asked, as they always did, what parish we belonged to. But we were also the couple who mailed out the ME newsletter and helped organize the non-liturgical parts of city-wide gatherings. It was a peculiar mixture of sticking out and blending in.

Another place my spiritual cynicism hampered my participation was Overeaters Anonymous. In an attempt to deal with my eating issues—my weight has spiraled in a hundred-pound range almost all of my adult life—I wandered in and out of OA numerous times. At one point, in 1987, I went to an out-of-state food rehab program that required a 90-in-90 commitment (ninety OA meetings in 90 days) when I returned home.

At the food treatment center the therapists had presented the spiritual aspects of the program laced with enough cognitive psychology to make it palatable to me. However, the world of neighborhood OA meetings where regular people—in all states of mental health, religious beliefs and intelligence—led the meetings was an entirely different matter. I felt I had no choice but to define my own spirituality very strongly or become swallowed up in theirs. And I couldn't define my own.

This was a challenging time. I was working full time. The children were teenagers. I was seeing a therapist regularly for clinical depression and juggling the sizable side-effects of anti-depressive medications against the modicum of relief I felt from them. I was struggling to get my eating under control. Coming face-to-face with the spiritual issues of a Twelve Step program almost pulled me under. I could handle the food plan; I couldn't handle the concept of turning my will and my life over to the care of God as I understood Him. The God I understood was either too frightening or too illusory.

I lasted almost 90 days. I found some meetings where real recovery was happening. I got a sponsor. I read the literature. I tried to pray. I listened much more than I spoke. But in the end, my alienation from the God of my understanding and my inability to trust the God of their understanding made it impossible for me to stay. In a group where the unifying premise is faith in an intercessory Higher Power, someone like me, who continued to question God's day-to-day presence, wasn't just an annoyance. Eventually I became a threat.

One evening, in an OA group specifically for people following the strict food plan I'd learned at the rehab center, some fervent believers began to verbally attack a woman who challenged the plan's strict weigh-and-measure-all-food parameters. I jumped to her defense, stating she had every right to ask questions, and quickly became another target of their verbal attack. One woman actually said, "I'm glad both of you are on the same side of the room so your diseased thinking won't contaminate all of us." Things eventually calmed down, but on the way home from the meeting, I decided the believers were correct. I didn't belong.

The next day, when I broached the question of my quitting OA with my therapist, her reaction surprised me. I was sure she was going to talk me into staying with it. Instead she said, "Connie, I'm so relieved. You're losing yourself in that group. Your sense of humor is gone. Your self-hate is at an all-time high. I know Twelve Step programs are the answer for a lot of people, but I don't think they're right for you—at least not right now."

As we continued our search, Ross and I also attended some workshops at Omega Institute of Holistic Studies in New York. The institute's goal to create dialog between the fields of science, spirituality, creativity and healing seemed like a perfect fit for us.

In one of the Omega classes I came as close as I'd come, before Hellinger work, to finding a crack in my protective wall of cynicism. We attended a workshop with Harville Hendricks and his wife Helen Hunt, coauthors of *Receiving Love* and *Getting the Love You Want.* I liked Helen's contribution to the weekend. She was amazingly honest, vulnerable and caring. When she offered a course on women's spirituality the next summer, I decided to give it a try. I thought she might just be the person who could help me understand and be open to spirituality.

Unexpectedly, I was the odd man out again. For the other women in attendance, the workshop focused on merging their spiritual beliefs and practices with their emerging sense of who they were as women. I was the one in the group without a spiritual practice to share—the one with only spiritual questions.

The difference between my experience with Helen and the OA folks was that Helen and the others didn't find my questions a threat. They simply shared their stories and their own paths. Helen adapted the visualizations in the workshop to include the seekers as well as those who had already found their answers. Additionally, meeting someone as brilliant and open as Helen, who had found a spirituality that worked for her, gave me at least a small flicker of hope in the possibility.

The other experience that kept me afloat for the next 15 years was my discovery of Joseph Campbell in 1988. By this time my frustration and confusion were at an all-time high. I bounced among these three concepts:

Disbelief—there is no God. Anger—there is a God and He chooses not to answer the cries of someone who is searching for Him. And self-hate—there is a real and loving God but I'm doing something so wrong I can't connect to Him.

It was a Saturday. Ross and the kids were out. I was clicking through the channels (which, in the late '80s—before cable and remote controls—meant standing by the TV and manually cycling through all five channels) when I heard a man's voice say, "The Bible is poetry. .... When people try to read it as prose, that's where they get into trouble." I stopped clicking and sat down. As I watched the rest of Bill Moyers' interview with Campbell, I was awestruck. I just kept taking deep breaths and allowing his words to wash over me. I wondered if finally, finally, someone was saying something about spirituality I could embrace.

Joseph Campbell spent his life in the study of beliefs, mythologies and religions of every culture on the globe. He believed each was, given the temperament, geography and culture of a people, an attempt to reach out to the Transcendent. None was more right or wrong than the other. Rather, each was its culture's best attempt to understand the Incomprehensible.

He reiterated what numerous anthropologists had said: all religions were, to some extent, manmade creations. But he went a step further. He said all of them were true in this sense: They all pointed to God, to a Transcendence far beyond our abilities to categorize.

I was dumbfounded. I felt such relief. In just those few words, Campbell gave me hope. I remember thinking, *"Maybe I'm not a horrible, arrogant person because I keep rejecting the Catholic Church. Maybe I'm not terrible and stupid because I can't find the One True Religion."*

When the PBS pledge break interrupted the interview, I pledged whatever amount gave me the entire *Power of Myth* series. I couldn't wait to watch it, to share it with Ross and our friends. Over the years, Ross and I bought just about every version of Campbell's lectures and books we could find. We had Campbell's audiotapes for the car, videotapes for the TV, and books on both our nightstands. When the PBS series was reissued on DVDs, we gladly put aside our well-worn VHS tapes and ordered it.

If this was the best answer I could find, perhaps it was good enough. Joseph Campbell, while he didn't give me a sure place to rest or a way to fill my heart with peace, at least understood my questions. I wasn't alone in the search.

That's how I survived until 2005 when I discovered Hellinger's Family Constellations.

Section 3

Moving Forward

Chapter 11

The Day-to-Day Times

When a man begins to have a vision larger than his own truth...
he begins to become conscious of his moral nature.
~ Rabindranath Tagore

The philosophy behind Hellinger's Family Constellation work is multidimensional and complex. Many of Hellinger's basic tenets fly in the face of today's conventional psychological wisdom—and emotional comfort levels. Using love as the guiding force in all relationships, he challenges our accepted notions of guilt, innocence, blame and forgiveness. He shows how perceived innocence and righteous behavior are often the cause of, rather than the solution for, long-standing problems.

Every time I try to describe or summarize these concepts at the beginning of a workshop, I grapple with how to express the basics in a helpful way. Sometimes, especially when I'm speaking to therapists, I use other writer's words. Dan Booth Cohen, author of *I Carry Your Heart in My Heart*, has an amazingly thorough definition: "The Family Constellation process is a trans-generational, phenomenological, therapeutic intervention with roots in family systems therapy, existential phenomenology, and the ancestor reverence of the South African Zulus." At other times I use the profound yet succinct definition from Heinz Stark's book, *Systemic Constellation Work is an Art*: "Love is the essence of Constellation Work; all serious problems come from unconscious love and are solved with conscious love."

They are helpful starting points. But somewhere in *my* interpretation of *their* analysis, I'm aware that I'm just piling words on words to try to express something that can only be understood fully by experiencing the concepts. And when this happens, I go back to telling stories—my story or the stories of others who experienced the richness of the concepts as they affected them—as one particular insight turned their lives around.

So that's what I need to do now. There are references to the books I've found most helpful at the end of this book. But now stories, not definitions, are what we need.

~

From the beginning, I knew Hellinger's work was not for the fainthearted. It was challenging on all levels—emotional, intellectual and spiritual. For Hellinger, love is not a soft, fluffy Valentine's Day emotion. Love is a law stating that no one is left out of the family system without dire consequences. It also requires that we give up our victim status and accept the parts of us that are like the perpetrators we have chosen to condemn. The insights I gained while working with Mark around this issue of giving up my victimhood led to a very different approach to my depression.

In the past, I felt unable to fight the onset of a depressive episode. When fear and hopelessness struck, I held on until they passed. I just gritted my teeth and told myself I'd make it through. My efforts went into functioning despite the depression. However, as I integrated Hellinger's insights, I began to recognize how my thinking brought on some of my depression and how I could change my

116

thoughts to rid myself of those feelings. I started to look for my own *victim thoughts* and began to refute them. As I learned to let go of the victimhood and anger I'd carried for so many years, I felt my physical as well as emotional energy coming back.

Another of Hellinger's principles concerned understanding guilt and innocence differently. His premise is that what we often feel innocent or guilty about is not what is intrinsically good or evil but what goes against the family or group's conscience. For instance, going to college, which would be seen in most families as logical and expected, could be seen in others as conceited and as rejection of family.

This concept challenged me to see my own actions and interactions with other people in a very different light. I began to understand that my view of a given situation often was just that—my view—tinted by the lenses of my accumulated opinions, theories and reactions. It wasn't Ultimate Truth

My relationships with almost everyone changed—just as they had with my mom after my first Constellation. From my new perspective, I made very different decisions.

One early incident, although small, illustrates this shift. Ross and I were at the zoo with the grandchildren, my daughter Lisa, and my daughter-in-law Leslie. As we were looking over the wall at one of the animal enclosures, Ross, who already had one of the grandkids on his shoulders, bent down and picked up another one. I immediately panicked, fearing he'd lose his balance and one or both children would fall out of his grasp and over the walls. From my perspective, he was acting irresponsibly. In my fear, I snapped at him to put them down and act like an adult.

Ross, whose focus was on the children all enjoying the zoo, resented both my doubt about his strength and my comment about his maturity. He angrily maintained he was perfectly capable of holding two children at the same time. When Lisa tried to defuse the moment, I snapped at her too. A few moments later he put both of the kids down. It had been a quiet confrontation, probably one Leslie didn't even notice, but it left an uneasy feeling between Ross, Lisa and me.

In the old days, I would have carried the hurt feelings for the rest of the day, or—with some feeling of superiority about how *I* didn't want to be the one to ruin the day—I would have acted like nothing happened and been quite judgmental if Ross and Lisa couldn't forget my outburst and do likewise.

This time, however, I saw it differently. When I opened myself up to seeing the incident objectively, I realized I was the one at fault. I'd become angry because Ross wasn't doing things the way I thought was best. With just a slight shift in focus, I understood that Ross hadn't done anything wrong. He'd just done something in a way that I wished he hadn't. I had to let go of my self-righteousness.

When I walked away from the group and let the truth sink in, I couldn't hold on to my anger. After a few moments, I rejoined everyone, waited until the kids and Leslie were distracted at the next animal exhibit and quietly apologized to Ross and Lisa. Ross just nodded and went back to playing with the grandchildren, but Lisa stopped dead. "You know, Mom, when I saw you walk toward us, I was all ready for round two. I certainly didn't expect an apology. Thanks."

I doubt either of them remembers the incident, but it's still with me today. It marked the day I started to understand how often I judged situations—and tried to manipulate them—from only my perspective, assuming mine had to be the one-and-only correct one.

Naturally, I didn't accept all of Hellinger's principles hook, line and sinker. There were lots of days I'd fight with a concept I'd read.

Hellinger's philosophy was not touchy-feely; his words were often strong and inflexible. On the other hand, when I gave them some time to grow within me, when I allowed myself to soften around them, I often found his harsh truths to be much kinder than the soft truths of others.

One of the most profound changes in my attitude came about when I read a talk Hellinger delivered in Garmisch-Partenkirchen in 2004. I'd been cruising the Internet for quite a while, reading snippets of things about and by Hellinger and knew I should stop soon and start dinner. I scrolled down the screen and saw I had just a few paragraphs before I got to a new section, and decided the end of this selection would be my stopping point.

As I continued reading, I stood up to get ready to go downstairs. And when I got to the lines below my knees buckled—just like in the cliché—and I fell right back into the chair. Hellinger said:

> I'll explain in an example. A client complains about his parents or about the hardships of his childhood. Originally we had pity or compassion with the client and thought: "Well, we'll help him." But now, if I think philosophically, there is nothing bad. It cannot be.
>
> If there is a creative force behind everything, then there is nothing that can be in opposition to it. So now I look at the client's situation philosophically and expect him to do the same and to say: **"Whatever it was: Thank you. I take it as a source of strength.** I take these parents as the special ones who gave to me this special source of strength, which has been essential for my life."

"Jeez," I thought, *"if I believe this, everything in my whole life will change—again. And if I don't believe it, do I really believe in Hellinger's*

work at all? Here it is—his philosophy concerning parents and children, distilled to its purest essence. I can either disagree and leave Hellinger's path or I can agree and take the next steps down the road."

I sensed the enormity of that choice. If I accepted this idea, it would mean my reaction to all my childhood—to the bad as well as the good—had to be the same: Thank you.

Wow.

As I started downstairs to the kitchen, I began questioning the premise. It had to be too radical to be true! *"No, I'm sure there's a major flaw in his logic somewhere."* But as I began cooking, the one thing I couldn't escape was the immense potential in Hellinger's words.

"OK, Con," one part of my brain said, *"what harm would it do if you believed this? If, instead of seeing everything that happened as the cause of your problems, you could see it as the source of your strength, would you be better or worse off? Better, right?"*

"Yeah, but...." another part of me replied.

"And can you really ever change the past? No. Despite your thoughts and fantasies about it, your past is just that, your past. It was what it was—no matter how you wish things had been different. So with that reality in mind, is it better to fight it or accept it?"

"OK, it's better to accept it, but..."

"And if you're going to accept it, is it better to accept it as a gift for which you can be thankful or a curse that remains a burden the rest of your life?"

"Well, a gift, of course, but..."

And then, my wonderful mind very bravely stepped out of the way and allowed my body to feel what that would feel like. For just a few seconds, I simply felt the effect of Hellinger's words in my body.

"Whatever it was, thank you. I take it as a source of strength."

It felt good and strong and peaceful—so good that I had no reason to go back to the alternative way of thinking.

By the time I'd finished making supper that evening, Constellation work had given me another gift. I just let go—not 100%, but to the degree I was able—of a ton of hurt and self-pity and justified self-righteousness. I embraced the idea, not because it was the right thing or the smart thing to do, but because it felt so damn good when I did.

I also made one further change. As I continued to understand and practice Hellinger's principles, my physical and emotional energy continued to increase. After a few more months, I started to wonder if my extremely high dosage of antidepressants was still necessary. I wasn't anti-medication. Antidepressants had been a lifesaver when I'd really needed them. But now, more than ten years later, I wasn't sure I still did.

At this point, I wasn't seeing a therapist regularly, so I carefully researched the methods of safely reducing my dosage and began the slow process of very gradually reducing my intake of fluoxetine from 100 milligrams a day to 40. I did it cautiously; it took several months. But I did it with no ill effects and my energy continued to increase.

CHAPTER 12

A WHOLE NEW WORLD

Our mind is capable of passing beyond the dividing line
we have drawn for it. Beyond the pairs of opposites
of which the world consists, other, new insights begin.
~ Hermann Hesse

The spiritual aspects of Family Constellations crept up on me subtly. This work challenged my 40-year stance of rejecting anything I couldn't explain logically. It had been easy, before Constellations, to tell myself that others who found evidence of the spiritual in their lives were simply forgoing logic for the sake of a comforting illusion.

This wasn't true of Constellations. With Constellations, I wasn't creating something inside me that was spiritual. The spiritual *something* seemed to exist outside of me and my need to believe in it. Sure, when I chose to be open to the energy present in those rooms, I experienced something I couldn't logically explain. But even when I chose to be my old cynical self, when I doubted the concept of Constellations, something *still* happened in the workshops. Every time I attended one I witnessed total strangers correctly manifesting the emotions and circumstances from a client's past. People were touched. People healed.

I wasn't just interpreting objective facts in a spiritual manner. Something spiritual happened—independent of me. The Constellation process didn't rely on my faith. It didn't rely on my getting into a place where I could skew reality to match my belief system. It happened, objectively, outside of my control, over and over.

In a Constellation workshop a few months after my first Constellation, for example, I was chosen to represent the grandmother of a client named Gabe (a pseudonym). Mark lined up representatives for the grandmother's children. By this time, I'd read enough to know that when the children are set up in front of a mother, the mother's interest generally goes to her children. However, as the representative of *this* mother, I just couldn't look at them. As usual, I worried I was doing something wrong and the Constellation might crumble because of me. My mind raced: *Should I do what I think is appropriate and face the children or go with my feelings and keep my gaze elsewhere?* As I fussed, I remembered some advice I'd read: "When you aren't sure, don't act. Just wait until you become sure." So I waited. I just stood looking away from them. I was pretty uncomfortable.

A few minutes later, Mark asked Gabe if his grandmother had any other children, perhaps ones who had died young. Gabe said yes. He didn't know their names, but he'd been told there were at least two babies who had died soon after birth. As soon as Mark set up representatives for the two dead children, my attention—as the grandmother's representative—went directly and unwaveringly to them. My body, not just my head, turned to face them. They were the recipients of all of my emotional energy.

As the Constellation unfolded, it became clear the woman I represented had been so caught up in her grief over her lost children that she couldn't be there for her living children—including Gabe's father. This struck an immediate chord for Gabe and he and Mark went on to resolve the family entanglement. It was a good

Constellation but one that left me, as usual, both puzzled and in awe of the work. I still wondered *"How did I know to react the way I did? Where had the information to look away from the children come from?"* Certainly not from my logical brain.

Other people I knew had similar experiences. Time after time, representatives expressed emotions and thoughts both real and recognizable to participants they'd never seen before.

In a close friend's Constellation, I watched Sally (a pseudonym) take on the unusual characteristics of my friend's mother. As Sally represented the mother, she shouted and held her ears as Mark spoke. She disparaged Mark, my friend and the rest of her family. It was surely atypical behavior for a representative. *And* it was an accurate representation of the woman I'd known for 20 years. How did Sally, whom my friend had never met, know to act this outlandishly—and accurately? I had no explanation.

Another example involved my son, Ken. He'd finally agreed to come to Pittsburgh and have a Constellation done. When we met at Mark's office the night of the workshop, I could see he was there more to please me than because he was eager to have a Constellation experience.

Soon after the first Constellation of the evening got under way, Mark asked Ken to step in as a representative for the grandfather of a client I'll call Gloria. Despite his doubts, Ken agreed. Within seconds of entering the Constellation circle, Ken began to feel some really strong emotions. As he looked at the person who represented his wife—Gloria's grandmother—he felt immense hated for her. He stated, with astonishment, he was having a hard time controlling his impulse to strike her.

As the Constellation unfolded, we found out Gloria's grandparents had married just before her grandfather was shipped overseas in World War II. Although she was pregnant with his child, the grandmother fell in love with someone else. When the grandfather returned to the States, she immediately asked for a divorce. Ken's representation of the distraught and angry grandfather had been spot-on. And just like his mother, Ken was amazed and confused by what had happened in the Constellation. Where had his anger come from? Why was it so absolutely correct?

I couldn't stay away from the workshops. They fed such a need within me. Something happened in the Constellation field that was real and healing and—it took a long time for me to admit it—sacred. Again and again, something spiritual happened right before my eyes and I struggled to either understand or refute it.

Occasionally friends asked why I had such a compulsion to attend, why I cared so much. To me the answer was monumental. If Constellations were real, they would be no less than the complete negation of the way I'd lived for the last 40 years—and the answer to the deepest yearnings of my life.

If Constellations were real, the fabric of human life involved more than just what we could see, hear and understand with our senses. If Constellations were real, the spiritual world was real—and approachable. And if the spiritual world were real, there might be the possibility of a God who interacted with mankind. If Constellations were real, I could find the answer, at 58 years of age, I couldn't find at 21. After so many years without a spiritual base, I could once again have what I thought was impossible. I could go back to my very first quest as a child—my search for a loving and knowable God—and this time find a truth that would withstand the doubts and skepticism I'd come to think were unassailable. If Constellations were real, I could have a place in the spiritual world to put down my feet without fearing the entire surface would crumble and leave me with nothing but a cavernous hole.

Naturally, the self-protective part of me wanted to go no further with this illogical work. *"I've been wandering through most of my adult life, unable to find solid ground. If the solid ground had always been here, why hadn't anyone (Anyone!) shown it to me before?"*

And beyond the anger, I think, was fear. *"What if I once again believe in something beyond myself? What if I make a leap of faith and find out, one more time, that this road leads nowhere?*

But another part of me, the part that had just awakened after years of Chronic Fatigue Syndrome, that had found something to cut through the depression and give life meaning, chased these new concepts like a puppy chasing a squirrel!

That summer Ross and I drove to North Carolina where I participated in a three-day workshop with Stephan Hausner, a gifted German constellator. I also signed up for the first U.S. Family Constellation Conference in Portland, Oregon and looked into going back to school for a Master's Degree in Counseling. I continued to read every book on Constellation work I could find, attended every workshop Mark facilitated and maintained my morning rituals. I began to meditate. I edged out the cynical part of me a bit more every day.

The Portland Constellation Conference astonished me. It often felt surreal. I attended workshops by authors whose books I'd just read. I found myself sitting at dinner with internationally-known facilitators and at lunch with people whose lives, like mine, had been totally changed by Constellation work.

There I met Suzi Tucker, Editor-in-Chief of *Zeig, Tucker & Theisen*, the publishers who introduced Bert Hellinger's books to the United States. A few weeks earlier, Mark told me Suzi would be speaking at the conference and manning the ZTT table. I'd emailed her and asked if she needed help with sales. Luckily for me, she said yes. As we worked together between conference presentations, she introduced me to some Constellation pioneers and I picked up odds and ends of the history of Constellations in the United States. More important, the conversations Suzi and I had between sales created the foundation for a deep and warm friendship.

The Constellations themselves were what amazed me most. Despite the international flavor of the conference, despite the range of facilitators and topics, every Constellation still looked, in essence, like the ones I attended in Pittsburgh. I think I expected Mark's Constellations to look quite different from other facilitators'—just as I'd expect two cognitive therapists' sessions to look different from each other because of their personalities. Yet in almost all cases, the rhythm, energy and results were the same. The field was created and, once established, produced similar movements and similar insights. Total strangers represented other people's family members with uncanny accuracy, and people seemed to experience life-altering changes in their perceptions.

My inner cynic began to wilt. In Portland I had to face the reality—not just the possibility—that there was some sort of force independent of the facilitator at work in this process.

After I returned from the conference, Ross and I made some big decisions. I told him I wanted to pursue Constellation work in earnest—to become a counselor and Constellation facilitator. He supported me completely, although it meant dipping into our retirement savings. I applied to grad school and signed up for a training workshop to become a Family Constellation facilitator.

As 2005 drew to a close, I boxed up the polymer clay and art books that had been my life as I recuperated from CFS.

CHAPTER 13

A SEA OF CHANGE

If we don't change, we don't grow.
If we don't grow, we are not really living.
~ Gail Sheehy

The year 2006 exploded with new beginnings. In mid-January I began grad school at a university about an hour's drive from home. I also began the year-long course in *The Principles and Practice of Bert Hellinger's Family Constellation Work* led by Mark Wolynn and Suzi Tucker.

My first graduate school and I were a poor match. The good classes were OK but not particularly challenging; the bad ones were worse than no class at all. It was a sad example of what can go wrong when administrators underestimate their students and tenured faculty take advantage of the fact that they can't be fired. I definitely felt I was paying for a piece of paper rather than learning. If this had been my only option, I probably would have simply left school without my MA. In the midst of a complaint fest with a fellow student, however, I learned about another program—seven minutes from my house—at a satellite of Waynesburg University.

I heard about it on a Saturday. I had an appointment to speak with Dr. Jim Hepburn, the dean of the school, on Tuesday. I signed up immediately.

Waynesburg was a different world. I felt both challenged and welcomed. Jim had a strong sense of integrity and a good knowledge of what makes an excellent teacher. He built a solid and caring faculty. The teaching staff consisted of counselors and psychologists working in the field. They genuinely cared about preparing us for the challenges of counseling. They set the bar high and loaded us with practical information.

It was a cohort program; everyone in a particular graduating class attended classes together in a strict cycle that would enable them to complete 60 credits, including practicum and internships, in six trimesters. Unfortunately they were beginning their third trimester when I enrolled. The only way I could catch up was to take 51 credits in the coming year. At 59, I had to seriously consider the time factor. If I didn't graduate fast, I'd never get a real job. I decided to go for it.

Although I joined the group two trimesters after everyone else, my fellow cohort members were welcoming and kind from day one. Things I worried might be a problem—my age, my weight, my lack of experience in the field—were inconsequential to them. From the first class, they accepted me as one of the team and were encouraging and supportive. I felt at home by the middle of the first trimester. Today I'm still blessed with friendships begun there.

After years of having too much time on my hands, I entered a world in which every minute counted. Psychology had been my undergraduate major and had remained a hobby. Over the years, I skimmed the surface of a lot of concepts and theories. Now I had to understand the essence of psychological principles well enough to prepare me to help real people. I was stretched by the experience and well served by my professors.

With Ross' unflagging support, I managed to finish with my cohort.

For six 3-day weekends in 2006, I also attended classes in the theory and practice of Constellations. I had no grad school classes on Fridays and some flexibility with my internship calendar. So I just wove the weekends into the schedule. Luckily, the reading I'd done in the ten months before the training held me in good stead for the theoretical base of the course.

Suzi and Mark were experienced facilitators and exceptional teachers. There was no down-time in their classes. They had an immense store of knowledge to share with us and they shared it generously. It was an intense learning experience in which the theoretical knowledge was enhanced with heavy-duty experiential work. We did hands-on work as clients, representatives and, in the last few sessions, as facilitators.

One of the real gifts of that training was the difference in Suzi's and Mark's facilitation style. The contrast gave us a broad base on which to build our own style. Another gift was the 11 people who took the training with me, and whose lives provided the fodder for many of the experiential aspects of the learning. Everyone came to class ready to be challenged and vulnerable. Everyone took risks. We all supported and respected each other. Again I made friends who are still important in my life today. One woman, Carla, lived just a few miles from me, and we carpooled. We were about the same age, had Italian Catholic backgrounds and were definitely Daddy's Girls. Often, after eight hours of class, we'd stop for dinner and talk another three or four hours, relating what we'd learned to ourselves. Talk about blessings. Our friendship, which naturally enhanced our lives, also improved our understanding of the work.

However, the biggest change in 2006 happened unexpectedly on January 28th. My mom suffered a debilitating stroke that left her completely paralyzed on her right side and unable to speak. As Ross and I rushed to the hospital, I don't know which of us said it out loud first, but we were both thinking the same thing—how grateful we were my mom and I had worked things out between us before this happened.

We went from hope to despair to hope so many times during the next nine months. Only one thing remained constant the entire time. Although Mom couldn't speak or move her right side, her brain continued to function well.

I still remember that first day in the hospital. About a dozen of us gathered in her room, unsure of how much the stroke had affected her. As we all hovered around her bed, Mom kept motioning for my youngest sister, Duffy, to move closer. Mom seemed really concerned about something. We all leaned in a little, thinking she had something important to share. Finally, as Duff moved very close, Mom struggled to stretch her good hand out—and straightened Duff's sweater. Then she smiled, fell back and relaxed. From then on we knew that, behind the paralysis and inability to speak, Mom was still Mom and still very aware.

She brought the full force of her personality and strength to her recovery. From the beginning, she worked harder at rehab than the physical therapists required. If they wanted ten reps from her, she always gave them twelve. Mom also worked hard with the speech therapist and recovered a tiny portion of her ability to speak. While she couldn't say even the smallest *intentional* sentence, she could recite things she'd learned by rote when she was a child. For example, she could sing Happy Birthday, occasional bits of old songs and say the Hail Mary and Our Father.

This ability brought her so much joy and some wonderful moments with each of us children. At the beginning of each year, Mom always wrote all of the family birthdays on her calendar. Now Mom's husband, Ed, kept her informed of them on his daily visits. So when we'd come to visit her on our birthdays, she would always proudly sing to us. Then, both she and the birthday kid would cry.

This rote ability also led to two of my favorite memories.

I'd taken Mom for a walk around the nursing home grounds in her wheelchair on an early spring day. We'd been out about 15 minutes when the skies got dark. As the storm quickly approached, I hurried back to the building. Knowing I wouldn't make it to the main entrance before the rain started, I entered a side door. I went down an unfamiliar hallway and ended up at the nursing home's chapel.

Thinking Mom would enjoy going to the chapel for a while, I pushed her wheelchair up the middle aisle to one of the first pews. She gave me a look that said, "Now, sit down here beside me, young lady." I sat. After a few moments, I thought this might be a good time to practice her speech therapy by saying some prayers together.

"Mom, do you want to pray out loud?" Her eyes said yes.

"OK, let's do it."

Together we said an Our Father and a couple Hail Mary's. When we finished, I glanced over to see if she was ready to leave and noticed an interesting expression on her face. It was definitely the look of "Gotcha!" Immediately I understood. For the last 35 years she'd been telling me she prayed every day that, before she died, she'd see me back in church, praying. This rainy day, despite my best efforts to prove her wrong, she got an answer to her prayers. We both burst out laughing.

A few months later, after she'd suffered another serious stroke, she lost a good deal of her ability to sing and pray out loud. Then the phrase *"No Way!"* became the staple of her vocabulary. She'd use it to mean everything—yes, no, up, down, hello, goodbye, I'm hot, I'm cold—everything. It was her one-stop communication shop. As with her first stroke, she again had trouble chewing and swallowing and needed to eat the puréed meats and veggies she hated.

One afternoon, as I helped her with lunch, she really fought me hard. As soon as I got a spoonful of that brown and green mush anywhere near her mouth, she pushed me away with a vigorous "No Way!" After about eight or nine tries, she suddenly burst into song. "NO WAY in the manger, no crib for his bed," she sang. Her eyes lit up with delight. She'd made a joke and she knew it! I put down the spoon, took off her bib and on that summer day, we both sang several loud choruses of her newly-minted Christmas carol, *NO WAY in the Manger*, as I wheeled her back to her room.

The song became our inside joke. After that day, no matter what else we did during our visits, at some point we'd sing our song together—and she'd always smile. Toward the end of her life, as her ability to speak decreased even more, the only place in the song she'd join me was on the word *hay* as I sang, "... The little lord Jesus, asleep in the hay." But she always smiled.

On the other hand, her awareness sometimes made things harder for her. I remember one day trying to decode what her annoyed stares at the window meant. "Do you want to go out, Mom?" That wasn't it. "Do you want me to open the window?" Definitely not. "Do you want me to close the curtains.... pull up the shade.... pull down the shade?" She was really getting frustrated with me. Finally I walked over to her wheelchair, bent down to her level and looked at the window. "Oh, do you want me to take the dead flowers out of the arrangement on the windowsill?" Bingo!

Damn. It must have been so frustrating to be able to think so clearly and be unable to communicate what you were thinking. As a kid, I'd read about people in iron lungs, who were able to move only their heads. At the time, it was the most horrible existence I could imagine. But, this was much worse. At least the iron-lung people could talk. Being trapped inside her body, with her brain functional but without the ability to communicate, was horrific. I still shudder when I think of it. I admired Mom's determination and will to keep trying. I'm not at all sure I would have had her fortitude in those circumstances.

Our initial optimism as Mom stormed through the first months of physical therapy was short-lived. She did manage to return home to Ed for a short while, but after little more than a month, she suffered another massive stroke that made home care impossible. Fortunately, my sister Mary, the nurse who had chosen Mom's first excellent rehab facility, got her into the Catholic nursing home where Mom had once served as a Eucharistic Minister. The first few days were hard for all of us—especially Mom. But because she knew so many of the staff, she soon relaxed into their care.

Every day I spent with her, from January to her final day on October 11th, felt like an unbelievable gift. I never drove up to a hospital, rehab facility or nursing home without realizing how lucky, how unbelievably damned blessed, I was that the Constellation work had given us a loving and deep relationship for her last years. My mom had been hospitalized often during my life. Complications seemed to surround even the simplest illness or procedure. And just like my brother and sisters, I faithfully visited her every time. But in truth, before the Constellation work and our reconciliation, I was there because it was my responsibility. She was my mother. I was a dutiful daughter, so I showed up and did all the *right* things. Did she sense my emotional distance? I now have no doubt. I'm sure my mandatory filial devotion led to a lot of the tension between us.

How different it was during her last illness. Before the stroke, we'd had a good relationship for almost a year. We'd spent time together really talking. We enjoyed being together. After her stroke, we grew even closer. When I visited her, I came because I wanted to be with her. As I watched her work in rehab, I genuinely admired her strength and perseverance. When we played poker together, I loved watching her cheat to let me win a hand if she felt she won too often. I loved wheeling her down to the big glass cage in one of the rehab facilities and watching her delight as she viewed the baby birds.

For so much of my life I'd resented the attention Mom got wherever she went. Now I celebrated her strong personality that—right up to the end—got her special consideration from just about everyone who came in contact with her. I could tell the staff really liked her. So did the other residents. As I wheeled her around the halls, other patients would stop us and pat her hand. Their families stopped and talked with her. When we were in her room, little old nuns would wheel themselves up to her bedside and say a prayer for her. Hospice volunteers who came to say the rosary would always stay and talk with her—often sharing intimate stories and feelings of their own. They could sense she heard and understood them. Until almost her last day, she'd reward each one with that twinkle in her eyes that made even her crooked smile beautiful.

Mom and I spent the last day of her life together. On October 11th, I went to my internship at the drug and alcohol outpatient facility as usual. The morning's program was full. However, as sometimes happens in these facilities, the number of patients dropped drastically for the afternoon program. When I returned from lunch, we had two clients and three therapists. I was definitely superfluous. So, knowing that Mom's time was getting short, I asked my supervisor if I could rearrange my schedule to visit her that day.

When I got to the nursing home, Mom was still coherent enough to recognize me but she was highly agitated, unable to get comfortable. From my experience with the deaths of Ross' mom, uncles and aunt, I knew she was in her final days. I sang a couple rounds of "No Way in the Manger," with Mom now unable to chime in on even the last word. Only her eyes let me know she still recognized our joke.

Once more I held her hand and told her how much I loved her and how glad I was she was my mom. And then, truth be told, I just rambled. I told her stories about the grandchildren, how things were going in school, how I felt about working in a drug and alcohol facility. Anything I could think of. One of the hospice volunteers came in to say the rosary with Mom and stayed and talked with both of us. I was amazed at how close she had become to my mom—especially because they met after Mom had lost her ability to speak.

I left close to dinner time so Mom could drift off a little before Ed came for his evening visit. As I kissed her goodbye, I had no idea it was for the last time. Less than four hours later I got the call from my sister saying Mom had died. I'll never forget the gratitude I felt as I realized we'd gotten to spend her last day together, that a fluke in my schedule had allowed her to have someone with her that entire afternoon.

Ross and I rushed to the nursing home. As I hugged her lifeless body one last time, my thankfulness for our last two years together replaced my sadness.

My first two phone calls that evening were to Lisa and Ken. My third was to Mark. Standing alone in the deserted nursing-home dining room, tears streaming down my face, I thanked him one more time for working with me, for the miracle he had helped bring into my life. I thanked him for the best two years my mom and I had in my adult life. I reminded him of what he'd said the first day I met him. "If you give this approach a chance, I can assure you that you'll come back some day and say to me, 'Mark, I'm so grateful we did this work while my mother was still alive.'"

I did. I was. I still am.

CHAPTER 14

TWO HUNDRED CONSTELLATIONS LATER

At the boundary we arrive at insight.
~ Bert Hellinger

I facilitated my first Constellation in late summer of 2006. By this time, I was in the middle of grad school and Hellinger training and had witnessed almost 200 Constellations with numerous facilitators.

My facilitation was a one-on-one Constellation for Regina, a neighbor of my friend Emily. Emily asked me to go to the physical rehab center where Regina (a pseudonym) was recuperating from a near-fatal car accident. She'd shattered her pelvis and broken her leg in a crash caused by her driving drunk. Emily thought Regina needed some special motivation to give her the strength to face the grueling months of physical therapy ahead and to come to grips with her alcoholism.

My hands shook as I got out of the car at the rehab center. I knew Constellations worked, but I didn't know if I had what it took to facilitate one well. I breathed deeply as I talked myself into the building: *"Hey, I've done everything I know how to do. I've reread tons of Hellinger, gone over my notes, talked to both of my instructors, and, in meditation, called on my family and Regina's family to be with us as we worked. It's time to just take the next step—time to do the work."*

I relaxed as soon as I met Regina. From her electric wheelchair, she gave me a mini-tour of the facility. We chatted a while. Her easy way with the staff and quick self-deprecating laugh were endearing. It was easy to focus on her and forget my apprehension.

After the tour we went to her room. I explained how one-on-one Constellations worked and gave her some background on Constellations in general. She was eager to give it a try.

We both took a minute to switch gears and center ourselves. I asked the traditional Constellation questions to get a feel for her goals and past family dynamics. We set up a Constellation on the table beside Regina's bed using small wooden figures to represent significant people—her mom, dad, and her sister, Dana. Her sister was deceased. Regina told me where to place each one in reference to her issue—healing in body and spirit.

Up to this point I'd been OK. I had been walking on familiar ground. I'd done the steps I'd been trained to do and asked the questions I'd learned to ask. I'd kept my fear in check to be of service to Regina and her family. But with everything set up, I found myself at the end of charted territory. I could feel the panic forming in the pit of my stomach. I felt as if I were on the edge of a huge expanse of land, knowing I must move forward but totally unable to decide where I should place my foot next.

One more time, just as I was about to open my mouth and begin, I took a deep breath, focused on our families and asked for their help. And in that brief moment, in that one deep-breath's time, everything shifted. Before I could say a word, Regina began to cry. I closed my mouth. The next words, the next steps, were Regina's, not mine. And with such gratitude I wanted to cry too, I simply stepped back and let Regina and her family lead the Constellation. The absolute truth, although she remembers it differently, is that I did very little more.

Regina's words and experiences carried us along. She said things to me that she'd never said to anyone before, including herself. She made connections to past events in her life—to people in her life—that had never been clear to her. For the first time she allowed the full force of her sister's death to hit. She acknowledged her unexpressed fear that Dana hadn't died from an accidental drug overdose, but had committed suicide. She allowed herself to express both her intense anger with Dana for dying and her own guilt for not recognizing the depths of Dana's pain.

At one point, she looked at me, tears streaming down her face, and said, "Connie, you're killing me here. You're making me go where I don't want to go." And all I could think was, "*I had nothing to do with getting you to this place. Some force way beyond me—the knowing field, your own subconscious, the energy of family members long dead, your sister—is at work here. Not me.*"

But I said none of that. I said almost nothing. I just sat and let the images and the tears come. We witnessed them together. My only job, for a while, was to hold the space for her to see what the Constellation offered.

When she finished, I did what I was trained to do. I gathered the images she'd brought to the surface and laid them out in front of her. Then, working with what she now knew to be true, we together reframed them into a healing Constellation image.

Just as Mark had done in my Constellation, I led Regina through a guided visualization. In it, she told Dana how much she loved her and how, despite her fears and sadness, she honored her as her sister. She affirmed that Dana would always have a place in her heart. Then, confirming her own desire to continue living, Regina asked

Dana to bless her, to be happy for her as she continued to live—as Regina chose not to follow her into death.

The words weren't easy for Regina. I witnessed her courage as she pulled them from somewhere very deep inside. The tears returned but they were different. Now they were tears of acceptance and love. She chose, in that moment, to accept her sister into her heart and to forgive both Dana and herself for their very human weaknesses. She made the decision to respect and honor her own life—to go on with her life despite what her sister had chosen.

Then the Constellation was over. The feeling in the room shifted; the intensity disappeared and we were both back to our normal selves. I gave Regina some homework—a few short sentences to say twice a day—to continue to affirm what she felt and said in the Constellation. I suggested she not talk too much about what happened—just allow it to settle inside her. A few minutes later, an orderly knocked on her door and Regina left for another round of physical therapy.

As I walked to my car, three thoughts vied for attention in my brain. First, I truly admired Regina's courage and honesty. We could not have gotten to that place of healing if she hadn't given her entire heart to the process.

Second, I was amazed by how the Constellation had unfolded. I recalled the things I'd done to set it up. I remembered asking the questions and setting up the figurines. But mostly I remembered the distinct feeling of not knowing what to do next—of coming to the end of my knowledge—and then, of witnessing the Constellation process take over.

The thing I feared most had happened. Despite all my preparation, I'd reached a point where I didn't know what to do next. And, and, and—it hadn't mattered. The family energy—the knowing field I'd experienced so many times in Mark's workshops—had been present in that hospital room with us. I still didn't understand it, but I knew I'd experienced it. Some force beyond me had worked with us.

Third, although doing this kind of phenomenological work felt a lot like walking a tightrope over the Grand Canyon without a net, I knew I wanted to do it.

My work with Regina marked the end of my major doubts about Constellations. I'd experienced them from every angle, in every role, and knew something real happened in them. I couldn't precisely describe or measure this *something*—but it didn't matter. I based my acceptance on things I could objectively verify. People in Constellation workshops were real. Both the person requesting the Constellation and the representatives in the circle existed outside me. They registered in my left brain; they could be seen, heard, and touched. Their experiences were verifiable. My own experiences as a client, representative and facilitator were real and verifiable. It was foolish to deny them.

I assumed I now understood the essence of Constellation work.

CHAPTER 15

THE CIRCLE OF GENERATIONS

The past is never dead. It's not even past. All of us labor in webs spun
long before we were born, webs of heredity and environment,
of desire and consequence, of history and eternity.
~ William Faulkner

Then experiences I couldn't readily explain began happening outside the Constellation workshops, outside the realm of outer verification. They happened to me alone, in the private work I did around my parents and grandparents. Again, Constellation work challenged my cynicism.

According to Hellinger, the proper balance in a family is upset when a child—often acting out of innocence and the desire to make the family better—goes against the natural order of love and takes on the role of the adult and caretaker to parents. This is especially true for Daddy's Girls and Mamma's Boys—children who, in their love for a parent, sometimes see themselves as the real love in that parent's life.

I was definitely a Daddy's Girl. I adored my dad. For most of my life I believed my dad could do no wrong and all of my parents' problems were caused by my mom. In my view, I thought my job was to make things more bearable for Dad, whom Mom didn't fully understand or appreciate. I was the one he talked to about poetry and politics. I shared his love of science fiction and mythology. Especially in my late teens, as my parents' marriage started to crumble, I saw myself as the one who *really* understood and loved him.

In one of our follow-up sessions, Mark pointed out the results of this kind of thinking.

"Con, holding this image of your dad not only kept a wedge between you and your mom, it keeps one between you and Ross. If your dad was the perfect man, what does that make Ross? If you continue to want Ross to be more like your dad—and therefore less like himself—how can you ever expect Ross to feel safe with your love?

"And this stance affects more than Ross' perceptions, it involves yours, too. As long as you see your dad as bigger than life, as the only man who really loved and understood you unconditionally, you're going to have real problems totally opening your heart to Ross as his wife."

Sadly, it made sense.

I decided to change how I felt about my dad, even though he'd been dead for almost 30 years. Mark helped me to write a letter to Dad. In it, I chose to see him as just a man, a normal man, and to see our relationship realistically—a regular relationship between a normal father and daughter, not one I'd idealized into mythic proportions.

> Dear Dad,
> I did everything to make you my partner. I tried to supply what I believed Mom couldn't. And I tried to ease your loneliness by being the best one for you.
> I did it, Dad, from my love.
> But it had consequences. And now I see them.

Loving you like that kept me from growing up, from becoming a full woman—a woman open to love her husband as his partner.

I lost so many years with Mom and I lost so many years of possibility with Ross.

Dad, thank you for helping me to see you as my father and not my emotional partner. Please help me, Dad, to allow Ross' love into my heart. Please help me to fully feel the presence and the beauty of my husband's love.

I love you as your daughter,

Connie

I read this letter every day after I read the one to my mom. As I did, I could feel the space in my heart, which I'd reserved only for my dad, begin to open up. I began to see Ross in a new way. I began to view traits that had irked me, because they weren't like my dad's, for what they really were—good, strong and mature attributes that made our marriage richer. Dad was a quixotic dreamer whose dreams often failed. All my life I'd loved and idealized him for that. Ross was a stubborn, disciplined, determined realist—and I'd often resented him for being one. Now I began to appreciate the gift in those traits. They gave our family emotional as well as financial stability. Ross' solidity enabled us to give our children a stable home and support as they chose their careers. It gave me the freedom to pursue my dreams. Hellinger work began to change our marriage in a very positive way.

I continued to experiment with this letter-writing practice, adding Ross and other relatives—living and dead—to the list. Eventually numerous letters became part of a ritual I used to start my day. As soon as I got up in the morning, I went upstairs to my office, logged on to the computer, lit a candle, and reread the letters. At first I did it more as a form of therapy than communication. I got my thoughts down on paper, saw how they evolved and examined new ways of thinking about my relationships. The letters to my mom and to Ross, especially, were just that—therapy. Ross was often in the next room. Mom was just a phone call away. These were my way of testing ideas in my head and heart.

However, as I continued to work in this new space, I sometimes sensed *responses* to my letters—especially from my dad. The first couple of times this happened I just assumed they were my own subconscious thoughts bubbling to the surface. But I soon noticed these thoughts and images weren't following my normal daydream pattern. They didn't simply reinforce what I knew or point out logical next steps. They gave me a little something more—ideas I wouldn't have thought of on my own and, sometimes, something I'd rather not consider.

One of the first messages from my dad shocked me. It came after I'd been reading my letter to him for a couple weeks. As I finished my morning ritual, I got a quick image of me dumping out the urn containing my dad's ashes. I immediately dismissed the thought. Those ashes were one of my prized possessions. I kept the urn on a bookcase in my study, surrounded by books I thought he would have liked. (Before he died, Dad owned a used book store—the fulfillment of one of his life-long dreams.) It felt wrong and disrespectful to even consider getting rid of his ashes.

But the image just wouldn't go away. It stayed with me all morning. Finally I felt compelled to go to the computer. Right after my old letter to Dad, I typed:

> Dear Connie,
> Letting go of the ashes will be a gift to me. It won't hurt me
> at all! It will be a gift to both your mother and me. In a way you

can't understand, it will be freeing for me. I'm glad that you're finally able to do it.

I'm so happy that you're becoming a woman. Now you can write.

Daddy

Trust me; that message didn't come from any part of me I knew! I would never have thought to write this in a million years. I certainly didn't want to do it. And what did it mean, *"finally able to do it"*? I'd never considered doing it at all!

I looked at the urn. (Ironically, it sat on a shelf surrounded by Hellinger's books.) It meant so much to have that tangible link to my dad with me. Now it seemed—if I believed this Constellation stuff—my dad wanted me to part with it. At first, I rejected the whole concept out of hand. It was just a stupid idea! Then I burst into tears. Somehow, in the totally irrational, emotional part of me, the message felt real. And I felt I needed to act on it.

I waited a couple more days hoping the feeling would lessen or go away. It didn't. The next weekend, Ross and I took the urn and drove several hours from home. I didn't want to release the ashes in a place I was familiar with, a place I might be tempted to return to. We pulled off the interstate and drove down an unfamiliar country road until we spotted a stream in the woods. Then, with Ross waiting by the car, I walked into the woods. I sat down at the edge of the stream and said my farewell to Dad's ashes and my old relationship with him and released them. I cried, but not as hard as I thought I would. In all honesty, I felt numb as I watched the ashes slowly float away. But that evening, still a little stunned as I snuggled into Ross' arms, I sensed a feeling of love and caring between us I'd never felt before.

So, perhaps because of the power of that first experience and the good it seemed to produce in my life, I went against my normally cynical nature and stayed open to these kinds of messages.

Once I made the decision to be open to them, more came. On the whole, they were good messages, and often seemed to carry with them the personality or interests of the sender. For example, messages from my paternal grandmother, who, like me, had battled depression most of her adult life, dealt with overcoming depression and realizing the love that surrounded me even when I didn't feel particularly lovable or loved. The few messages from my paternal grandfather, a WWI hero, unabashed patriot and strong believer in God, were always filled with calls to live up to my commitments.

From one of his messages:

> Honey, find your passion. This is what gives you the strength you're looking for. You can't hook strength onto the wind! Find what you believe in. And then cherish it, revere it. Stand firmly for what you believe in. Stand humbly before God. This is where the strength comes from.

Grandpa was also a great jokester, with a fondness for bad puns. The next one reflected that side of his personality. For months I had been thinking about having a pendant engraved with the Hellinger words that had changed my life—*Whatever it was, thank you.* But I kept postponing it. I felt guilty enough taking money from our savings for grad school. I didn't want to spend more on a piece of jewelry.

One day, I found myself typing this message from Grandpa:

> Get that necklace made. You need to show your *mettle*!!!!

Another message from my dad, almost a year later, has become a foundation block I still use every day. It came halfway through graduate school as I was trying to decide where I should do my second internship. I'd worried my way into quite a frenzy. After all, I was 59 years old. Time was whizzing by. I couldn't afford to make a mistake. I had three opportunities and wanted to make sure I made the best possible decision. Every day, I did a mental checklist of the alternatives in my head: *"Internship A will give me this experience, Internship B will give me that experience, Internship C seems to be what I really want, but it's not the most practical. I don't know what to do."*

I began the remarkable intellectual dance I always did when I was confused. I let the problem build until I had worked my way into fear and frustration, ending with the most negative thought I could imagine: *"Maybe I shouldn't even be in grad school so close to retirement age! By the time I get in enough hours to be licensed, I'll be 64 years old! It's really far too late to begin anything! Maybe I should just realize the folly of this before I put more money into tuition. Maybe the best thing is to quit, right now!"*

I went to bed thinking it might be better to stop halfway than to continue wasting money.

The next day, with the problem still churning away on the back burner of my brain, I began my normal morning ritual. I lit a candle, logged onto the computer and read my letters. After I read the letter to my dad, I felt a strong need to type this:

Work with the work in front of you.

That's it. I typed it into my journal, right after my most recent letter to Dad.

I went on to read the next letter, but my eyes kept being drawn back to that sentence. *"OK,"* I thought, *"it's good advice. I've got it."*

151

However, the more I tried to move on, the stronger my compulsion was to read it again. Finally I typed it in caps, in a large font, in blue, printed it out and tacked it to my bulletin board.

Over the next few days, I saw it every time I glanced up from my computer. The phrase grew on me. Slowly, it helped me put things into perspective. After a while, rather than getting into a frenzy every time I thought about the internships, I realized I couldn't make a decision until I took further action on each option. In all three cases I needed to call someone, send out some information or clarify something.

So instead of fussing and simply restating my options, I made the phone calls and filled out the forms. As soon as I did, I realized the big reason for my procrastination. I wasn't at all happy about not being in total control of the results. I'd been waiting until I could find a way to get—with 100% certainty—what I wanted before I took action. In this situation, that wasn't ever going to happen. I simply needed to act, to work with the work in front of me.

As I further relaxed with the letter responses, another phase started. Sometimes, after my morning ritual or when I tried to keep my mind clear to meditate, tiny visualizations would pop into my head. Unlike a movie, where a scene is acted out in front of me, these were flashes of pictures followed by words explaining the pictures. And as I stayed focused on the experiences, the flow of the pictures and words became more and more seamless.

The first of these visualizations happened one evening in February, 2007 about four months after my mom died. I had just started my last semester of grad school and was doing an internship in an outpatient clinic for people with severe mental illness.

It was the first in a series of three related visualizations that took place over several months. All three took place in the same meadow. As each began, I stood with my mom surrounded by generations of my female ancestors.

I sensed this image was important. So in between the flashes of pictures, I typed what the women said to me:

> We know you and love you personally, Connie, not just you as our representative here on earth, not just as the child of our children. We've been where you are. We aren't angels who have no feeling. We're women, just like you. We've felt what you feel. We understand. Our feet have walked your roads. And, just as you feel concern and respect for your clients [at the clinic], we feel respect and love for you. This isn't some esoteric exercise. **This is flesh and blood loving flesh and blood.** We understand you. We love you, Connie.

As I typed, my heart ached with gratitude and wonder. But there was still a part of me thinking, *"Maybe this is my own creation—my way of creating a bond between Mom and me after her death."* Then the next scene appeared.

A very short, arthritic old woman broke away from the group and came up and patted me on the butt. After that, she walked in front of me and looked up with eyes so brown and deep I needed to catch my breath. I could feel her wisdom and love. She smiled and said, "We have you covered there." At first I didn't understand. Sensing my confusion, she said, "Take some risks, honey. We'll cover your ass!"

I laughed so hard I started to cough. No part of me—not even my subconscious—would have dared to create a punch line for what had been such a solemn vision.

153

After I took a couple deep breaths and centered myself again, the vision continued:

> "We understand you from our depth. We approach you with humility and love, but also with wisdom and power. Don't underestimate this; don't underestimate us."

These words, this experience, did not come from a place I knew. The next vision occurred several weeks later.

I was again in the field encircled by women in the family. As I stood, each of the women brought flowers to me. They placed a wreath on my head; they handed me flowers; they put leis around my neck. When I could hold no more, they brought out a long sleeveless coat. As they put it on me, I could see it was made of roses and scraps of cotton cloth. It was heavy and smelled wonderful. I didn't look closely at the robe but I had a sense of hundreds of pale yellow and pink roses on the top and darker roses near the bottom.

I wanted some words here, too. I wanted them to say something I could write down and reflect on. But this was strictly a visual image. When I asked for words, they simply motioned for me to really look at the coat—to notice the scraps of cloth as well as the roses. I glanced at the coat again but, on that day, I didn't look at it for long. I was too immersed in the scent and beauty of the roses.

~

The third took place several months later, at the end of the Second U.S. Constellation Conference in October, 2007. This conference experience was so different from the first one two years earlier. I'd completed my Hellinger Training. I had my MA in Counseling.

I wasn't a starry-eyed new kid. So I guess I was open to a deeper experience. But I still wasn't prepared for what happened.

The second workshop of the conference really touched me deeply. In a talk called *Facing Grief,* Brigitte Sztab, a Constellation facilitator from Washington, spoke about her own grief and how the lessons she'd learned from Constellation work had guided her through it. There was a crystal clarity in her talk. There was nothing guarded or self-serving in her words. She shared far more than intellectual knowledge. I could hear both the raw vulnerability of her pain and the first inklings of healing.

This workshop set the tone of the conference for me—and stirred a nagging fear in me. It's the fear I think every parent and grandparent always tries to keep far, far under the surface—the fear of losing a child or grandchild. And try as I might, despite the fact that this had not been the grief experience Brigitte had spoken about, I couldn't keep those feelings from popping up again and again during the conference.

By the time I attended the last workshop three days later, I was overwhelmed with tons of new information and experiences. I felt a little drained and glad the last speakers were facilitators I knew and liked. I settled in to listen and perhaps gain just one more insight. But toward the end of the talk, something triggered a reaction that had been building inside me since Brigitte's workshop. An innocent comment about vulnerability collided with the hidden fear I'd been carrying and I was suddenly caught in a downward spiral of uncontrollable terror and grief. Tears streamed down my face. I felt embarrassed. I wasn't someone who cried in public. Even when I participated in truly heart-wrenching Constellations, I remained dry-eyed. Now tears flowed uncontrollably.

After the talk, ignoring people I'd wanted to say goodbye to, I just turned around and pretended to be looking out a window until everyone left. I went outside and sat on a chair facing away from the walkways and waited for the tears to stop. They didn't. Perhaps 15 minutes later, I remembered the book table I'd been manning and worried there might be some folks who wanted to buy books before they left the conference. This brought the crying to a stop. I wiped away the tears and headed to the main hall.

When I walked into the main conference lodge, it was empty. Everyone else had gone to the closing ceremony. In my strange state of—whatever it was—sorrow, grief, emotional breakdown—I had completely forgotten about the closing ceremony.

Once I knew no one needed me, the feelings of intense grief came back. I would have gone back to my room and taken a nap—cried myself to sleep. But it was the final day of the conference; we'd already packed our belongings into the car and left our room keys at the desk. I looked for some place to go as the tears began again. I spotted a cluster of chairs on a little mezzanine away from the main lobby. Clutching my notebook, I headed there.

For the next two hours, I just cried and journaled. At first the tears dominated. Then, once, when I closed my eyes, the most amazing thing happened. The visualization of my women ancestors gathering around me in the meadow came back again with striking clarity. I picked up my pen and alternated between visualizing and writing. This is a summary of my notes from that afternoon:

> I am again standing in the field wearing the same robe of flowers and scraps of fabric. Now the tone is much more somber. One of the old women says, "This time, Connie, really look at the fabric in the robe, not just at the flowers."
>
> As I look down, I see that the scraps of material intermingled with the darker roses aren't simply decorated fabric. As I look more closely, I see the colors on the cloth are made of blood and

mud and grass stains and dirt. So much blood and dirt—fresh blood, dried blood, dried dirt, fresh mud. I now realize they had been there the previous time, but I'd been so focused on the flowers, I hadn't noticed.

As I continue to examine the scraps, pictures begin to flash before my eyes. I begin to see women in horrific circumstances, facing the death of a child. I see mothers holding children who have died in the night; I see them watch their babies gasping their last breaths. And as I watch, I share their pain. Now I feel the pain of women who lived through what I only fear. In flashes that hit my chest like thunder, I experience the feelings of women who have lost their children. I feel their grief as if it were mine. I recognize these feelings. They're what I've felt at the worst of my deepest depressions. The difference is, in those past depressions, the pain had no reason, no connection to what was going on in my life. Now as my experience merges with theirs, the pain makes sense.

Now the screaming banshee I couldn't quiet during depressive episodes takes on meaning. It becomes the wail of a mother who has lost not just a child, but *another* child!

The pictures and feelings keep coming faster; the sorrow of the women surrounding me overtakes me. My chest aches as the images seem to crash into my heart. I experience—I'm no longer just seeing—image after image of women wailing as their sons are torn from their embrace, abducted to fight for some cause they don't understand—and are never, ever seen again.

Now I see one scene after another of women watching as the life drains from their children before their eyes. I see children with distended bellies and eyes burning with delirium lying in heaps of straw or on dirty mattresses, and watch their mothers stand by, unable to rescue them from their fate.

157

I can't stop the images or the feelings.

Now, I see young mothers dying. In these last minutes, their worst pain is knowing the horrors their children will face without them. Their despair crashes into my chest, making it hard to breathe.

The women keep coming, each with more pain than I think is possible to hold. And yet they hold it.

I see them kneel beside makeshift graves and gutters where a dead child lies covered with flies and maggots. I watch as they get up and turn back to life. I watch them return to their living children, to their broken husbands, to their hopeless futures— and carry on. I witness the deadness in their eyes—and watch them move on despite it. I watch as they pick themselves up and return home—as they rock infants, soothe frightened children, and move through the drudgery of jobs that always need to be done.

I watch them do what I know I could not do. I watch them endure the unendurable.

As the visualization started to fade, I understood these images were my ancestors' gift to me. And more deeply, I finally understood that their *lives* were their gift to me. If these women hadn't pushed on in the face of unimaginable pain, in the absence of all hope, I would not exist. Writing this now, I know these words are inadequate to describe the reality I experienced that day.

I'd been to hundreds of Constellations, completed my training and facilitated workshops. But this was the first time I *really* understood Constellation work. This was a life-changing image, a life-altering message. I realized we are all here today because we have been carried on the backs and in the hearts of our ancestors—men and women of unfathomable courage and perseverance.

For the first time in my study of Family Constellations, I truly understood the rightness, the absolute necessity of bowing in gratitude to the generations preceding us. Without their immense courage and strength, we simply would not be.

As the tears kept flowing, I realized the most important aspect of Constellation work couldn't ever be read or studied. It could only be experienced. I knew that none of what I'd learned from all the books, from all the workshops, from all the classes was as important as what I'd just seen. For the first time in my life, I understood the immensity of the gratitude we must hold for the family members who came before us. Our lives are built—not metaphorically, but in reality—on their love and courage and willingness to continue to live.

After these visions, I gave up the notion that I was creating them. They come from a place I'd never been and brought me to a totally new place in my own journey.

CHAPTER 16

FIRST PRAYERS

Praying is not about asking; it's about listening...
It is just opening your eyes to see what was there all along.
~ Chagdud Tulku Rinpoche

Before my first Constellation, I didn't pray. I searched. I reasoned. I envied people who believed God was real and approachable. I loved the e.e. cummings poem, *i thank You God for most this amazing day* and had a copy of it on my office bulletin board. I wondered what kind of experience made him write it. In an odd way, it gave me hope. But I didn't pray.

After my Constellation experiences, prayer seemed logical. Something or Someone was at work in the Constellation world—in the world beyond my senses. Something or Someone was behind all the changes in my life. Acknowledging this force felt like a reasonable step, but I didn't know how to do it. I definitely couldn't go back to the prayers of my youth.

For several months I simply said the prayers Mark recommended. They were unthreatening enough for me to say with some sincerity.

"May I be led.

May I keep my heart open.

Please, let me not be limited by what I know, but made vast by what I am open to.

Please, make me an instrument for what is needed."

I was comfortable with them because they weren't directed to anyone in particular. At this point, the best I could do was ship them off to an impersonal and hopefully benign universe.

A few months later, I created my own prayer in the middle of a restless night. After several hours, this is the best I could come up with: "OK, teach. I'm ready to learn."

It wasn't much of a prayer, but it felt like a giant leap of faith for me. By saying it, I acknowledged that Someone I couldn't see—OK, possibly God—was real and could possibly teach me a better way to live. I opened myself up to acknowledge and respect that entity—and I conceded I was willing to learn.

But the prayer also held a lot fear within it. Each time I said it, I held my breath. I worried if, since the gifts of Constellation work were so immense, the price I'd have to pay for them would be equally high. I assumed I was setting myself up for some tough lessons. My old magical image of the taskmaster God—the one I thought I'd rejected so long ago when I left the Church—was still with me.

I didn't get what I expected. I sometimes had to work hard at letting go of old beliefs, seeing things from another perspective and allowing my feelings to surface—especially the dark and angry ones. However, truth be told, the learning came incrementally. There were more good times than bad, more simple lessons than difficult ones. Sure, there were days of tears and insecurity and confusion. All in all, however, the road was pretty gentle.

But this didn't stop me from remaining fearful of what was around the next bend. *"Yeah, yeah,"* I thought, *"I'm being spoon-fed right now. But soon the real lessons are coming—and they will probably rip me in two."*

I used this prayer for nearly a year until an exercise we did with Suzi Tucker in the Hellinger training class gave me some insight into the prayer's negativity—and into Suzi's insightful way of handling spirituality. The more I'd worked with her in the training, the more I liked and trusted her. She balanced her brilliance with common sense and a quietly wicked sense of humor. She stood firmly, but unjudgmentally, in her spirituality. I thought she might be a good person to help me get a better handle on mine.

A few days later we scheduled a phone consultation. After we did some Constellation-like exercises, Suzi suggested I set up a visualization for myself that evening. After our conversation, she wrote this email to me:

> Tonight [in your visualization], I want you to visit little Connie [yourself as a little girl]. I want you to see her standing between her mother and father. I want you to look into your mom's eyes, your father's eyes, and into that little girl's eyes. Look with love and see that they look back with love. Really look, Connie. Just fill up with looking. Let [your parent's] parents come in too, and their grandparents, as many as it takes. Tell them all: **I am here now. Finally, I am here. I have grown into a woman now. I am here and I will stay.**
>
> I want you to write a new prayer from THIS place, this place where you already have everything you need, this place that is steadfast and true.

This was early 2006, before the meadow visualizations, when I wasn't used to trusting visualization work. So to heighten my chances of doing it right, I decided to wait until I was exhausted. I theorized that, if I were tired enough, my ever-chattering brain might not have the energy to get in the way.

Long after Ross had fallen asleep that night, I got up and went upstairs to my office, lit a candle and set to work. I guess my theory had some merit because the visualization came easily. In no time, I saw an image of myself as a young child of maybe four or five. It was easy to picture my parents as they looked then and easy to talk to the little girl I used to be. I wrote this about the experience in my journal the next day:

With tears streaming down my face, I talk to little Connie. I tell her that her fears were never realized. (As we talked, I remembered the fears I'd had as a little girl—fears of another world war that would destroy our lives, fears that I would grow up and no one would love me, fears that I wouldn't have a family of my own.) I tell her I now live a life better than she could have imagined. I have a life richer than buried treasure—better than gold and rubies—better than the best ending to a fairy tale. I tell her that I have a husband who loves me deeply—who loves me more than he loves anyone else in the whole world. I tell her that I have two beautiful children, and three grandchildren, who are about her age. I assure her that the bad things she feared never happened!! We were never caught in another world war. Everyone in our family grew up and grew old. . . . We cry together for joy.

Then I look to Mom and Dad . . . I see the love in their eyes. I thank them for being my parents, for being the very best parents for me. Then, I see both sets of grandparents . . . great grandparents, Aunt Mary, Aunt Ann and Uncle Ray . . . more and more ancestors . . . until my heart is full to overflowing. I thank them all for their love and support.

And then, when I don't know what more to do, what more to think or say, they say to me, "Take the candle, go downstairs, tuck yourself in and go to sleep. We'll take care of the rest." I do. I fall asleep in minutes.

I don't wake up again until about 7:30. I wake up smiling. As I open my eyes, I'm aware of my new prayer:

Thank you for the overflowing abundance. I'll live from here.

My heart aches from the good feelings.

That prayer held me in good stead for a long time. The work I did with Suzi helped me see things so differently. Praying from gratitude and abundance felt so much better than praying from neediness and fear. It was a good beginning. Granted, the prayer still wasn't directed toward anyone in particular. But I could say it without wincing and, for me, that was a very big step forward.

CHAPTER 17

A DEEPER BROADER LEARNING

One sees clearly only with the heart.
Anything essential is invisible to the eyes.
~ Antoine de Saint-Exupery

When I finished grad school in late spring, Ross and I took the family to Disney World with some of our inheritance from Mom. The grandchildren were the perfect ages—Hannah and Steven were six; Liam was five—still young enough to treasure getting Goofy's autograph and having dinner with Mickey.

After we returned from Florida, I developed bronchitis and missed my graduation ceremony. I think my body needed a break from the non-stop activity of the last year and a half. When I recovered, I began to get the house in order, relax a little and catch up with friends and family I hadn't talked with in months. We chose to have a slow-paced summer. I decided to postpone serious job hunting until Ross returned to the university in the fall.

That's when the unforeseeable adventure began. A couple weeks after graduation, I got a phone call from Joan Clipp, the editor and founding publisher of *PolymerCAFÉ*, a craft magazine I'd contributed to when I worked in polymer clay. Joan had sold the magazine and was stepping down as editor. When the new owners asked her to suggest her replacement, she gave them my name.

Initially, I rejected the idea. I'd just put a huge dent in our savings to become a therapist. I'd spent every waking moment of the last year and a half studying both counseling and Family Constellations. How could I justify taking a job in a totally unrelated field? Didn't I owe it to myself—to our retirement savings—to work in the counseling field? I thought Ross would think so too.

But he didn't. Ross knew how much I loved to write and edit. He understood my fascination with the creative process and the people who chose to work with polymer clay. Before my Constellation, I'd even researched the idea of writing a book about polymer clay artists—why they chose this non-traditional medium, how they pushed the boundaries of something often considered a child's craft material to make striking art. Now I'd been given another chance to follow that dream. Ross wanted me to at least consider the option. He was right. As soon as I allowed the possibility of editing the magazine into my consciousness, I got excited.

When the new publisher called me, I agreed to write a synopsis of my ideas for the magazine and meet her for an interview. I wasn't a hundred percent sure editing the magazine was the right choice, but I didn't want to turn away from it without taking a few more steps down this path. I also remained in touch with classmates as they found new jobs in the counseling field. I kept my options open.

In keeping options open, however, I allowed myself to enter a place that tends to be dangerous for me—one full of indecision and lack of structure. I had been strong and determined when I knew my goals—graduate with my cohort, get excellent grades, complete Constellation training, learn to lead group therapy and overcome my fear of working with severely mentally ill clients. Then I hunkered down and forged forward until I accomplished all of them. Now at a crossroads with no specific duties or goals, I began to falter. I felt the first inklings of depression begin to creep in.

One morning, to keep myself out of a possible tailspin, I looked for one positive goal I could work on as I considered my career options. I decided to get my eating under control. I hadn't gained any weight during grad school, but I hadn't lost any either. No matter what new job I chose, I needed to be healthier, lighter and more vibrant. I went to Sunny Bridge, my favorite health food store, to stock up on some protein powder and supplements.

As I stood in the diet-food aisle pondering the eternal question—whey or soy protein powder?—a saleswoman I'd never seen before approached me.

"And what is it I can help you find today?" The odd phrasing of her question elicited a slightly facetious answer from me.

"Ah, I believe I could use some inner peace, please." We both smiled and I asked the whey versus soy question. After she'd given me the pros and cons of protein drinks, she circled back to my original statement.

"So, what's the inner peace comment about?"

I answered flippantly, "Just the normal stuff. I'm 60 years old and still trying to figure out what I want to be when I grow up."

Her reply wasn't glib. Instead, she asked some perceptive questions. As we moved from the diet aisle to the supplements, I found myself explaining my career dilemma. Fifteen minutes later, as I checked out, I thanked her and said she surely wasn't your average salesperson.

"I'm also a life coach." She reached around the counter and took her card from a display of brochures and business cards: *Abundant Life Coaching, Robin Janis.*

"If you think I can be of assistance, just let me know."

Several days later, I gave her a call.

Robin and I worked together, once a week, for several months on both the weight and career issues. I was a challenging client. Although I always did the assigned homework, I often came to our sessions with immense anger and frustration. I hated my inability to make the decisions necessary to move forward on either matter. I handled it by becoming enraged with myself.

Eventually, Robin made an insightful suggestion.

"Connie, I think your real issues are deeper than job choices and weight loss. That boulder in your gut needs more than a life coach can offer. I'd like you to consider doing some craniosacral work with my chiropractor, Dr. Jonas Marry. He's tremendously gifted in working with the big questions."

I was familiar with craniosacral work. As I understood it, it involved the subtle manipulation of bones in the head and spine to detect and enhance the flow of cerebrospinal fluid. I'd had a few sessions with a therapist several years before and remembered they produced some strong emotional, as well as physical, reactions. I trusted Robin's opinion. I made the appointment.

~

Jonas' office had a homey feel. On the longest wall in the waiting room, a large painted tree held about a hundred photos of patients—adults as well as children. There were toys and a child-sized table and chairs in a little nook beneath the tree. The receptionist greeted me warmly and several of the other waiting patients smiled at me. It was busy—all five of the treatment rooms were in use—but not rushed. Jonas went between the rooms and the front desk, checking on the arrival of X-rays for one patient, getting a set of home exercises for another, stopping occasionally to compliment the artwork of one of the children in the play area.

Two things surprised me that morning. First was Jonas' age. Robin had spoken of him with such respect, I assumed he would be an elderly man, or at least someone my age. Actually, he was the age of my children. The second was Jonas' intense focus. When he closed the treatment room door, he shut out the rest of the world. I was aware of other people in the waiting room. Jonas acted as if there were none. We talked until he fully understood why I wanted to do craniosacral work. He answered all of my questions thoroughly and thoughtfully.

He then gave me a quick explanation of how he worked, of his understanding of how the human body is designed and how it heals.

"In this practice, we're not just aiming for health—for an absence of disease. We're aiming for wholeness, for a maximum expression of the life force inside each of us—body, mind and spirit. We don't want to just get rid of a pain; we want to find out what's causing it and clear the path to healing—to allow wellness and wholeness to take its place."

I know I didn't grasp the full significance of what he said that day. I'd grown up thinking chiropractors worked with neck and back injuries while medical doctors worked with everything else. In high school, when I slipped on the ice or dislocated my neck while sleeping on a new set of extra large hair rollers, our chiropractor promptly "*snapped*" me back to normal. Even as an adult, I went to a chiropractor to ease the pain of arthritis in my back. I had no understanding of the philosophy behind the work.

Besides, when we first met, Jonas' philosophy of chiropractic wasn't particularly important to me. I hadn't made the appointment to get chiropractic treatment; I had a regular chiropractor. I'd come for craniosacral therapy. I knew this kind of adjustment affected the emotions—and that's what I was looking for, something to deal with my ever-present emotional boulder.

Under Jonas' care, I experienced the results of the craniosacral work in numerous ways. Sometimes it produced a deep feeling of relaxation. I'd feel my whole body unclenching and my heart opening up. At other times, the work brought up strong emotions—both positive and negative. Occasionally I'd get a flash of deep sadness that caused uncontrollable tears. At other times, I'd have a feeling of peace so deep I didn't want to move for fear of losing it. Sometimes these feelings led to profound insights; sometimes they didn't. At times I felt nothing in particular during the adjustment but noticed major shifts—mental, emotional or physical—a few hours or a few days later. In other words, the craniosacral treatments were energy work and energy work is hard to define. All I knew was that I felt better—calmer, clearer—after them than I did before.

As we talked during our sessions, his philosophy became increasingly important to me. Very briefly, the basic premise of chiropractors like Jonas can be summed up in this sentence: The power that makes the body heals the body. They work with the innate intelligence of the body—the instinctual force that keeps our hearts pumping and our lungs breathing. Their adjustments don't find the bone that has "popped out" and "pop it back in." They work by manually clearing subluxations—interferences in the nervous system—that block the flow of innate intelligence throughout the body.

As my understanding grew, I learned that illnesses I didn't think were in the realm of chiropractic, such as colds, ear infections and psoriasis could also be affected by adjustments. Jonas stressed that—because mind, body and spirit are inseparable in each of us—adjustments, not just craniosacral work, affected every part of a person. Soon Jonas became my only chiropractor. He was treating the whole package.

As we continued working together, we also shared ideas and books. A CD I borrowed from him deepened my understanding of

Bruce Lipton's ideas about belief and healing. Jonas introduced me to Joe Dispenza's work. I introduced him to Joseph Campbell and Bert Hellinger's writings. We discovered common ground in Candace Pert and Lynne McTaggart's studies. We often discussed how changing our beliefs, attitudes and intentions affected every aspect of our lives.

Eventually I noticed something. While I simply thought about my beliefs, Jonas lived his. He noticed it too. He challenged me to use what we were discussing in my day-to-day life. For example, at one session we discussed my dilemma with the *PolymerCAFÉ*. The day after my interview, Ruth Keessen, the publisher, offered me the job but not at a salary I thought was fair. I declined because we couldn't reach a financial agreement. I felt caught in a double bind: I couldn't accept the job for that pay, yet I really wanted to take it. I thought I'd simply have to chalk it up to one of life's lose-lose situations.

Jonas saw it differently.

"Or, Connie, you could experiment with all the concepts we're discussing. What if your thoughts do influence your life? Could you test this premise on the magazine job?"

"Well, not on the magazine job. That's already gone."

"Is it? Let's try this: Make sure it's the job you really want. Then set your intention to get it."

"But I've already turned it down."

"Did you turn it down or simply not accept the offer?"

"OK. I didn't accept the offer."

"So, sit down and figure out what you need to earn to ensure you're fairly paid. Set your intention to get the job for that amount. Then—this is the hard part—let it go. Don't fuss. Don't try to figure out how it can happen. You've already done the footwork. The publishers already like your proposal for the magazine. Just set your intention and let it be. You have some editing jobs that will keep you busy for a while. You don't need to have an answer tomorrow. Experiment with this. Keep your options open. What have you got to lose?"

I gave it a try. Nothing happened for several weeks. As the editing jobs came to an end, I started to look seriously at counseling opportunities. Then, while I was attending a seminar on counseling trauma victims, Ruth left a message on my cell phone. I returned her call at the lunch break.

"We've interviewed some promising candidates, but we still like your ideas for the magazine best. What would it take for you to say yes?" I mentioned the amount I had affirmed. She agreed to it. I hung up the phone, went back to the classroom and completed the workshop. I left with a certificate of completion—and a new job as a magazine editor!

I accepted the *PolymerCAFÉ* job in December—just a few weeks before Christmas. My first issue needed to be at the printer in February. I had no choice but to hit the ground running. I revved up my courage and called Kathleen Dustin, the polymer clay artist I most admired, for an interview. I asked every clay artist I knew to consider writing an article. Then I called a ton of artists I didn't know. Soon I was just as busy as I'd been the year before.

Despite their holiday plans and commitments, people came through for me. Two friends from my local polymer clay guild rearranged their schedules to create a project, photograph step-by-step tutorials and write articles for my first issue. No small feat. Kathleen generously created the time—and the heartfelt depth—for a great interview. She also gave us unlimited access to her art archives.

The production and design folks at the magazine were amazingly kind and patient with a novice editor. They filled in the gaps in my knowledge of magazine layout. They graciously listened to my suggestions for format and style changes, accepted them and then improved on every one. I'm sure they also juggled other magazine assignments to accommodate our tight schedule and my inexperience. We made the deadline.

By mid-March, I held my first issue of the magazine in my hands. It felt good—but not as good as I'd expected it would.

By the third issue I began to suspect I didn't want to be a magazine editor for the next several years of my life. I loved working with the contributors. I met some wonderfully creative and interesting people. Learning their stories, talking to them about how and why they created their art excited me. I really enjoyed helping first-time authors turn their ideas into articles. I even liked the pressure of meeting the deadlines. Yet something was wrong. Despite our conversations before I became editor, the publishers and I had some essential differences in our vision for the magazine. I wanted it to become more artistic; they definitely wanted a craft magazine. But more significantly, as time passed, I realized my heart was no longer content with polymer clay.

Studying Constellations, counseling, and the new frontiers of healing with Jonas fed my hunger to work with the questions I'd carried inside me as long as I could remember. How do people live purposefully and joyfully in this confusing world? How do people cope with life's pain and promise? How do we heal? Where does spirit fit into the equation? Where does *my own* spirituality fit? At 61, I realized I couldn't keep ignoring them.

I gave Ruth two issues' notice. I stayed with the magazine for a year. After that, I needed to work in a field that allowed me to find the answers to these questions.

~

My ever-deepening work with Jonas brought the spirituality question into clear focus. As a chiropractor, Jonas saw himself as someone who helped his patients reestablish a healthy nervous system, normalize brain activity and create a clear connection to their spirit. That was his job. Beyond that, he saw himself as a servant of God who acted as a conduit for the ultimate healing force of the Creator. For him, *innate intelligence* meant God. He became a chiropractor because he thought it was the best way to become a healer. He was someone living in the real world—with a wife and children and a career—who also had a very real and deep connection to the spiritual. As we worked together, I came to realize how much I wanted a spirituality like his.

Jonas had an amazing gift for accepting people exactly where they were—and offering just a little bit more than they asked for. If a patient came in looking for relief from a touch of arthritis and a little commiseration about the last Steeler football game, he was just the man to see. He happily joined in on Monday morning quarterbacking sessions as he made adjustments. As I sat in my treatment room awaiting his arrival, I'd overhear tons of animated conversations about sports, martial arts, guns, Little League, gardening and the vagaries of Pittsburgh's weather.

He was also an enthusiastic teacher. If someone wanted to know what to do to help themselves toward better health, Jonas offered explanations on how the nervous system worked—often with visual aids—and suggested exercises or nutritional changes to enhance their healing.

He also had the desire to share his spiritual path with others who were searching. I knew craniosacral work often impacted emotional blocks—that's what I came looking for. Jonas gave me that. However, as we got to know each other better, he offered assistance in understanding the spiritual pieces that were also blocking me. I wouldn't have even considered asking him for that.

Jonas confronted my basic approach to life. There were two recurring themes in our discussions. The first had to do with my emotional self-protection.

"Connie, I can sense the blocks inside you—the walls, the fortresses, you've built to keep yourself from being hurt. Please understand, by keeping out the pain, you also keep out the good emotions—the love, the joy, the peace you're looking for so earnestly. If you shut the doors to one emotion, you block all of them."

I experimented with this concept—very tentatively, very cautiously. I became more vulnerable, more honest. I allowed myself to feel all my emotions, not just the "good" ones. Instead of blundering forward when I felt scared, I first admitted the fear. Instead of telling myself I shouldn't feel angry or sad when something happened to hurt my feelings, I owned the sadness. Sometimes, with people I really trusted, I even voiced the hurt. Over time, I found I liked this new approach. The tears came more quickly—often at odd moments, like the day Steven read me a story from his third grade reader about a little girl living through the Depression. But the laughter was heartier too.

The second theme often came in the midst of our discussions of the latest discoveries about healing:

"Connie, you're asking questions that are too big for your mind alone. These are heart and soul questions. You're not going to find the answers if you limit yourself to just your brain. Western science makes a big deal of annotated studies and double-blind tests, but sometimes real wisdom comes from what can't be weighed or measured or charted."

When he said this to me I opened my mouth to argue with him but, in half a second, I realized how silly that would be. I'd come to his office for energy work. I'd begun this part of my journey—the most rewarding part of my life—because of Constellation work. Could I explain or measure either of them with only my brain? I no longer lived a life based solely on intellectual theories of reality. Why continue to act as if I were?

Just about every book on holistic healing talked about this shift. They stressed the need to broaden our base from the Western mechanistic view of the world to a more organic, intuitive view. The first dozen times I'd read this theory, I wrote it off as New-Age-Feel-Good mumbo jumbo. Now I realized that sometime in the last few years—somewhere in the world of Constellations and craniosacral work—I'd made the switch. I now searched with my heart—and maybe my soul—as well as my brain. Once again, I acknowledged I'd entered into the world of spirituality.

I also realized I'd found a mentor. Jonas had become the guide who made it safe for me to delve deeper into the spiritual. He was at home there and invited me to join him.

CHAPTER 18

THE SWORD

*A writer is dear and necessary for us only in the measure
of which he reveals to us the inner workings of his very soul.*
~ *Leo Tolstoy*

As I wrapped up my final issue of the magazine in late September, Jonas asked me what I wanted to do next. I told him I planned to get a real job as a therapist as soon as possible. What better way to work with the big questions than to help others? Jonas offered a different view.

"Connie, I've known you for over a year now. And every time you talk about writing—writing your own book—everything about you changes. Your eyes light up. Your voice becomes animated. You glow. Are you really going to look for another job before you at least consider writing that book?"

"Yeah, I know, I know. I want to write, but it feels so irresponsible. It's not as if I have anything profound to say. I'm not even sure what it would be about. Yes, it's what I want to do—it's always been—but life is not about doing what you want. I can't decide to take time off again. I did that after grad school and look where it led."

"It led to an interesting year editing a magazine. Was that really so bad? Why the rush to find a job? Are you guys starving to death, on the verge of losing your house? Is Ross pressuring you to find a job?"

"No, but..."

"Then why not consider, just for a few weeks, being the writer you've always wanted to be? I'll tell you what. Give yourself three weeks. At the end of this time, give me two chapters and a title page. I promise to read them and we can discuss them. That way you'll have the structure and time limit you're looking for, and you'll also give yourself the gift of seeing if this is the time for you to write."

Considering his overflowing schedule, it was a generous offer. I made a commitment to spend the next three weeks actually writing something—not just thinking about it.

When I came for my next appointment a week later, he casually asked, "How's the writing coming?" By then I'd written several first drafts, each a page or so long—a serious one, a light-hearted one, and one requiring more research—none of which I liked.

My tone of voice registered my frustration. "It's coming. It's coming. I made the commitment, and I'll keep it. I always keep my commitments to you, don't I? You'll have the chapters by the deadline, just as I promised."

He looked me straight in the eye. His voice was calm and caring, but his words were strong.

"Don't bother. If you're going to give me something you write because of a commitment, I don't want to read it. I don't have the time or the interest."

Before I could get my balance back enough to reply, he continued.

"Connie, do you know how a samurai faces his opponent? He stands up and raises his sword above his head, just like this."

Jonas stood in a warrior stance and raised an imaginary sword, in both hands, straight above his head.

"In this stance, every part of him is exposed to his opponent. *And*, it's the stance in which he is most powerful against his opponent. It's his best strategic posture. To be truly in his power, the samurai must also be at his most vulnerable. He must stand with every part of him, with every vital organ, open to attack. Anything less is not only an act of cowardice, it's a stance that guarantees he'll be killed.

"If you really want to write, this is where you have to be. Totally committed, totally vulnerable. Anything less and it's not worth writing."

At that moment, a current ripped through me. This isn't a figure of speech. Something electric shot through me. I felt it in my muscles, my brain and my heart. Something buzzed, got hot, and then dissipated.

He was absolutely right. All my first attempts—not just the ones this week, but all the books I've ever begun—were attempts to write and still be safe. I'd begun how-to books; I'd started novels. I had tons of half-finished short stories. I had notebooks and computer files filled with first drafts, with new beginnings. All of them had one thing in common; they were written without vulnerability, without courage.

Suddenly it became clear. If I wanted to write a book worth reading—hell, worth writing—it couldn't be any of the ones I'd been experimenting with. They were too safe. They were just intellectual exercises. If I wanted to write the book of my deepest dreams, I'd have to begin again and write from a samurai stance.

Jonas then went into his other office and brought out a replica of a life-size samurai sword. "Take this home with you. Get the feel of it; see how you feel when you hold it. Use it in your meditation."

That night, I wrote in my journal:

Today, suddenly, I walked into a sacred space. When Jonas said, "Hold your samurai sword above your head" I felt a shock run through me. This [fear] has been the writer's block that has stopped me for the last 35 years!

Now, as I consider writing from this stance, I feel completely different. Getting a story down, getting it out of my brain and onto paper will be a big deal. Whether it goes anywhere from there is not the issue. If I write to be read—to be clever or bright or helpful—I'm lost. If I write to be honest, I've got the book.

I now know what I have to do. I have to make this decision. I can leave the serious writing for another time or choose never to do it. And that's OK. Or I can write my book as a samurai warrior would. Anything else is a waste of my time. If I choose to do a book, I must choose absolute honesty and courage.

No wonder I've been hesitating. This is a much bigger cliff than I'd imagined. But my body knew. It's been inching away from this ledge all these years. I've come up to this moment a hundred times, and each time, I've used another excuse not to continue.

"I'll write when the kids are older, when the credit cards are paid off, right after I've taken care of my weight, my marriage, grad school, or painting my study. For now, I need to diet, sleep, or tie down those free-lance editing jobs. Let's do workshops; let's spend quality time with the grandkids; let's edit a magazine; let's edit someone else's book. Let's keep very busy."

I've been running away from writing a truly honest, no-holds-barred book all my life. I've done a dozen jobs that weren't quite right for me rather than face the immensity of this job—the exquisite focus and pain and courage of telling an honest story.

My writing can be either totally and completely—fiercely—honest, or it can be fluff. I can use the next two weeks to begin to make this decision, to try it on.

One thing I know already is that I love this sacred space. This space of courage and staying true feels damn good. It feels clean and solid. The other thing I know is that I can't write a *safe* book and remain [in this sacred space].

For the next two weeks, I wrote. I got up every morning and, after my morning ritual, I stayed at the computer and wrote—something. I'd read enough *How To* books to know the basics. Put something on paper, write what you know. Don't stop and edit. Just keep writing. I added the samurai insight and wrote from my heart—unedited, vulnerable.

At the end of the two weeks, I put on a title page: *Dumping the Magic: A Retired Skeptic Re-examines Spirituality and Healing.*

I handed the first draft of the initial two chapters of this book to Jonas, as promised, on October 21st. When he gave them back to me at the next appointment, I could see by the highlighting and notes in the margins that he'd read them thoughtfully. Still, I wasn't prepared for the intensity of his reaction:

"The ideas in these chapters are important. They're spirited and thought provoking. And you write in a way that's accessible, that can touch people. Connie, there are so many people who are struggling, who have given up hope of finding something meaningful in their lives. Writing this book can be a real gift to others who are searching. I hope you continue."

I'll be brutally honest. I wasn't sure he was right. I wasn't at all sure my very quirky journey would resonate with anyone else. However, Jonas wasn't someone who flattered or gift-wrapped his truth. I had taken the risk and been as honest as I could be. He was genuinely excited about what I'd begun. I'd been looking for something to write about. Now someone I admired thought this could be it.

It made sense to try a couple more chapters. After all, I was sure the significant parts of my journey were behind me. I could just write about them and intertwine a bit more about the latest theories in the holistic health field.

When I got home, I scoured my bookcases for books I could refer to as I delved a little deeper into the subjects. I scanned a couple looking for experiments I might do with beliefs, affirmations, neuropsychology and maybe meditation.

I wrote myself a note in my journal:

> The cutting-edge science is now proving that [the concepts] the wisdom traditions always taught are true. Writing about how this truth affected my life could be cool. Maybe [I'll] jump onto the Internet and get involved in the experiment Lynne McTaggart talks about in *The Intention Experiment* or begin by cracking the spine of Ramtha's *The White Book* that changed Joe Dispenza's life. Or maybe I'll just finish Dispenza's book and not skim past the parts that describe brain physiology. Speaking of skimming, I'll really read Candace Pert's books and try to actually understand the scientific parts. Glancing over at the dozen or so Hellinger books on the shelf, maybe that's where I should begin—begin with the parts that changed my life and REALLY analyze what happened there. Maybe if I document things well enough, it could be an interesting book.

For about a month, that's what I did. I read more. I took notes on what I read. Jonas and I talked more about spirituality. (I was OK if we referred to it in terms of "The Universe.") Our craniosacral work continued to bring up emotionally charged issues. Life felt good; progress felt steady.

Until November 18th. After that, all bets—with the book and with my life—were off. Once again, I had an experience I couldn't deny—and couldn't explain.

CHAPTER 19

NOVEMBER 18TH

The opposite of needing is—allowing.
~ Jonas Marry

On Tuesday, November 18th, Jonas and I began the appointment as
we usually did, talking a little, joking a little. When he asked what
I wanted to work on for this cranial session, I came back to the
weight issue. The extra 100 pounds I carried really interfered with
my life.

"Shall we deal with the weight loss from the viewpoint of pleasure or pain? From which end of the spectrum?"

"Hey, if I've got a choice, I'll go with pleasure."

"What gives you pleasure?"

I named the normal people—Ross, the kids, the grandkids, my
friends.

"No, what makes you feel pleasure *inside yourself?*"

I dropped my casual tone immediately. We'd moved from small
talk to work. I thought for a while. I wanted to be completely honest. Nothing came to mind. I felt tears begin to well up. I thought
to myself, "*This can't be right. I'm being overly dramatic. Of course there
are things inside that make me happy, give me pleasure.*" I thought
some more.

After a minute or so, Jonas broke the silence, "Is this something you don't want to get into, something you don't want to deal with right now?"

"No, it's not that. There's just nothing *inside* me that gives me pleasure."

"OK. Stay sitting where you are, right there on the table. Just sit up straight; square yourself up."

Jonas came over to the table. He took my right hand and asked me to place it over my heart, where I felt my heart chakra would be. He placed his hand over mine. He then placed his left hand on the back of my head. That was it. The craniosacral treatment began just like that. I tried to breathe into whatever happened.

For a while, nothing did. I kept repeating in my mind the only thing that felt right. "*I'm allowing. I'm allowing. Thank you. I'm allowing.*"

Then a feeling came into my chest, then into my heart, then all around me, of love. I'd experienced something similar during previous cranial work, but not this strong. The feeling totally captivated me. I felt as if I were breathing some sort of different kind of air, something that seemed to fill me with both contentment and a longing to feel it more deeply.

I knew I needed to be present to more than just this technique. I needed to allow myself to shift my focus from what was going on outside me and move my attention more inside. "*Fortunately,*" I thought, "*Jonas is so centered, so familiar with this place. He can hold it for me—he can be here and ground me, allow me to go beyond him. OK, I choose to be open to what is beyond Jonas—to be touched by whatever he is the conduit for.*"

The experience deepened. While I continued to be aware of the room and Jonas, they were now in the background. Jonas moved his hands to my shoulders. I slowly removed my hand from my chest so my heart could be open—totally open and unguarded—to what would come next.

Then it happened. I felt really loved. Loved like I'd never felt before—no, like I hadn't felt in almost a lifetime. Maybe like the love I felt with my dad when I was a baby or from Grandma Bordone when I was a very little girl. I breathed more deeply, trying to pull the feeling into my lungs, into my heart. I wanted to inhale it so deeply my lungs would burst.

The feeling grew more intense—beyond Dad, beyond Grandma. At first I tried to figure out if I'd felt it before, but I stopped as soon as I realized thinking about it took me away from the feeling. I stopped trying to understand and just felt.

I needed to lean back, to surrender into the force both surrounding me and filling every fiber of my being. I needed to allow this force to be in charge. I leaned back. My head bumped into Jonas. Feeling his strength behind me, I felt safe enough to let go some more.

The experience deepened. The words I'm using now don't come close to the feelings. So deep. So rich. I felt I was falling into the color burgundy. The more I fell, the deeper the color, the more intense the feeling of love became. For a while, that was it. I just sank deeper and deeper into an all-consuming, totally wondrous feeling of being loved. I inhaled it with every part of me. I let it wash over me and into me. I pulled it in with my skin as well as my breath. Whatever that burgundy color was, I felt enfolded in it—and totally cherished.

Yet my mind couldn't keep still. Soon I saw something else. As I was sinking, I saw a frame around the burgundy. I knew the frame was the love I'd known all my life—the love I'd received and the love I'd given, and it, in comparison to this burgundy, was like translucent red plastic. It had the quality of the cheap plastic made for a throwaway toy you got at a carnival or a fast food restaurant. All my life, I'd had the plastic. Now I had this—this magnificent, all-encompassing, totally deep and caring burgundy love.

I began to cry. I wish I could say they were tears of gratitude, of awe. But they weren't. They were tears of sadness—deep sadness and regret because I'd lived all my life with plastic—that I'd loved my children and Ross and my grandchildren with this plastic love. Because I'd only known the plastic.

Jonas' hands shifted from my shoulders to my head. The feeling deepened. The color grew deeper. I had a more profound feeling of being wrapped in, being encased in, unconditional love.

I tried to cry quietly, tried not to sob so loud that people in the other treatment rooms could hear. If I'd been alone, I would have howled in pain.

Minutes later the experience was over. I was back in the room, back to real life again. As I opened my eyes, Jonas sat down across from me. I felt so grateful he was staying in the room for a while, so grateful we could talk about what just happened.

"Jonas, if I could feel this, even for just a few seconds a day, I'd never overeat again."

"I know. And you can, Connie." He paused for a second, gathering his thoughts.

"What I want you to know is that all you experienced today came from you, not me. I didn't give you anything. Honest, Connie, I didn't give you anything. I just helped you to open the door. Everything else was inside you. It was just—I'm going to have to say this in terms of God. Can you handle that?"

I impatiently waved aside his hesitation. I needed to hear what he was going to say. "Jonas, I'm so far beyond doubting God right now. Please. Just tell me."

"You experienced the love of God—the love that has always been there, waiting."

Up to this day I'd always been frustrated by these particular words. I'd never experienced God's love directly, not even in the convent. In the past, when I got to these words or similar ones in inspirational books, I stopped reading. If a motivational speaker used a phrase like this, I turned off the CD and never listened to it again. In the past they described something impossible for me to comprehend, let alone believe.

But not today. Today, after all these years, these words were about *my* experience, *my very real* experience. Today I didn't fight them. Today I embraced them. I just wanted to allow them to keep resonating inside me. I just wanted to hold on to the experience.

"Connie, today you found the key and unlocked your heart. And for right now, that's enough. The only important thing for you to know is the key is yours. No one else holds it for you. You may not be able to find it again right away, but just know it's yours. It's in your house. It may get misplaced. But it's in your house. It's yours."

"So I can feel this again? Even for a few minutes?"

"Connie, I've been in that space for days at a time."

My greedy heart wanted it too. "For days?" I wanted it for days— for days and days and days.

"But let me tell you. It's not a place where you can communicate well with other people. I was young when this first happened to me. I didn't know how to deal with it."

Jonas then tried to explain how he felt when he had these experiences as a young boy. I listened intently, looking for clues to fully comprehend what he was saying, but his words just slipped off my brain. Finally, I stopped trying to hold onto them. I just listened, hoping some part of me understood. I so appreciated his sharing, his trying to make this experience comprehensible to me, to make it easier for me to stay on this path. I felt a gratitude I couldn't contain.

"Jonas, I don't know how I ever could, but if there's ever a way for me to be a conduit for you as you have been for me..."

"But you already are. I experienced this with you. There can't be this much Spirit in the room without my experiencing it too." (These aren't the right words. They're not exactly what he said. They're just as close as I can come, as much as I can remember from that moment.)

After Jonas left, I sat very still and soaked up the fragments of the experience still remaining in the room. I sat in a holy place. I didn't want to ever leave.

Nothing after this was ever the same.

CHAPTER 20

THE GREEN WORDS

When I was a child I spoke as a child, I understood as a child,
I thought as a child;
but when I became a man I put away childish things.
~ I Corinthians 13:11.

I wrote about this extraordinary experience in my journal soon after I got home. I didn't journal again for several days. I wish I had.

I have just the vaguest memory of the next few days. I know I felt very different—the words *fresh* and *new* and *shiny* come to me, but they're clichés and terribly inadequate. Oddly, I felt very young— not like a baby but maybe five or six years old—old enough to be really grateful for the love, old enough to realize the privilege of being cherished. My heart felt better. Another cliché fits here—I don't know how else to say it—I felt I was looking at the world through different eyes.

Friday, I saw Jonas for my regular adjustment. I was still overwhelmed with excitement and gratitude and assumed Jonas would be in the same euphoric space. I'd anticipated that we'd talk about Tuesday in glowing detail for the whole session. Jonas, however, didn't get caught up in my excitement. He was definitely happy and grateful to have been a part of what had happened but not giddy with excitement. His reaction surprised me—and quickly grounded me.

Wow. For the first time, I realized Jonas lived this way every day—constantly in the presence of God and miracles. For me, November 18th was a life-changing, once-in-a-lifetime experience. For him, it was something he'd prayed for and expected to happen. He simply accepted it as part of his normal life. Interesting.

Following Jonas' example, I tried to get back into some sort of routine. The next morning, after meditating, I went to the computer to write in my journal. Suddenly I began typing something, nonstop, that I didn't think I was creating. It was the closest I've come to automatic writing, I guess. I was fully conscious. I could have stopped at any time, but it seemed something was dictating the words. It felt similar to the short bursts of inspiration I sometimes got after I read my letters to my family, but it was only words, no pictures. It felt as important as Tuesday had been.

In the course of pulling this book together, I've often come to facts that I debate about including. Usually it's because they're embarrassing or highly personal or just plain weird. This is one of those parts. I've had the hardest time deciding whether or not to include it.

At various stages of the book's development, I've trimmed this message, censoring what I felt uncomfortable including. Some of it didn't make sense out of context, some felt too personal, and some felt simply strange. It was awfully long. On this final go-round, however, I've chosen to include it all. It's part of the story—part of my journey.

So I'm reproducing the text as it came to me, leaving in the ungrammatical shifts in person and tense. Occasionally I've added a word or two in brackets if the meaning seemed unclear. I've deleted only references to specific people and added, as footnotes, explanations for some of the allusions:

Get up and do the work you were given. This is my Love too. I keep giving you what you ask for, and you keep squandering it by old behavior. There's no need for the food binges now that you know you are loved. There's no need for the collapse. Do the exercise that you need to do and you'll have the energy you so desperately crave.

The job is simple. The answer is simple: "Get up and do the work you were given—the work you begged to have."

The drama of you prostrate on the floor in gratitude is of little value if you don't do the work in front of you. It really is that simple. Do your work. You know this is real. Your body can't handle much more of this abuse. After the drive [last winter when you almost slid off the road] you now know you want to live. You can't continue to act like someone who wants to die.

No drama. Action. That's the lesson of your work with Jonas yesterday. He couldn't be pulled into your drama. It didn't even occur to him. He does his job—every day, with consistency and constancy. You want to see my Love again, do your job. This isn't a threat or bribe. This is the natural law.

Do we suspend the laws for a child? Of course. But you are no longer a child. You are a knower. With that comes the responsibility to act as an adult. The laws of life are now here for you in full force. You can use them to walk further down the path, or you can misuse them and suffer the consequences. The path will remain.

Connie, now that you understand, the right action—the only action—is to work with the work in front of you. (Sound familiar?)

You can't learn to walk if you keep insisting on being carried. And the life of a walker is so much more exciting and free than that of a child who waits to be carried. The metaphor [of your life] needs to be played out in your body. You need to learn to walk again as Milton Erickson did[1], and with the same wondrous results. Learning this now will enable you to learn it in a new way.

This is the posture: commitment and curiosity. This is a learning experience, not an arbitrary boulder thrown in your path. This is the Boulder of Learning. Treat it as the gift it is!

Change your attitude now. This is the experiment, the boot camp, the apprentice's wax-on/wax-off task. Do it well. You'll build on it. Do it with pleasure, with joy, and you'll learn so much from it. This is the gift of this cave.[2] You've found it.

The old convent prayer: "All that I have and all that I am you have given me. I surrender it all to be disposed of according to your will. Give me only your love and your grace, with these I am rich enough and desire nothing more." You now have them both Connie. But you can't use them if you keep throwing them away.

The time is NOW.

"What is it that gives me energy to live the life I crave to live? What takes that energy away?"[These are the questions you need to ask yourself.]

Each minute is a choice, not of drama, a choice—of curiosity, of challenge, of learning. Of fun and hard work. Of hard work that, with the right attitude, is fun and rewarding.

---

1   After contracting a severe case of polio in his late adolescence, Milton Erickson, the father of modern medical hypnosis, had to slowly teach himself to use his limbs and to walk again. He did so by watching the younger children in his family as they learned to walk, breaking their actions down into the smallest possible elements, and teaching himself to mimic them. Later in his life, he credited a good deal of his success in creating groundbreaking hypnotic procedures to his habit of observing others with tremendous intensity.

2   This referred to one of my favorite quotes from Joseph Campbell: "The very cave you were afraid to enter turns out to be the source of what you are looking for. Where you stumble, there lies your treasure."

You have been given the gift of the generations. You have worked to achieve the honor of doing [this job]. Now you understand the price. The universe rewards a-thousand-to-one your efforts. Not bad odds, Chickadee. And such a terrible gift to squander.

You are, right now, above the fray. You can see beyond the crowd. You can waste this gift—as many do, Connie, don't be deceived, many do, as you know—or you can carry it with reverence in your heart and [in the] actions in your life. It can't be carried any other way.

This is huge. This is real. You could lose it if you choose to act like a baby, like a small vulnerable child. You are neither. You are an adult. Remember the quote from St. Paul: "When I was a child...:" Look it up. Make sure you have it 100% right.

Constancy, consistency, love, humility, gratitude, curiosity, and wonder. This can be your life. Or you can go back to [lying on] the couch and questioning. You've asked. You've received. Now it's your choice to accept, to truly take this gift. For you, [physical] exercise is your way of kissing the ground in humility and awe. Do it every day with the respect and humility you would use to bow to the universe. This is our gift to you as you begin.

Love, Love, Love—

And your gratitude is expressed with food, with your food choices. Don't be naive; your body needs these changes NOW if you are going to do the work you so much want to do!!! We can work a thousand ways. But if you want the way you've chosen, it must be NOW and now and now that you make the right choices for this particular life. Connie, this is serious. The abuse can't go on. This is your gratitude. This is your tool. This is your way of choosing this road a thousand times a day.

Here is the secret. The problem with food—with having to make choices over and over every day—is also its gift! Now, you have the opportunity to truly express your gratitude and willingness a thousand times a day!!!!!!

You have a wonderful opportunity to grow a thousand times a day!!! Every sip of water, every rejection of junk food, every choice of good food, every effort to make this [choice] into a new life plan is a way to express your gratitude, humility and your love. What a gift! A thousand genuflections a day. Because now you are choosing to walk on holy ground ALL the time....

The rules are different now because now you can see them. You're no longer playing the game and getting arbitrary results because you don't understand them. It's not that the game is less challenging now that you know the rules—it's MORE challenging now because you know the rules. Now the fun begins!

Will you slip? Possibly.

Can you use it as an opportunity to learn and grow? Always.

But you **can't** learn constancy and consistency [by always slipping]. Bundle [your] constancy and consistency with gratitude and humility. This is the learning you are seeking now. There is no Thank You that is adequate without right action anymore! The days of Santa and Tooth Fairies are gone. The days of the real adventure are here.

You can feel it in your heart. You know it is true for you. You can keep the gift alive—or, quite realistically, not metaphorically—you can let it die.

And there is always help if you ask. Help not just to carry you through [the challenges], but help to strengthen your muscles, to get your balance, to learn to walk forward on the chosen path with abundance and joy.

Right action doesn't get you into heaven; it creates the heaven on earth in which you are privileged to live.

Some days it will be easy and light, as it feels right now. But you are changing core actions, core beliefs. Sometimes it will be very hard. But it will never be impossible! If you hang in, if you do **even the smallest right action**, the power to do the next will be there. This is the law. This is how the universe works. The smallest right action has the seeds of the next one inside it. If you do one, no matter how small, the force for the next will be there.

Remember the dream [you had several years ago about protecting your child by simply refusing to respond to the abductors with violence]? You couldn't lose your child if you didn't play by the abductor's rules, if you stayed true to your commitment to remain nonviolent. [The same is true now.] If you don't play temptation's game, you cannot lose yourself. Remain true to the way you now know and you'll always have the energy for the next moment of remaining true. This is so important. And so is its opposite: giving up on the right action puts you back where you've been for the last forty years. The small missteps CAN lead to a draining of your energy for the next steps. These are the rules. This is the reality.

You can keep ignoring reality and insist on being carried when you get yourself into a jam. You can act like a child, and you'll **always** be rescued, over and over. This is the way to be with a child. Or you can accept the world of an adult, with its freedom and growth and privilege, and act like an adult.

Connie, [unlike November 18th] this isn't from or through or because of Jonas. Then, you got to this [level of openness] with his help. He held the lantern on the path for you. Now, you're at the place of YOUR truth. This is yours, not his. He has no interest in it. He did his job. That's where his interest rightly lies. This is yours.

That bond of dependence [on Jonas or anyone else] is useless to you now. It's the magic! Dump it! Now, walk the path as an adult. He'll still walk with you. He'll still lift his lantern to help you. But what you see now is yours!

[Like a child,] you can run with each new shiny stone you discover to the grownups and get their approval, or you can take the stones, examine them, learn what you need to from them, discard the useless [ones] and build with the useful—as an adult would do. Which is more fulfilling? You can choose the more fulfilling.

I don't know how long I just sat and stared after I finished typing. My heart swelled with gratitude. But I was also confused and disoriented. I read and reread those paragraphs a dozen times that morning. There were concepts in them I'd never thought of before. I understood different pieces every time I read them.

I continued to reread them every day for weeks. When I needed a shot of motivation, I went back to them. Eventually, to find these words quickly in my journal, I changed the color of the text to green so they would stand out. After a while, I just thought of them as The Green Words.

On the day I received them, in that surreal glow of the 18th, I couldn't imagine doing anything but following their advice. But, as a matter of fact, I often didn't. I still don't. I still have difficulty with the food and exercise issues. If ever there was a case of "the spirit is willing but the flesh is weak," this was it. What seemed so clear in print that morning was often unreachable in practice. It demonstrated clearly the separation still inside me.

After I had this experience, I bounced between thinking the message was odd but interesting to believing those words were The Ultimate Truth—with all the ineffable infallibility that implies. Now, three years later, I see them as simply an inspiration, a message appropriate for me then, coming through all the filters and hang-ups I had then, in words and feelings I could accept.

Some of the message—especially the occasional harsh tone—I now disagree with. Now my ears are attuned to a gentler voice, and I act on its motivation more quickly and consistently than I did The Green Words. Still, I go back to them. Some of the message still bowls me over; some continues to challenge me. As I continue to change, different parts surprise and inspire me. Some parts I gratefully use every day. And this is still true—I believe the message came from a place beyond me.

Chapter 21

Life Unfolding

Before enlightenment, chop wood and carry water;
after enlightenment, chop wood and carry water.
~ Zen Proverb

An odd thing seems to happen to us after a transcendent experience—however we get it. First, we're really, really grateful. It's so wondrous, so fulfilling, so life altering, we can't begin to express our awe and gratitude. Second, we really want to experience the feeling again.

I remember hearing Cardwell Nuckols, a well-known research scientist and addictions therapist, lecture on his battle recovering from a life-threatening drug addiction. His transcendent experience came with his first hit of cocaine. His experience was so strong, so magnificent, he spent the next ten years—despite jail time, despite threats to his health, despite losing his family and almost his life—trying to recreate it. "With that hit, suddenly, I knew God; I felt the core of life, and was unable to stop my search until I found it again. And the fact that no other hit of coke ever gave it to me didn't stop my trying. I was always sure the next one would."

I felt the same way about November 18th. My heart physically ached each time I remembered being unimaginably loved—of being in the arms (not the mere presence) of God's love. I couldn't believe my good fortune—and I wanted to have that feeling again. I was willing to do anything—everything—I could to find it again. In that state, I was the antithesis of thankful.

For the next several weeks this battle between overwhelming gratitude and frantic grasping dominated my every waking moment. Each day, as I meditated, I tried to be mature. I had enough theoretical knowledge of spiritual experiences—from books, the convent, other people—to know running after them, trying to recreate them, was the sure-fire way to keep them at bay. I knew that was the recipe for creating a horrible cycle of wanting something so badly it leads to the inability to experience it. But I also couldn't figure out what I was supposed to do.

On good days I remembered what Jonas said within seconds of my experience. "Connie, this has always been inside you; God has always been this close. You've just learned to allow yourself to experience His love." I calmly believed November 18th had not been a fluke. I assured myself that once some sort of connection had been established, it could be reestablished. I knew other people sometimes had recurring experiences. I just had to stay out of the way—keep my greedy ego from closing the connection by desiring it too much.

I began to again pray the Ignatius Loyola prayer I'd learned in the convent:

> Take and receive, Oh Lord, my entire liberty. All that I have and all that I am You have given me. I now surrender it all to be disposed of according to Your will. Give me only Your love and Your grace. With these I am rich enough and desire nothing more.

What a different meaning it had now. In the convent, I'd thought I was the one doing the giving. I thought it was a holy, somewhat unfair deal in which God got the good part. Now, as I understood what Ignatius had received in exchange for the paltry little gift of his liberty and his life, I realized who had the better deal. Ignatius had been, indeed, rich enough to desire nothing more. On good days I thought it was more than a fair trade to give everything, including a limb or two if necessary, for God's love.

On bad days, though, I became a crazy person. My meditations were a mish-mash of pleading, pouting and trying to be as humble as I could be. "Please, please, please, I'm as open as I can be. If there are rules, just let me know what they are, and I'll follow them to the letter." I felt six years old again, trying to coax God out of hiding.

After a few weeks I chose the most mature prayer I could. *"Not in my time, but in Yours."* I figured I was still sending the message I was ready—night or day, any place, any way—but I was also willing to wait until God's time, whenever *that* would be. Some days I truly meant it. I believed this was the beginning of a long and beautiful relationship and I had to respect God's timing. Other days I just said it because, like it or not, I certainly couldn't make November 18th happen again. My best approach was to stay open. What else could I do?

Sometimes I just skipped morning meditation so I didn't have to deal with the immensity of my desire.

For better or worse, I also needed to talk about it. Not a lot, not to a bunch of people, but I needed to make it real outside my own head and heart. At the very least, I needed to tell Ross what had happened. This was the man with whom I'd shared every day of my adult life for the last 40 years. He had to have noticed something was going on inside me. On the days when I allowed myself to appreciate the gift of this experience, I smiled more, fussed less. I got things done. I was steady. I appreciated the little things Ross did and let him know it. On the other hand, with my heart so open and unprotected, I tended to be much more sensitive to everything. I cried more easily; I got angry or befuddled more quickly. He had to be noticing something.

I waited almost a week. Then one morning as we drove to our favorite diner for breakfast, I shared what happened on the 18th. Ross listened intently. When I finished, he stumbled through a clarifying question or two, tried to give me some advice—and then hesitated as he realized he had no knowledge of what I was going through. Finally, he stopped talking completely. I surely understood. Beyond just repeating what happened, I certainly had nothing to say.

Later, after we were settled into a booth, he thanked me for sharing my experience with him. It was an odd conversation, full of stops and starts. Neither of us had ever talked about this kind of thing. It bewildered both of us. But somehow, through all of our stuttering and pausing, Ross and I made a connection. It reminded me of how I felt right after the World Trade Center attack on 9/11, when things were raw and real and not yet political. Someone said then that we, as Americans, stood together shoulder to shoulder, so close that not a speck of light could be found between us. That's how I felt about Ross' support. We were both confused and dazed by what had happened. Neither of us knew where this might lead, but he was determined to stand by me, no matter what. I'm a very blessed woman.

I also told my friend, Carmen. She cried. I cried too, so relieved and grateful for her reaction.

"This is because you've had this experience yourself Carm, isn't it?"

"Yes, and I'm so truly happy you've had it too."

Neither of us said much more. We just sat across from each other in my living room and smiled. Then, slowly, we drifted back into everyday conversation. But the bond we established, the closeness of a shared experience of life, cemented what had already become a very deep and warm friendship.

I was also grateful everyday life took up so much of my time. I was glad I wasn't in the convent or on some sort of spiritual retreat when this happened. I had a short deadline on a manuscript I was editing. Thanksgiving and Christmas were coming and I had to make the normal preparations. I couldn't lollygag and fixate on this new path. I had real-world stuff to keep me busy. I needed to appreciate it, be grateful for it and get back to my everyday life. Once I got past my early morning meditation frenzy, the rest of my day filled in nicely. The Zen saying, "Before enlightenment, chop wood and carry water; after enlightenment, chop wood and carry water" seemed like good advice to me.

Besides, I had my routine. I met with Jonas twice a week. Every Friday he did a standard adjustment to support the healing of my knees and hips, and every Tuesday he did a craniosacral adjustment that worked on the mind/spirit part of the Body-Mind-Spirit equation. We also had time to talk as he worked—time for me to ask the burning questions I always accumulated between sessions. After all those years of trying to figure things out on my own, I genuinely loved having a mentor in my life.

~

Then life happened. Not to me, but to Jonas. In early December Jonas had a family health crisis that rocked his world. He needed to close his office for over a week to be with his family. When he returned, I expected to see a preoccupied, anguished man as he worked his way through the crisis. I remembered how distracted I had been at work when there had been a difficult situation at home. But this was not the case.

When he walked into the treatment room, I could see the exhaustion and concern in his eyes. But I could also sense his strength. He was ready to get right back to work. I was the one who needed to ask how everything was going, to put the focus on what he'd been facing for the last weeks.

"What you said in your email was pretty darn accurate, Connie. I was devastated the first three days after everything happened. I was so angry, so hurt, so confused, I couldn't pray. I couldn't find God anywhere. I was stripped down to my bones. Then I realized I couldn't go on like that. I couldn't really be there for my family if I continued like that.

"So, finally, I did the only thing I could. One night, when I was lower than I'd ever been in my entire life, I just surrendered. I told God, 'I trust You with my life—with my wife, with my children, my practice, my home, everything. It's all Yours. Do with it what you will, and I will follow.' And I meant it.

"And, Connie, as I did, everything changed. It changed in an instant. Suddenly, I could feel God's love again. As I prayed, the room I stood in just filled with love. And then I could feel the love grow. As I stood in awe, this amazing, all-encompassing love filled the room, the city, the country, the world.

"After that, Connie, the anger and doubts were gone. I was at peace—perhaps the most profound peace I'd ever known. Now I know, in the deepest part of me, that everything will be all right—that everything already IS all right. I know there will be challenges in the next months, but I also know we'll be OK."

I didn't know what to say to him. I had been prepared to be supportive—to offer him the strength of my friendship and caring. But he was already standing strong. It was the first time in my life I'd experienced his kind of faith.

In the months to come I continued to ask how things were going. But I did it because I needed to know, not because he needed to tell me. He knew everything was working out just as it should.

CHAPTER 22

YEAR'S END

The sacred is in the ordinary. It is found in one's daily life,
in one's neighbors, friends and family, in one's own back yard.
~ Abraham Maslow

It's our tradition to celebrate Christmas whenever we have all three grandchildren together. So, in fairness to the other grandparents, every other year we celebrate Christmas either before or after the official calendar date. This year we celebrated "our" Christmas Day on Sunday, December 28th. On Monday, since Hannah was in town, I'd scheduled an appointment with Jonas for her. This appointment also gave Ken a chance to meet Jonas.

When we arrived at the office, the receptionist confirmed both of our appointments—mine and Hannah's. This surprised me a little. I knew I had a cranial scheduled for the next day but hadn't remembered an adjustment appointment.

She glanced at her computer screen. "It looks like you rescheduled your Friday adjustment because of Christmas."

"Sure, sure, that's right." It made sense and, since I felt a little achy from the holidays and my over-the-top sugar consumption, an adjustment seemed like a good idea.

Jonas spent quite a while working with Hannah and discussing Ken's recent back injury (Ken had fallen down his basement steps and cracked a vertebra). I knew he'd have a busy day after the holiday weekend, so I anticipated a quick adjustment.

After Jonas adjusted me, he asked me to stand. Thinking he was just checking my posture, I stood up. However, when he placed his hands on my spine, both of us knew this was not just a posture check. Immediately I felt everything inside me shift. As I breathed deeply, I could feel my heart begin to open. Again—as strongly as I had on November 18th—I felt the presence of something beyond me— something wondrous and loving—coming into me. I began to let it happen. Then, I stopped the process. I could hear Ken and Hannah talking in the waiting room. I realized Ken would have to leave soon to get back to work. I knew Ross and Leslie were at home making a big post-Christmas breakfast. If I were here too long, we would have to rush the meal. So, after only a few minutes, I just opened my eyes and let the energy dissipate.

Jonas didn't miss a beat. When I stopped, so did he. But he also sensed my confusion—my feeling of being torn between the spiritual and the practical.

"Don't worry, Connie. You got what you needed from this. Don't focus on what you didn't experience. Focus on what you did. You got enough. Keep your focus there."

I agreed. Whatever began before I opened my eyes felt transcendent—felt almost as awesome as November 18th. But I didn't have the maturity to follow Jonas' advice. Short-circuiting my experience and returning to everyday life so abruptly left me unbalanced. I really made a mess of the rest of the day.

When I returned to his office on Tuesday, I skipped the polite small talk. "OK. Yesterday. What the hell happened yesterday?"

"What do *you* think happened, Connie?"

I tried to find the words. "Well, I guess my heart opened again, much like it did on November 18th. I just felt it stretching and stretching. My chest ached—a good ache, like being in love. It felt so wonderful. I wanted to hold on to it; but then I screwed it up. That's what I need to talk with you about."

Jonas laughed. "How do you think you screwed it up?"

"Well, in about a dozen different ways! Looking back, I'm really angry with myself for ending the experience so abruptly. What was I thinking? Surely a rushed breakfast wouldn't have been too high a price to pay for a transcendent experience.

"Then I kept messing things up. I really wanted to talk with Ross about what happened here. I knew we couldn't talk right away, with everyone scrambling to have one final meal before Ken and Les left. But when they were on their way home, as we drove the grandchildren to Phipps Conservatory to see the Christmas Flower Show, I thought I'd have a chance. All three of them were together in the back seat of the van, listening to a Bill Cosby CD, giggling and enjoying each other's company. They didn't need us.

"I tried a time or two to talk with Ross, but he was still in Grandpa mode. He kept his attention on the road and on them. Finally I got angry and started to cry. I knew I was acting like a spoiled four-year old, but I wasn't ready to let it go. I really wanted to share my experience with him—even if he thought it wasn't the appropriate time or place.

"I stayed angry as we toured Phipps. Oh, I was Nurturing Nana to the kids—taking pictures, joking around, trying to identify all the different flowers with them—but I was cold to Ross. I rebuffed his every attempt to normalize things. Damn. I was so angry with him.

"Several times I'd realize how childishly I was acting, and I'd cool off and apologize. But then the anger would unexpectedly burst through again.

"Jonas, I am *not* good at this spirituality stuff. I didn't understand what happened. I didn't know how to handle it maturely. I'm being given these amazing gifts—and I refuse them—and then I pout! How can I be spiritual and a jerk at the same time?"

Jonas leaned in as he spoke. "Here was my intention when we worked yesterday. I pictured you letting go of the neediness—of needing the food, the outside validation, the outside acceptance that can stand in your way on this new path."

"Well, obviously I screwed that up. I was a quagmire of neediness!"

"You can look at it that way—or you can see what happened between you and Ross yesterday as a logical outgrowth of the changes you're undergoing. How will you know something is gone if you never experience its absence? How will you know you've changed if you never face a situation similar to one you faced in the past? Maybe you can see yesterday's reaction as your opportunity to learn what you're letting go of, what you're ceasing to need. From now on, you'll be aware of when and how you experience your neediness. Then you can acknowledge it, humbly accept it as how you used to live, and let it go."

Part of me got the message; part of me struggled with it. I decided to just give myself some time for things to settle. Besides, Jonas wanted to talk about what happened in the office yesterday and I was more than willing to discuss that!

"Connie, yesterday we did what the Gospels say, 'When two or more are gathered in My name, so too am I ....' I sensed you were ready for the next step. You accepted the work as soon as I began. I trusted that, if you were ready, we should begin. It seemed foolish to postpone the work, to censor the flow of God's spirit just because it wasn't a day scheduled for craniosacral work.

"I'm doing this more and more in my work now. I offer my patients what I sense God can do through me. Some people accept it eagerly, some ignore the invitation and others recoil from it. I understand it's not my place to judge whether or not to make the offer. I just make it. The rest is between the person and God.

"Now, you and I can continue to work like this. We can set an intention together for our work and then allow God's energy to complete it. We can just humbly get out of the way."

We continued to talk as I lay down on the table.

"Connie, what's your biggest intention right now?"

"So many of the big ones are already beginning to fall into place, I'll have to think a minute."

After a few moments, I answered.

"OK. I don't even know if this is something we can use as an intention. I'll just say it and you tell me if I'm on the right track. I guess the hardest thing for me to imagine is the book—being completed, being successful. I can't even say the word 'successful' in the same sentence with 'the book' when I try to set my intention."

"That's because your intention is too small. It's too small for this much power. I've said this before: people are waiting for your book, for your story. That's not the issue. Let's make this experiment huge. Let's set our intention for something that's really big. Let's set it for you to have the humility to just let the book flow through you."

I sensed the difference immediately. Jonas' intention was much bigger—much deeper—and much more exciting.

I decided to just relax and let things happen. My body loosened with each subtle adjustment Jonas made to my skull. I noticed the difference in my muscles. I began to sink into it.

After a while, Jonas moved his right hand to my chest, right below my throat, where I sensed my heart chakra. I immediately felt the energy deepen. I remember thinking, *"No, I can't have another amazing experience. I just had one yesterday."* But I dropped that thought quickly and went back to allowing it.

As I breathed, the electricity built inside me. My heart opened more. I knew I had to do something to confirm it—allow it to increase. I placed my left hand on Jonas' hand. The process deepened. I breathed deeply, almost as if I were trying to catch my breath. Then I sensed the flash of a triangle of energy—with Jonas and me forming the two points of the base—and a huge in-pouring of energy at the top. I felt it flowing to Jonas too. It wasn't like November 18th. I didn't feel the sensation of being loved. Instead I felt the sensation of immense energy.

When Jonas removed his hand, I moved mine, too. Quietly, he told me to return my hand to my fourth chakra. "This is yours. Feel it as your own." A few minutes later, as he left the room, he added, "Rest with this, Connie, as your own."

After Jonas left the room, I stayed on the table for a long time—maybe a half hour, probably longer. Drifting in and out of the feeling, finding words, losing the words in feelings, needing to open my eyes and get acclimated to the outer world, needing to dip back into the inner world again. It felt quite different from November 18th, when I simply didn't want to leave. This time, the experience was too overwhelming to integrate. I needed to give myself a chance to catch up with what I'd experienced, allow my senses to settle a bit before I dared to walk or drive a car.

Just as I was getting ready to sit up, Jonas came back into the treatment room. I was surprised to see him. Generally, if we needed to talk things out—if I needed to ask questions—we did so at our next session.

I was delighted to see him. I already had tons of questions. As I sat up, he sat down in the chair beside me. But before I could get one question out, he began, "Thank you for letting me be part of this experience." I started to protest, then realized he was right. We'd both experienced something.

"This was huge, Connie. This was a thousand times bigger than November 18th. Can you feel it?"

"Honestly, no. It felt big, but not bigger than the 18th. That day, I sensed God's love. This was fantastic, but…."

"Connie, on November 18th you stepped over the threshold—out of the darkness into the light. Today you moved through another threshold within the light—to a new place. This is…" I could see him trying to find the right analogy. "This is the equivalent of what Pentecostals would call being slain in the Spirit. This was an important shift. You're different now."

I have to admit it; I didn't feel what he felt. I sensed his exhilaration, but I didn't share the depth of his experience.

"Connie, this kind of experience lifts all of us up. I'd recommend that you talk a lot less for a while. Just let yourself grow into an appreciation of this. But you also need to teach this. I know this may not make sense…"

"But it does."

As he said those words, I'd flashed back to a poem I'd written in the convent more than 40 years before. It was about a mute Christian who sang the most melodious songs and told the most enchanting stories—without saying a word.

"I think I understand that part, Jonas. We all teach by truly living in a way that reflects the gifts we receive. As for the rest, I'm willing to allow the rest of the understanding to come in time."

We thanked each other again. I walked out of the office a little confused, very grateful, and looking forward to what might happen next.

I came home to an empty house for the first time in four days. Ross was driving Hannah and Liam back home and would be gone for several hours. I collapsed on to the couch, in part exhausted by the holidays, in part because my senses were still on overload. I slept until Ross returned home. This latest movement needed to grow in me slowly.

Two days later we celebrated New Year's Eve—2008 had been quite a year.

CHAPTER 23

AFTER THE RAINBOW

For standing in your heart is where I want to be, and long to be,
Ah, but I may as well try and catch the wind.
~ Donovan

December's triangle-of-energy experience grounded me for quite a while. I stopped worrying and started living. January felt like my honeymoon time, my rainbow. I walked on the spiritual sunny side of the street. Everything brought me back to God. Meditating with consistency—always my biggest challenge—became easier. First thing in the morning, last thing at night, I sat, I breathed, I tried to remain still—to open myself to the God I now knew loved me. Often the meditation itself wasn't easy and, considering how many times I had to pull myself back to focusing on my breath, it wasn't what I would call successful. But I meditated consistently.

And, sometimes, the meditations brought me just where I wanted to go.

January 19
Today it happened, without Jonas! I felt God's love and presence in my life. Now that I know it's possible on my own, I feel much more at ease and grateful.

I read books Jonas suggested—Christian books I would have never glanced at on my own. As often as not, I found inspiration in them. I also read books of my own choosing. With new eyes, I reread Jack Kornfield and Steven Levine to get some insight into meditating better. I fell in love with the poetry of Rumi, a 13th century mystic. I got out Joseph Campbell books and DVDs and relished new insights from an old friend.

Jonas shared one of his prayers with me, "Lord, your servant kneels before your creation, ready to serve." I loved it. Saying it as part of my morning prayers brought me into a sacred space where I lived my days. Cooking, editing, talking with a friend, snuggling with a grandchild or smiling at the checkout clerk in the supermarket—all were done from this sacred place of service and love.

I felt an increased closeness to past generations of my family. Often after a cranial, as I rested on the table for a while, I felt my women ancestors around me, supporting me, continuing the healing the cranial work had begun. I sometimes got inspiration from them at the end of my morning rituals. This is one I found especially helpful:

> January 21
>
> Connie, what you need to see, what you haven't seen before, is this is how the past generations made it [through hard times], by praying for help and getting it. Despite the rules and regulations of the Church, people had a personal connection to the Source of help. That's how it's done. Connie, you're not [doing this] alone.

I couldn't imagine a situation my newfound spirituality wouldn't get me through. Feeling God's love in my heart, coursing through my veins, seared into my soul, what could I possibly fear?

In the afterglow of November 18th, I became a new creation, ready to face any problem—spiritual, physical, emotional, financial, mundane or profound—with God's grace and my newfound courage. I assumed my healing work was complete. I presumed my need for therapy was a thing of the past. I figured it was time to learn to do soul work, not emotional work.

And then I imploded.

Three months after November 18th I hit the wall and crumbled.

What I hadn't counted on was losing the realization—the feeling, the thought, the understanding—that God truly loved me. One day it was there. The next it was gone. And I didn't know how to get it back.

Fear and grasping dominated my mind for the next several months. The fears I'd banished from my mind after November 18th became real again. I felt myself, once more, in some dark hole of unbelief. In spite of all I'd been given and all I'd experienced, I couldn't maintain my spiritual balance. I felt abandoned. I couldn't get rid of the fear that tests, trials and horrific times were coming.

Despite everything, I still feared God—the God of my childhood, of the Church and the convent I thought I'd left behind a lifetime ago. The roots of the old beliefs were deep and wide.

So were the old fears. I thought of Job and how God could do to me what He'd done to him. If God knew my heart—and He certainly did—He knew the way to test me wasn't by taking away my things. Things could come and go and I'd still be OK. The best way would be to take away the ones I loved. On a very visceral level, my fear of losing a child or grandchild became entwined with my fear of continuing in this relationship with God. And knowing my fear was illogical didn't do anything to eradicate it.

Of all the things I wrote in my journal those months, this excerpt is the most telling:

> Sometimes I think there are too many leprechauns and mag-ic-bottle genies in my mind when I think about God. I'm always looking for the trick, for the joke that leaves me desolate, with no more wishes and no pot of gold—again.

I'm grateful I journaled so extensively then. If I hadn't, I think, standing where I am now—slightly downstream of those turbulent transitional days, out of the fury of Level 6 spiritual white water—I'd have a tendency to brush them off as merely uncomfortable. In truth, they were acutely painful and confusing.

Every day I was either totally up or totally down. I felt I was living on some fiendishly designed roller coaster where the hills and valleys had been so compressed I could never catch my breath. I'd come home from a cranial and be on top of the world. I'd wake up the next morning and, unable to meditate well or confused by my spiritual reading, I'd become totally crushed and disillusioned. The next day I'd have a good meditation or read something that gave me clarity and I'd feel my heart lighten—until, three hours later, when I came up against a thought about harm to my children or Ross. Then I'd totally reject any sort of spirituality and find myself confused and bereft.

I was confused for months. After 40 years of standing on the outside of a spiritual life, looking in, I was now on the inside. But inside of what? The phrase "stranger in a strange land" kept coming to mind. I didn't know how to safely navigate the terrain of a spiritual life. I didn't know the consequences of any of my actions. I didn't know what would make me feel confident and what would make me feel desolate. I didn't know what God expected and how I could do the things that would put me in His favor.

I struggled with a whirlpool of unanswered questions: *"Is this the time to dig deeper into understanding or to blindly believe? Is this the time for trying harder or having more faith? How can I be doing all the right things and still feel this lonely and discouraged? Is this the darkness before the dawn or a never-ending black hole"?*

I still felt grateful for the gift of November 18th, but I couldn't figure out how to hold on to the realization it was real. I felt vulnerable and on edge most of the time.

"Was the love I felt that day really God's love or some sort of brain aberration? Have I taken one inexplicable experience and made it into a totally absurd belief system? Maybe believing is better than living in a world of perpetual cynicism, but not when you don't know the rules."

Ironically, my day-to-day life, which was going well, added to my internal discomfort. Ross and I were both working in jobs we really liked. The children and grandchildren were all healthy. Naturally, some people I loved had problems, but they managed them with only occasional support from me. No one needed my full-time, undivided attention. I didn't particularly like that. I would have preferred a nice, clear-cut, outer-directed crisis—one I could have thrown myself into with abandon, one that would have allowed me to lose myself in its all-encompassing, unthinking embrace.

Without a crisis or a looming deadline to serve as distractions, spirituality issues took center stage. The chatter in my mind—questions, doubts, theories, fears—was interminable:

"What's wrong with me? Why can't I just be grateful for good times? Am I so perverse I can't appreciate my blessings and be happy? Do I really think my choice to be spiritual will cause harm to my family? What am I, some three-year-old narcissist who assumes the world revolves around her? Do I really think I have this kind of power?"

I was either on the mountaintop or in the deepest gutter. The following two quotes from my journal are typical of almost everything I wrote for the next several months.

February 4, 2009
And today, again, the experience of the opening of my heart.
. . . Right now, I can feel the sacred ground under my feet. I can feel my heart chakra open to the point of aching. I can feel my family, the generations and generations before me, with me. I feel the same sense of healing that I feel in Jonas' office when I have a cranial. I'm learning to get to this place without his help.

February 9, 2009.
Maybe November 18th was an aberration, a trick of my needy mind.
What do we have a right to as humans? Do we have a right to feel loved? Maybe this is too much to ask. Maybe this whole journey has been a trick. Or maybe it's just me, my negativity.
Maybe my idea of God is too mixed up with my ideas of wishes and magic. It seems like I'm always flinching, waiting for the trick, waiting for God to finally demand the price for the past months of happiness.

~

Working with Jonas now also fueled my fears. After his family crisis, he had changed. When we first met, he'd seemed to be in a space where he accepted all forms of spirituality. We discussed Buddhist concepts and Chinese healing theories as frequently as we did Biblical teachings. Now his focus was different. When I pressed him for guidelines, he consistently urged me to read the Bible.

"Connie, reading the Bible, immersing myself in God's word, is what got me through the terrifically difficult months I've just faced. I can't offer you anything better."

I knew he was being honest. I'd watched him grow in strength and faith. It seemed like a logical choice for me too. I wanted what Jonas had. My mind wanted to accept his path, but my body couldn't. The harder I tried to go down Jonas' path, to read the Bible as my source of spiritual nourishment, the more ill at ease I felt. My neck and shoulder muscles would tense. My back would ache. I couldn't read the Bible without reliving all the doubts, fears and confusion I'd felt before I left the Church.

I gave it my best effort—not out of virtue, but out of desperation. I bought a *New Living Translation* version of the Bible so I didn't get caught up in archaic language. I followed Jonas' advice and skipped the Old Testament and went right to the New. I took deep breaths and prayed to see things with beginner's eyes.

I made it through the first couple chapters of Matthew with just a few twinges of fear and old thinking. I breezed through the Sermon on the Mount. However, when I hit the last verse of Chapter 5, "Be perfect, even as the Heavenly Father is perfect." I felt the discomfort begin. The words brought me back into the rigid, black and white, impossible days of my childhood and the convent—trying to be perfect and always failing. They brought me back to the world of feeling unworthy and unlovable, unable to ever get anything right.

By the time I was midway through Chapter 6, the unanswered questions that had plagued me my whole life were back in full force. When I reached the end of the chapter, the quote about the birds of the air and the lilies of the field did me in. *"Yeah, yeah, yeah,"* I thought. *"The birds of the air and lilies of the field are less precious than man, but all three—birds, lilies, and most of all people—are not safe in this world. No one is taken care of by the biblical God! If these words are a source of comfort to some people, they are not to me.*"

I tried several more times, with other parts of the New Testament. But the more I read, the more the accumulated contradictions and feelings of unworthiness from the last 50 years bubbled to the surface. The old perfectionist God of my youth, who kept a running tally of all my sins, who couldn't be trusted, who was always unsatisfied with even my best efforts, who judged harshly and wasn't there in time of need, shouted at me from every page. I couldn't open the Bible without those feelings returning.

By midmonth I was completely in the weeds. I couldn't get my bearings. I tried an alternative. I got a copy of the Gospel of Thomas, one of the early Christian Gospels discovered in the 1940s in Egypt, hoping to find a version untainted by my past experiences. But its call to transcend my humanity was more than I could handle. As I typed what follows into my journal late one night, I couldn't control my tears—and I couldn't understand why I was so emotional. I only knew I couldn't transcend the world. Since my Constellation experiences, I'd finally felt connected to the world, to my life. I really didn't want to give that up.

> February 17, 2009
>
> Now, the old thoughts are demanding all the air time in my brain. I just can't choose Jonas' way. I can't be a Bible person. I'm just starting to like being in the real world. I don't want to be a Not-of-This-World-person. . . .
>
> If I'm being completely honest tonight—and that's the only option—I'd choose . . . being fully human over Jonas, God and transcending my humanity. Maybe in the light of day, I'll feel differently. But for right now, this is where I am and where I choose to be . . . I can say, from the place where I am right now: "God,

if I have a choice, I choose to live in the world, with honesty and humility, and the fullness of my humanity. I choose to be human. I choose not to transcend, but to become more fully human."

The next morning, however, unable to face the feeling of emptiness that came from "choosing the fullness of my humanity," I returned to the spiritual path. I picked up the Bible. I meditated. I prayed for help. Occasionally I felt balanced for a day or two. More often the Bible readings left me confused and on edge.

It was an odd time. Everyday life continued. I made a conscious effort to separate my spiritual life from the rest of it. I continued my job editing and indexing manuscripts. I organized a 40th birthday party for Lisa, with 50 guests. Ross and I took some macrobiotic cooking classes. We went on excursions together discovering new organic markets. We played cards with other couples. I cleaned and cooked and had wonderful times with the grandchildren. I met friends for lunch. During the day my life looked and felt pretty normal. But alone, early in the morning and late at night when I tried to pray or journal, I was coming undone.

March, 9, 2009

And now, I'm having more bad days than good ones—journaling less, crying more. The old problems of living in this world have returned in all their glory and I'm scrambling to stay afloat. Things are barely OK between Ross and me. I understand why. He's got to feel like he's living with a crazy person. One day, I'm all sunshine and roses, two hours later I'm screaming at him or demanding he just leave me the hell alone. . . . Things are sometimes shaky with Jonas. The daily hum I had in my gut is gone. Now, every other day, I just keep trying to patch myself back together. My best intentions and beliefs aren't enough to keep me above the fray.

I'm asking for help, trying to visualize better, trying to be a better person. . . . But I want to just eat or play computer solitaire. I'm back to self hate and sadness. What If I AM totally unworthy?

I'd then have some good days:

March 13, 2009

Woke up this morning with such gratitude—for Jonas, for Ross, for a God who seems to be lighting my path to union with Him.

Those days, however, were becoming more rare.

March 15, 2009

I know, right now, I'm living at about 20% energy, if that. I can't have an active day without crashing for the next two or three days. I seem to need a nap every day. I even prefer ending a good time, playing cards or going out with friends, to come home and sleep. This isn't good! I'm so afraid the Chronic Fatigue is returning.

The weirdest part—this all seems to be tied into my desire to truly feel God in my life.

Jonas and I were working hard to get me out of the downward spiral. Unfortunately, I just couldn't hold on to the knowledge he kept giving me. I'd go into his office and make it very clear to him, "Just tell me what I need to do, what I need to say, how I need to change. I'll do it. I'll do it 100%! Just tell me what it is."

Then he would say what he always said—the only thing he could say because it was *his truth*—in a different way, hoping that, with one more iteration, he'd put it in a way I could finally understand.

"Connie, you need to trust, to believe in God's love for you."

"Jonas, I try. But I can't. It's not that I don't want to. It's not that I need to be convinced it's a good idea. I'm totally willing to dump my intellectual reasoning and my ego. But I can't take the risk—emotionally."

"Then how do you explain your experience on November 18th?"

"That's the problem. I'm afraid it was the answer to *your* prayers for me—not my worthiness to be loved. You're the believer. I'm still not. I know I'm doing something wrong— *being someone wrong*. I just don't know how to be someone who can feel God's love."

Each time we had this conversation, I could see the concern and confusion in his eyes. He genuinely wanted me to be in the space where he'd found peace. I did too. I knew, beyond any doubt, his experience was genuinely life-enhancing for him, but I couldn't make it mine. I didn't know why. I didn't know what I was doing wrong, but I knew I couldn't make the leap of faith and just accept the idea that God loved me.

One day Jonas brought in his own journal and read me entries from several years ago, when he'd had the same struggle, asked the same questions. When he finished, he said,

"Connie, believe me. Where you are, living on the fence between believing and not, is harder than letting go and trusting God."

His thoughtfulness touched me deeply. I truly appreciated his concern. His patience amazed me. I knew I was fortunate to have such a caring mentor in my life. Yet, bottom line, I didn't know how to do what he asked. I didn't know how to *not* be afraid, to *not* mistrust. Forty years of not trusting in God was stronger than one November 18th experience, especially when I didn't know what I had done or said or been to allow that miracle to happen.

When I got home from his office, I wrote in my journal:

225

I hope Jonas is right. But I'm afraid he's wrong. I'm fearful that, after I jump, the arms will be withdrawn because I'm not acceptable. Then I'll fall, once again, into a pit of darkness so deep, so smothering, so covered in the tar of despair, I will never recover, never again take a breath that is not filled with coagulated darkness and pain and infinite self-hate. I've been to this place before. I know its geography intimately.

This is what Jonas doesn't understand: The pain of the fall into despair is worse than anything—even the decision to remain on the fence, unable to choose, unable to move. The pain of not choosing feels like a chronic ache, a debilitating arthritis throughout my body and soul. It makes every day laborious and exhausting. But the anguish of falling and not being caught [would be] excruciating. That would feel like being burned alive—and unable to die. Oddly, here, in this place of not choosing, I maintain some flickering spark of hope. If I don't choose, I can have hope that he's right. If I choose and am unacceptable, I have nothing but pain and despair.

I went back to my old way of thinking:

If you can't get there by doing and you can't get there by working hard, and you can't get there by being worthy—because we're either ALL worthy or ALL unworthy—and you don't seem to get there by allowing and waiting, how the hell do you get there? I'm tapped out.

I found new ways of doubting the reality of spirituality:

Why this damned search? Why can't I just be delighted out of my mind with the freaking great life I have? Wonderful husband,

healthy and happy children and grandchildren, good job, financial security—what the hell else do I want??!! But still, [I have]
this need, this unceasing, gnawing need to know there is a God
who loves us—who loves me.

Maybe this is just a brain aberration—that's my fear. Is
needing to experience the love of God the road to spirituality
or simply a sign of mental illness? I feel like a freak, like a crazy
person. Other people don't seem to care about finding God.
They would look at my life, at all I've got, and wonder why the
hell I can't simply be content having such an enviable life. And
I wonder it too.

. . . This is what I want to, need to, know. Is this real or simply
a child's dream. Others would say the miracles are all around me,
[they] would ask how I can doubt. But it takes no effort for me to
doubt. It's my reality. It's my way of seeing the world. WHAT is
wrong with me!!!!????

The emotional rollercoaster continued for months. Then, somewhere in those months, on one of the good days, Jonas made a suggestion that gave me hope. He shared another of his prayers with
me—the one he said when he needed guidance: "Lord, I don't know
what to do next, but You do. You lead, I'll follow."

It was simple, practical and didn't require me to squeeze my beliefs and emotions into places they couldn't go. I used it daily and
the fog began to lift a bit. I thought of it as my Swiss Army Knife
Prayer—something for every situation, for every emergency, for every doubt.

*"Lord, I don't know how to end these fears, but You do. Please teach
me the way.*

*Lord I don't know what to read, but You do. Lead me to the books; I'll
read them.*

Lord, I don't know how to be spiritual, but You know what I need. Show me the way and I'll follow it.

Lord I just don't know, but You do...."

Sometimes, when I had the presence of mind to pray that prayer and remember to listen for the answer, an answer came. But presence of mind was not my trump suit for those months.

Things got a little better, but I was still unbalanced a good part of the time. My brain still whirled with doubts and confusion. I couldn't go back to denying God's existence; I couldn't stop aching to experience His love again *and* I couldn't get myself into a place where I could remain steady for more than a few days.

By the end of March I was back down again:

March 25, 2009

I'm 62 years old. I can't go on like this. God, if you're real, I need to know. If you're not, I need to know.

I'm so tired of wondering, of hoping. I don't know what else to do. I've used up every resource I know—if you're real, please show me!!!!!

Lord, I don't know what else to do, but You do. I give up!! You lead, I'll follow.

The answer to that prayer came in a way I never could have predicted—and it added a whole new dimension to my understanding.

CHAPTER 24

THE MIDDLE GARDEN

All of life on this earth is spirit/matter.
~ Carmen Stenholm

Carmen Stenholm was the third person I met who had profound spiritual experiences in early childhood. Interestingly, hers occurred despite the lack of religion in her home. She was raised in East Germany in the early 1950s, where religion was forbidden. Her encounters with the Transcendent were not shaped by the faith she grew up with; they were simply there as a natural part of her life.

Carmen and I became friends as I edited *Crack Between the Worlds*, her novel based on the lives of her great-grandmother, grandmother and mother. After an editing session, we'd usually have lunch or a cup of coffee. We often talked about spirituality.

When things started to go downhill for me during the first months of 2009, Carmen, who had been a therapist before becoming a writer, noticed. At first she just offered a listening ear. As things got worse, her therapeutic instincts couldn't be denied.

"Con, I really think you need to get some help with this—some professional help. You're skating on the edge of a pretty major depression."

"Carm, this is spiritual, not psychological."

Carmen smiled and sighed. "That's an artificial distinction, Connie. You're one person. Your spirituality and humanity can't be separated."

"Well, they feel separate to me. Besides, who could I go to anyhow? To a Christian counselor? To a priest? To some sort of psychic therapist? Who's going to understand both the spiritual and the psychological parts?

After an awkward silence, I finally said, "Carm, would you consider working with me?"

"I've thought about it, but I don't see how I can. We've become friends."

"Who else would you recommend? Who else would know what in the world I'm talking about? How do I go about finding a therapist who would respect the work I've done with the past generations of my family—with what happened on November 18ᵗʰ? Carm, what if we don't make it long term? What if we don't make it a formal therapy session? What if you just talk me through this one thing?"

She hesitated a long time but finally said, "OK, nothing formal, just one friend helping another. That's the only way I'll do it. And short-term. We'll just work on this one thing."

We stayed true to the agreement. We didn't work together long, but we sure worked hard. Carmen walked with me through beliefs I was unaware I had. She challenged me to think differently and stretch my intellectual and emotional muscles. These were no "how does that make you feel" sessions. Carmen broke new ground, made me look at things I had chosen to ignore and enabled me to see how the patterns of my beliefs affected my ability to integrate my spirituality into everyday life.

～

In our first discussion Carmen asked me to describe my current spirituality. I read her a piece from The Green Words. I assumed she'd agree with them completely. She didn't.

"Con. Don't you think the God in these words is a little distant, a little authoritarian?"

"Honest, Carm, I don't."

"All the talk of humility and reverence. Is that how you see God?"

"Of course. That's how we need to approach God, with great reverence, with great humility. There *is* no other way."

She paused for quite a while.

"Is this God distant or close to you? Does this experience match the one you felt on November 18th?"

"OK, I see where you're going. On November 18th I felt nothing but God's love, but that can't be all spirituality is about. It also has to be about my response to God, and I can't imagine any other way to approach God but with profound humility and reverence. We are all unworthy."

"Are you sure? We've talked before about the humility and unworthiness you learned in the convent. Did you ever feel you had a relationship with God in the convent?"

"Of course," I shot back. Then, after a little thought, "Maybe not."

Picture after picture of our lives as postulants and novices flashed through my mind. In each one, we were trying our best to be as good as we could be.

Another name for the three years of the novitiate was *formation*. The Church designated those years for study and prayer so those aspiring to religious life could learn to put away our *old selves* and allow God, with the help of our superiors, to transform us, to mold us into *new creations*, into women ready and willing to live our lives totally in service to God. I remembered an amazingly one-sided connection. We tried to be better. We imagined God accepted our efforts.

Was there a relationship with God? I'm sure some who stayed developed a close one. But, during my year and a half in the convent, I didn't. What I had wasn't a relationship; it was my trying to please God. And it was surely nothing like I'd experienced last November and December.

Carmen persisted. "Connie, did the God you experienced on November 18th feel close to you or far away?"

"Close."

"On that day, did God require unworthiness, require humility, or did He simply love you?"

"I thought God could only be approached with fear and trembling and admission of our unworthiness."

"And I'm suggesting, Con, that this could be part of the problem. It's just something to think about. Consider the possibility that your unworthiness—your need to hold God far above you, in great esteem—is one of the reasons you're having the problems with a relationship with God now."

The concept felt wrong and uncomfortable, but I agreed to consider it. Maybe my beliefs were standing in my way.

I respected Carmen and really tried to give her suggestion a fair chance. I experimented. I thought of examples of relationships with God where people spoke with this personal approach. I remembered *The Little World of Don Camillo* with the feisty priest chatting with Christ on the large crucifix in the church as he went about his duties. They joked. They argued with each other as friends would. Christ almost always won their debates but not without acknowledging Camillo's right to his humanity and, occasionally, giving him permission to kick some sense into his friend, Peppone.

I thought of Sonny, the wonderfully flawed preacher in Robert Duvall's movie, *The Apostle*, who spoke to God with a childlike informality: "I always call you Jesus: You always call me Sonny."

I recalled Malcolm Boyd's poems, which had an intimacy that both frightened and captivated my Catholic sensibilities in the 1960s. He started the first poem in his book, *Are You Running with Me, Jesus?* with the lines:

> I've got to move fast... get into the bathroom, wash up
> grab a bite to eat, and run some more.

You couldn't get more informal than that. But these examples were works of fiction and poetry. They weren't how real people dared to communicate with God.

For a couple days, I tried to imagine God closer, warmer and friendlier. I tried thinking and meditating with this in mind. I wrote the results of my experiment in my journal, but I couldn't get myself to be comfortable with them.

> What I got in meditation a few days ago—and can't allow myself to trust, or even write down until now—was that I should try substituting just one of the names I use in prayer for God with the word Friend. I still feel shaky thinking about it. It feels wrong! . . . Maybe during this week I can test it out, find out if there is a way for this to feel comfortable.
>
> To be fair, this is exactly what the message was:
>
> "Connie, if I let you experience My heart, as you've asked, It would explode you. You would no longer be. That's how much I love you. That's how much I love the world. Instead [of always using the word Lord], when you say your prayers, when you meditate, just one of those times, substitute *Friend* for Lord. You understand the depths of that word. You understand what it is to be a friend. That's where we can begin."

And I've run like crazy from this. It feels kind and gentle and—
untrue. But I'll keep doing it, for the next week. Damn!! This really feels hard! Like I'm again going into uncharted waters without
a compass or a paddle—or a canoe. But, on some other level, it
feels right, if for no other reason than to test my own powers of
discernment. OK, just for this week...

I tried. I couldn't do it, even for a week. It felt too close to blasphemy—too disrespectful of the greatness of God.

I also feared having an informal, friendly relationship with God
for another reason. I didn't want it because it might put me in
league with the non-fiction folks I didn't respect. I remembered
the real-life popes who condoned the Inquisition and jailed Gali-
leo for his arrogant heresy about the earth revolving around the
sun. I thought about the present-day evangelists who claimed their
friend God told them AIDS was His way of punishing gays and
Hurricane Katrina was His chastisement for the sinfulness of the
people in New Orleans. I thought of Ross' old friend, Phil. No
thanks! Keeping a respectful distance from God, keeping out of the
Divine-Revelations-from-My-Best-Buddy-God loop, felt much
safer and saner to me.

After a few more days of strong discomfort with the concept, I
just put it aside. It felt unnatural and egotistical to have the Creator
of the Universe as a friend.

Carmen next suggested we examine my view of spirituality in
general.

"Con, you can correct me if I'm wrong, but it seems you see the
spiritual world as something different from the real world."

"Yes, of course."

"And, it's more intriguing than the real world?"

"Yes."

"And you're most happy when your spirituality is good, when you feel you're working on the spiritual plane?"

"You've got it."

We talked briefly about my spiritual sidewalk/worldly gutter analogy.

"OK, now let's look at the last several weeks. You've been telling me you feel really miserable when your sense of spiritual connection is gone. Is that true?"

"You know it is, Carm."

"You've described these past weeks as a rollercoaster ride—either very high or very low. Am I correct?"

"Yes, and I hate it."

"Do you go through *all* your day like this, either very high or very low?"

"No. I live in the real world, too. I still have to edit manuscripts and cook and clean. I still spend time with friends and my family. You know—the normal stuff."

"How do you feel when you're doing the normal stuff? Is it the high of spirituality or the low of no spiritual connection?"

"It's neither. It just is."

"Equally?"

"Of course not. It's much more fun playing with the grandkids or going to lunch with a friend than doing dishes or cleaning the bathroom."

"Which is more satisfying, the spiritual part or the everyday part?"

"Carm, that's a dumb question. It's comparing apples and oranges. One's spiritual; one's not. I can't compare them."

Carmen picked up a pen and drew a long narrow rectangle in her notebook.

"Con, this represents your world—your view of where you live. Let's call it your emotional back yard."

She circled a small portion of the right side of the rectangle.

"This tiny part—this 10%—is the *good* end of your yard. Here you have your spiritual rose garden—your meditation time, your reading about spirituality, the Family Constellation workshops, your discussions with Jonas and other people about God and the times when you feel connected to your spirit."

She then circled about 10% of the left side of the rectangle.

"Here, on the other side, you have a garbage dump. This is where you go when you feel spiritually disconnected, depressed, or abandoned."

"Yeah, that feels right. So what I want to do is learn how to stay…"

"No. I don't think so. That's what you've always done—try to stay in the rose garden. Perhaps, instead, your challenge is to learn to notice and appreciate the other 80% of your yard.

"Connie, your split between spiritual life and real life is creating your discomfort. And it's not based on facts. There is no split. Our lives, right here and now, on this planet, on this Wednesday, on this day when it's raining, are our spiritual/human lives. There's no time when we're not fully spiritual—whether we're taking a shower or making a shopping list or praying. There's no time when we're not fully human—whether we're meditating or singing Gregorian chant or eating chocolate cake.

"I see you frantically trying to stay in your little spiritual rose garden. And when you can't, you assume the only place to go is straight to the junkyard. Then, you're unhappy until you can plot or plead or work your way back to the roses. But you're missing the rest—the entire middle of your yard."

I burst into tears. "But the good part of life is the rose garden, Carm. After all these years, I'm finally here. I'm finally in a spiritual place—at least some of the time. I don't want to give it up."

"And I don't want you to, Con. You don't have to give anything up. The rose garden is yours, always. You just need to realize the other 80% of the yard is yours too—and it's worthy of your attention. It's good too. It's spiritual too. All of life is spiritual.

"What you consider filler time—the time you spend doing everyday things—is *not* filler. It's the real substance of life. It's just as spiritual as the time you spend in pursuit of what you're calling spiritual. The distinction you made as a child—walking on the spiritual sidewalk rather than in the worldly gutter—is creating your pain. You've been dismissing huge chunks of your life as nonessential—as unimportant.

"In your frantic race to escape the dump and return to the roses, you've missed so much beauty of life. Just for a moment, think about this. Maybe the part of the yard you thoughtlessly race through in your desperate search for your spiritual garden is beautiful too. Maybe it has soft grass and pockets of cool moss. It may have little pockets of lilies of the valley and violets and a sparkling stream bounded by ferns. You don't know because you're too focused on it being *not-the-rose-garden*. I'm suggesting you need to expand your view of what is holy and sacred and spiritual. It might be worth considering."

Once I calmed down and thought about it, the image made sense. I could surely see how I'd spent so much of the last several months—of my whole life—devaluing everyday existence, making it only background for my Quest for Truth.

"Connie, your sidewalk metaphor has kept you from your life. Whenever you have been worried about falling off the spiritual curb or scrambling to get back on, you've been avoiding the beauty and potential in what you have been calling the gutter. Here's something I want you to consider: the sidewalk/gutter distinction is your own creation. It's not how the world really is. We don't climb above the world, and we can't fall off the high spiritual walk. There's no distinction between spiritual and worldly. All of life on this earth is *spirit/matter*. They can't be separated. Each is infused within the other."

I considered her argument. She was right about the first part. I'd always made the distinction between life in pursuit of spiritual fulfillment and life doing the background things before going back to the spiritual pursuit. But suggesting the filler was just as important as the quest—that the filler *was* the quest—felt like too big a leap.

"OK, Carm, I can agree, in part. But—here's the important part you're missing—the worldly things don't fill my soul. How can they be spiritual? How can doing a crossword puzzle or making a salad ever fill the hole inside me that craves the spiritual? Quite frankly, those things can't and never will. They *feel* like filler. I understand what you're saying, Carm, but I don't know what to do with the knowledge. Just making everything spiritual doesn't make it satisfying."

"Con, you don't have to *do* anything right now. Are you willing to just play with the concept? Consider it possible?"

"Sure, yeah."

"How about this: Just plant the seed of this possibility in your heart and mind. Try to see the spirit in the everyday aspects of life and the everyday in what you consider spiritual."

"OK, I can try it."

~

That seed took a lot of nurturing to even *begin* to sprout. I worked with the concept for weeks. I tried to see the spiritual everywhere.

Some parts were easy. We were coming into spring; it was easy to see God's love in the budding trees and blossoming flowers. Some parts were difficult and comically clumsy. I needed to once again learn that not every thought I had after an epiphany was an inspiration! For instance, after seeing an article in the newspaper about a local polka band, I fussed for weeks deciding whether or not I'd been divinely inspired to learn to play the accordion. (It's a story close friends still retell—with no small degree of relish and raucous laughter.)

But the concept did grow on me. A few days after my conversation with Carmen an odd image appeared at the end of one of my meditations and kept recurring, unbidden, throughout the next few days. It began as the image of a vertical tube—three-foot wide and six-foot long—that started above my head and stretched upward. The tube was there for just a while. Over time, it slowly began to rotate until, several days later, it was horizontal and went through my stomach from front to back. As it rotated, so did my perceptions. I began to be open to the idea that spirituality is not just about connecting with the transcendent God. It's also seeing—and appreciating—God in all of life.

As I looked for other beliefs connected to this one, a Bible quote popped into my head: "Whatever you do to the least of these, my brethren, you do to Me." Growing up, I'd always thought the quote described God's way of giving us a bonus for being good. You know, "Be nice to everyone, even the unlikeable, and I'll treat it as if you did it to Me. You'll get extra credit on your permanent record." Now I saw it from a different perspective. All of life is spiritual. God is in all of life. My new interpretation became: "Whatever you do, you do in relationship with Me, because I am in everything, in everyone."

By the time the tube became totally horizontal, I began to feel more at home with Carmen's ideas.

CHAPTER 25

GRANDMA AND ME

"We do not believe in ourselves until someone reveals that deep
inside us something is valuable, worth listening to,
worthy of our trust, sacred to our touch.
~ *e. e. cummings*

I truly appreciated the work Carmen and I were doing. Those first two insights—about 80% of the garden and God being in everything—felt significant.

But I knew we hadn't hit bedrock yet—and so did Carm. I could still feel the boulder in my gut. Mark and I had done some damage to it when I began Constellation work. As Jonas and I did the craniosacral work, the boulder cracked and shifted significantly. I thought I was ready for the next step in the demolition process.

"OK, Carm, where do we go from here?"

"You're not going to like the suggestion, Con, but I have to say it. We need to do some family-of-origin work."

"Damn, Carm, anything but that. I've done so much of that in the past. Isn't there something else we can do?"

"We can do all kinds of things, but if childhood issues are at the root of your distress, we have to discuss them."

Carmen believed I really didn't have the idyllic childhood I thought I'd had. I believed she was mistaken.

"Here's the objective reality, Carmen. No one beat me. No one ever did anything intentionally cruel. I wasn't abandoned. I had two parents who cared for me, a house, enough to eat, and a good education. By any standards, I was damned lucky. That's it. Let it go. Let's move on."

I did not want to do any more damned inner-child work. I'd done it before, with numerous therapists. I did it intensively for four solid weeks when I went to an inpatient food addictions rehab program in Florida. There, in group and private therapy, I dealt with my anger toward both of my parents and my resentment toward the priest whom I blamed for ruining our family. (I got to such levels of raw rage I actually drew blood while beating on an upholstered chair, expressing my feelings toward dear Father Tokay.) In the end I simply felt more angry and victimized. The work hadn't given me any peace of mind—and it hadn't helped me to stop eating compulsively.

I've always thought inner-child therapies gave people an excuse for not growing up. No one had a perfect childhood, but most of us made it to adulthood. Hey, my life was certainly better than most. I could list the friends who had it worse. Certainly my siblings had it harder than I did. I was married when my dad left the family. My youngest sisters were just 9 and 11 years old. They were the ones who had it hard, not me.

Even more, going back and digging into my childhood felt like a rejection of everything I learned from Family Constellation work. I could not afford to do that. My life changed 180 degrees with Hellinger work. Accepting my parents had saved my life. It was the foundation of all the good things that happened in the last several years. I didn't dare desert it to whine about my childhood. As I sat on the couch opposite Carmen, I clutched the pendant that held the words that clearly defined my new beliefs, "Whatever it was, thank you."

"Carm, I'm not fighting the fact I'm screwed up. I know I am. I know I've been fighting major depression all my life and I've come close to allowing it to pull me under more than once. I'm willing to admit that. Yeah, I know I don't feel terribly connected to my own life. Sometimes I'm not particularly happy to be alive. But still, Carm, what you're saying just doesn't make sense. It–really–wasn't–that–bad." *(If I speak slowly, maybe she'll understand me.)*

What really surprised me was that she, of all people, should say this to me. She actually had a horrific childhood. She had the classic traumas that take a lifetime of therapy to overcome. Inner-child work made sense for her. It made sense for my friend, Greg, who was beaten almost to death by his alcoholic father on numerous occasions, or for my friend, Tina, whose father molested her and her sisters.

I was ready to say this when, for just a second, I winced as I remembered that both Greg and Tina assumed the same sorts of things had happened to me. I remembered Greg saying to me, "You're so much like me, Con. Can't you see we have the same kinds of emotional scars? Are you sure you haven't just buried some childhood trauma?"

Still, I knew what I knew. My childhood wasn't bad. OK, I didn't understand where my scars came from, but Carmen couldn't be right. It just didn't ring true.

"Hey," I said to Carmen, "at least I got to have something wonderful with Grandma Bordone. At least I was the oldest kid, so I got the biggest chunk of my dad's time and attention."

But Carmen remained insistent.

"Connie, something was painful in your childhood. You were a bright, sensitive little girl. For a while, when your grandmother was alive, you had someone who loved you unconditionally. Then, suddenly, you had no one. Just from our casual conversations, I know you sensed from an early age you weren't what your mother wanted. Through the Constellation work you've come to see why and how your mom wasn't able to love and accept you just as you were. You've recently come to understand your dad was often emotionally unavailable, too. Once Grandma died, who did you have? Have you ever done any therapy work around your grandmother?"

"No. There was never any reason to. That was the good part of my life."

"OK. Then let's start there. What I'd like you to do is write down what you remember about your grandmother—how you felt when you were with her, what she did that made you feel loved. Email these memories to me before we get together again."

It was a good compromise—*positive* early-childhood work.

I spent the next two evenings thinking and writing about Grandma. The experience surprised me. I hadn't expected to recall those days with such clarity, to feel the emotions from almost 60 years ago with such intensity. I emailed my reflections to Carmen.

> Carm,
>
> These are the truest memories I have of Grandma. These events aren't prompted by old photos or conversations or someone else's recollections. They come only from my memory.

> **I am a toddler.**

We live with Grandma because she is too sick to live alone. She lives on the first floor. We live on the second.

I sit on her bed. Grandma smiles.

I talk. Grandma smiles.

She shares her Sen-Sen with me. Sen-Sen is odd and black and tiny. It's a little like licorice. It really doesn't taste good but Grandma loves it, so I love it too. When I snuggle into her arms, I feel like a baby bird in a soft, warm nest. I love this feeling.

If I am bad, I can stay with her. If I am good, I can stay. Her eyes shine when she sees me. I don't want to go back upstairs. I want to stay with her all the time.

It's always special when her friend, Jimmy the Tailor, comes to visit. He brings us M&Ms in a brown bag, instead of an M&M package. He gets them at a place called Murphy's 5 & 10. I tell Jimmy the Italian words Grandma taught me and he is amazed. He says I sound like a real Italian. They both smile at me a lot.

While they talk to each other, Jimmy lets me play with his special tailor's chalk. I can write on anything—my clothes, Grandma's blanket, even Grandma's clothes—and it doesn't ruin anything. I can use it anywhere and not get into trouble. While I'm drawing, I sometimes look up at Grandma. When she talks about me, she shines.

I am 3.

This is the best day of my life! I'm always happy when I think about it!

Grandma is feeling well enough to be out of bed. She's had a couple good days in a row. She invites me—just me—downstairs for dinner. We sit at her white enamel kitchen table. We eat breaded veal and green beans and salad. I use my best manners. Grandma talks to me like she talks to Jimmy. I sit up very straight in my chair. And then—this is the best part—after supper, when she begins to do dishes, she pulls my chair up to the sink. As she washes the dishes, I dry them!! I am grown up. I am just like her. I am her friend—just like Jimmy! This is my very best day!

I am 4.

Again, Grandma is having some good days. She's feeling well enough to babysit my cousin, Sandy, and me for an hour or so while Mom and Aunt Norma go shopping. They're taking Susie with them because she's a baby and too much for Grandma to handle.

I'd been misbehaving that morning and, before she left, Mom made Grandma promise not to give us any candy while she was gone.

As soon as Mom and Aunt Norma are out the door, I get out my little set of dishes and start setting up a tea party for Sandy and me. I'm sure if Grandma sees those empty plates, she'll forget her promise and give us some of the hard candy she always has stashed in her nightstand drawer.

"Hey Grandma, look, we're having a tea party. Come see. It's all set up. All we need is something to put on the plates."

Grandma barely contains her smile as she comes out of the kitchen to check out our table setting. She tries to look stern but there's a twinkle in her eyes from the very beginning.

"You know what your mother said. No candy! I promised and I can't go back on my promise."

Then she shows us what she is holding behind her back. A blue can of Planter's peanuts!! A far, far better treat than old hard candy!!! Sandy and I feast like queens. Grandma and I keep looking at each other and smiling. I'm so in awe of her! She'd figured out a way to keep her word to Mom and still completely undo my punishment. I feel so loved, so special. She is my very best friend in the whole world!

I am almost 5.

Grandma is dead. I know she has gone up to heaven to be with God. God missed her so much, He wanted to bring her home to Him. Grandma can look down from heaven and see me.

The rest is a blank.

I have no memories of funeral parlors or funerals. Did I go to the funeral parlor? Maybe. Were there tons of tears and relatives, and friends and food after the funeral? There had to have been. There always were at deaths in our family, and Grandma had been a very beloved member of the family.

My only clear memory is of a lot of people at our house and someone giving us kids cardboard animal cards with different colored shoe laces. We need to weave the laces through the holes around the animals, following the numbers—like dot-to-dot, but with laces rather than a pencil. My animal is a duckling. My shoelace is yellow. I have to help Sandy with hers. That's all I remember.

When we met several days later, I was totally unprepared for Carmen's take on what I sent her.

"Connie, I'm not saying this is true. But I want you to consider this: perhaps the death of your grandmother marked the beginning of your fear and lack of trust in God."

"What? That doesn't make any sense…"

"Just stop for a second and look at what you wrote: *God missed her so much He wanted to bring her home to Him.* You know, now, that's not how death works. But people in the 1950s, in your family, said those things to each other to help ease their pain. You weren't even five years old when you heard this explanation. For you, then, it was a fact. God, who knew everything, who knew how much your grandma meant to you, how much you two meant to each other, chose to take her away from you because He wanted her all to Himself. If that was how you understood death and God—and it probably was—do you think there may have been some anger and hurt in your little heart?"

My mind couldn't even take in her words. I wanted to disagree, ask her how she knew, ask her to give me proof.…

But my body was way ahead of my brain. Tears streamed down my face. Somewhere deep in my chest, her words registered. I felt the unlocking of a pain that had been there since before I could remember. My brain would wrestle with this concept for weeks—I didn't grasp its full impact for months—but my heart already suspected Carm had uncovered something very important.

When I got back home and wrote all this in my journal, I flashed back to the months I'd been working with Jonas. Whenever he'd asked me to describe the part of me that couldn't trust opening up to God, I always had the same image. I always pictured a little girl—about four or five years old—in a little white dress, huddled in a corner. Wow.

CHAPTER 26

INNER CHILD STUFF

my father moved through dooms of love
through sames of am through haves of give,
~ e .e. cummings

Carmen was wily. She knew I would meet her suggestion to work on "Mom issues" with insurmountable resistance. So she next asked me to write something about my dad.

"Nothing profound," she said. "Just catch some thoughts as they come bubbling up over the next few days. Then email them to me."

I struggled with this far more than with my recollections of Grandma. I knew the memories around Dad would be mixed and I really balked at bringing up negative information.

I quit a dozen times. It felt disloyal to the tenets I'd learned in Constellation work—disloyal to both my parents. I felt a lot better when I took responsibility for everything in my life, when "Whatever it was, thank you" was my only response to my childhood. I didn't want to go down the accusations road again.

I emailed Carmen and told her I couldn't do it. She wrote back insisting I keep trying. Eventually I wrote some things down, starting with the good memories. I spent several evenings in tears.

The rest of this chapter is my email to Carmen.

I'm a small baby.

The rules for child rearing in the 1940s dictated crying babies should be left to cry and children should be fed, on schedule, every four hours, lest they become spoiled. My mother believed in these rules and lived them. That's what rules were for!

My dad did not. Despite my mother's vehement protests, he held me, rocked me, walked me and fed me when I cried. Years later—when I heard my mother retell these events—she still resented him for "spoiling" me.

I'm 5 or 6 or 7.

I am home in bed with the measles or mumps or flu. I am bored and itchy and too hot under these dumb blankets. Mom insists I must stay under them. Finally Dad comes home from work. He brings mint ginger ale and comic books! He tells me—just me—story after story. He sings the tale of *Abdul Abulbul Amir*, acting out all the characters, acting out the duel.

> The sons of the prophet were brave men and bold,
> And quite unaccustomed to fear,
> But the bravest of these was a man, I am told
> Named Abdul Abulbul Amir.

Now, just reading the poem on the Internet, I'm in tears. Those were such wonderful times!

I'm 7.

We are walking to *McGinnis' Pharmacy* on a winter night to pick up a prescription for one of the little kids. It's a long walk—better than half an hour each way—and it's really cold and dark. I don't know why Dad has agreed to let me go with him. He'd be faster without me.

Walking with my hand in his—where it hasn't been for so long because now he holds the little kids' hands—I'm in heaven. I walk quickly, stretching my stride to match his. For this walk, he's all mine. When we get to the drug store, we both have a hot chocolate at the soda fountain to steel ourselves for the trip home. And then—the joy of the walk back home.

I'm 3 or 6 or 9 or 14.

Mom needs a break from us. Dad gathers us up and puts all but the babies into the car. We go to the museum or the zoo. Both are wonderful and free. We spend hours there. Even though we always see the same exhibits, I love it!

I am 8 or 10 or 12 or 19.

It's summer. Dad and I are on the back porch. He's reading. I sit down next to him on the glider. We talk. He shares what he's reading, or some Kipling poems, or the news, or something else grown-up. I contribute what I can. I know I'm kind of smart because he listens to what I have to say. He listens and discusses things with me.

I'm 6 or 10 or 12 or 19.

I have a problem. He listens intently and then always says, "There are several possibilities." He tells me what the possibilities are and together we decide the best approach. I never feel judged or condescended to. I feel completely heard and understood. I honestly think I could say to him, "Dad, I killed someone," and his reply would be "Well there are several possible ways we can take care of this." I truly believe that, if I killed someone and chose not to admit it, he would help me bury the body.

I'm 9.

Mary is born. Now there are four kids in our family. We can't afford another baby. Dad has to take a second job. Now he won't be home in the evenings. I'm devastated! "There must be something else we can do," I tell him. There isn't.

Supper used to be one of my favorite times. Dad would quiz us about what we learned in school. We joked a lot. We discussed current affairs. (Sometimes Mom would get on a kick and insist on good table manners or would read poems to us from one of her inspirational magazines. Mostly, however, it was Dad's show—and it was fun.) Now he eats supper as soon as he gets home from his first job. He's got about 20 minutes before he has to go to his other job—just enough time to change out of his suit and eat. This is the time for him and Mom to talk. There's no time for us kids, for me.

I'm 9 or 14 or 18.

It's summer. Dad is on vacation. We all beg for him to take us to a park to swim or go on the swings. Johnnie pleads with him to practice hitting or pitching a baseball. Dad's very busy doing things that need to be done around the house or just getting some peace and quiet for a change. There are vague promises of later. We almost never go.

I'm 12.

It's late summer. Susie discovered Uncle Joe—my mother's uncle—kissing me in the kitchen and has told my parents. I'm sitting alone in the bedroom Susie and I share, with the door closed. I'm pulling the tufting out of the chenille bedspread. I can hear the other kids and my dad downstairs in the kitchen.

My mother comes up to talk with me. She asks me what else Uncle Joe did. I don't know what to say. She's obviously concerned.

I'm getting embarrassed. I tell her he often kissed me funny, with his tongue in my mouth. I tell her we sometimes danced. She tells me, many times, it's not my fault! I shouldn't feel guilty! Uncle Joe did something wrong. She asks if I have any questions. I don't. I'm not sure what she's talking about. I just know I won't be going places with Uncle Joe anymore. Part of me feels good; part of me bad. I liked going to the movies and out for ice cream with him. It was fun taking long rides in the country, visiting people I'd never met before. I loved the attention. But now, in some way, I'm also glad it's over.

As I think about it, I guess the wrong part was us kissing and slow dancing together in the kitchen while Aunt Helen and her parents sat in the living room watching TV. The wrong part was probably my sitting really close to him in the car, with his arm around my shoulder as he drove with just one hand. I wonder if I should tell Mom these things or if I'll get Uncle Joe into bigger trouble if I do. I decide not to tell her more unless she asks again. She doesn't.

Mom and I talk for a long time. Finally, Dad knocks on the door carrying a plate of warm cookies. They're all for me. Mom and Dad leave me alone in the bedroom with the cookies. I'm so surprised and happy my dad baked them for me. I enjoy eating them without sharing them with the other kids. But I wonder why he doesn't come into the bedroom and talk about Uncle Joe, too. Dad's usually the one who talks with me when I have a problem.

I'm still 12.

It's right before a holiday—maybe Thanksgiving, maybe Christmas. Uncle Joe shows up with two big bags of groceries. Everyone treats him as if nothing has happened. I'm extremely uncomfortable. Even though it's cold outside, I go and stand on the back porch. I'm *almost* able to put what I'm feeling into words, but not quite. But there's a feeling—a feeling of being betrayed for the sake of appearances and family peace.

I wonder if I should feel angry with my dad. The more I think about the past summer, the more I've come to understand that what Uncle Joe did was really bad. And if it was bad, why didn't my dad punch him out, throw him out of our house and forbid him from ever coming back?

After my uncle leaves, I go back into the house and watch TV alone.

I am 8 or 10 or 12 or 19.

Father Tokay has come to dinner. He sits at the head of the table because he's a priest. Dad sits somewhere in the middle with us kids. My stomach hurts. It always hurts when I see my dad give up his place to this dumb jerk priest.

I'm 16.

I've just gone to my first concert. None of my friends wanted to go with me, but I needed to see Peter, Paul & Mary in person. I now have to get home from Oakland alone. That means a bus into town, a streetcar to the junction and the walk up the hill with the woods on one side. I've done the streetcar hundreds of times before, coming home from work at Murphy's a little after 9:00. Then, there were lots of people in town and sometimes others coming up the hill from the junction.

But now, it's eleven o'clock. Town is deserted as I walk from the bus stop to the trolley stop. I'm really scared. When I get off the trolley, the junction is deserted too. I race up the hill. I wonder why Dad hasn't offered to pick me up, if not in Oakland, at least meet me at the junction so I don't have to walk the hill alone. I vow never to tell my friends about this. I know *their* parents would have picked them up.

I am 19.

I've been home from the convent for over a year. I'm dating Ross. I'm in my bedroom, hunched over my desk doing homework. I'm alone because Susie is really intelligent and doesn't have to study much. Dad comes up and sees the copy of *The Kinsey Report* on my nightstand. He smiles and tells me, if I have any questions about sex, I can ask him. The only one I can think of is "Should I really wait until I'm married to have sex?" Without hesitation he says, "Yes, it's much better to wait."

I'm 20, just about to marry Ross.

My mother and aunt go to town to see a movie and have lunch on a weekday afternoon. They run into my dad and Barbara in a restaurant. My dad introduces Barbara to my aunt and my mother— except he forgets *my mother's* name. This is a big joke in the house for weeks.

I am 21.

It's summer. I'm pregnant with Lisa. Ross and I have come home for a visit. Things are tense. Dad and Mom have just had a huge fight about Barbara. He has sworn he's ended his affair with her. I'm on the back porch; Dad is in the back yard, below the porch. I lean over the railing to call him to dinner. He's writing something in a yellow tablet. My eyes focus on the writing before I call him. It's a letter to Barb.

I am 21.

It's February. Dad and Barbara come to visit us the day after I bring Lisa home from the hospital. At first I think the visit is tense because Lisa has been screaming since I gave her a bath a few minutes before they arrived. But that's not the cause of the tension.

255

After a few minutes, over Lisa's wails, Dad tells us he's going to ask my mom for a divorce and marry Barb. My hopes that my parents' separation is temporary are crushed.

When I finished this list, I felt disloyal and horrible and physically sick. I quickly emailed it to Carmen so I didn't have to look at it again.

CHAPTER 27

DOING THE WORK

Factual knowledge can be taught directly;
wisdom needs to be elicited experientially.
~ *Jeffrey Zeig*

Even after completing the email about my dad, I resisted working on family issues. Carmen must have sensed my resistance when I arrived for the next visit because she jumped right in as soon as I sat down.

"Con, I'm not asking you to revisit your childhood so you can assess blame. I don't want you to go back for the sake of reliving the pain. I want you to go back so you can *understand* why you have such feelings of abandonment and mistrust. Once you understand the why, once you know how your childhood interpretation of reality affected your belief system, we can work to change it.

"Some things can be changed without this step—but some cannot. You've made a lot of progress on other issues both with the Constellation work and the work you've done with Jonas. However, you need something more. Let's at least give this a chance."

After Carmen stated her case, she became quiet. She waited. In silence, I reviewed again what she'd been saying for the past few visits:

"Carmen is trying to have me understand—through no one's fault, through no one's ill intentions—I'd felt emotionally abandoned as a young child. I'd had a taste of real acceptance and love from my grandmother and my dad when I was very young. But after Grandma died, after my sisters and brother were born, I'd been left with a huge emotional hole in my gut.

"Carm's not telling me this to make me angry or to help me find excuses for my dysfunction. This isn't about blaming my parents and then 'reparenting' myself. She wants me to see how these experiences influenced my current struggle with trust and love. She wants me to see how and why I've shut myself down so I can open myself back up. She wants me to understand them so I can let them go. This is important."

"OK, Carmen, let's do it."

That day we began the deepest work I've ever done in talk therapy. As we proceeded, I noticed several things. For one, I experienced major time distortion. What felt like ten minutes to me was really an hour. Second, my mind seemed to be on some sort of comprehension delay. Words I understood as they came out of Carmen's mouth slipped off my brain as if it were made of ice. It felt like I was in Statistics class again. I thought I understood each sentence as she said it, but when I tried to put them together to form a thought, they became incomprehensible—and then disappeared. Third, I experienced acute feelings of pain and tension in my body as we worked. After a session, I often needed to go home and sleep for a couple hours.

One afternoon in early May, Carmen and I hit what I hoped was the bottom of the well. We were coming to the end of a rough session on abandonment. I was exhausted. I reached for the glass of water on the table in front of me. It felt really heavy; I struggled to lift it. I quickly took stock of my body. *"My neck hurts, my arms and legs ache, my stomach is tight. I want to crawl under a rock and sleep for a week."* I smiled. *"Yep, I must be doing some good work."*

As we began to wrap things up, I asked Carmen about something I could do before we met again. I knew the ideas we discussed needed to be worked with immediately and intensely or I would lose the insights. If things followed the pattern Carmen and I established, I could count on spending parts of the next several days in tears as I completed the assignments. They would be hard times but would produce more insights and healing.

"I'm not sure yet," Carmen said. "Everything that comes to mind feels trite for the depth of what you're working on. Give me some time."

My chin dropped. I felt panic set in at the thought of no assignment. Today's session had been painful. I didn't want to lose ground and have to start all over again. I needed to get it all behind me—into the reservoir of things I never had to touch again.

"Will you email me later?"

"I will, as soon as I think of the right assignment."

Carmen never did send the email. But I surely got the assignment—and within a matter of hours.

After we finished, I felt pretty raw. I needed to compartmentalize. I shut down the part of me with the tender emotions, knowing I'd get back to them later, in private. No sweat.

Then I went off to my favorite restaurant to meet two good friends—we'll call them Fran and Cindy—for a long-anticipated lunch. Our schedules had been hectic; this was the first time the three of us had been together in months.

We were eager to make up for lost time. We hugged and laughed and talked non-stop—pausing only long enough to garner hugs from Jeff, my friend and favorite waiter, or swoon over the crab bisque. We shared stories of our adventurous—or in my case, unadventurous—youths.

We reminisced about important events in our friendship. After lunch, we still had things to talk about. So Fran invited us to her house.

It was after four when I glanced at the clock in Fran's family room. I needed to go home. Ross was picking up Stevie after school and I wanted to be there when they arrived.

I grabbed my purse and slipped on my sandals. I walked over to the sofa where both of them were poring over one of Fran's art books. Usually they would have stood up and given me a hug goodbye.

This time, because they were so intently looking at the books, I just walked behind the sofa and hugged them as they sat. Cindy hugged me back and made me promise to call to set up another lunch date soon. Fran, interrupted in mid-thought, simply offered me her cheek, the way women sometimes do. I gave her a friendly peck and turned to leave.

I didn't give it a second thought. But my body surely reacted. Abruptly, Fran's slight gesture jolted me back to my childhood. Viscerally, I became a needy little girl, unloved and unworthy, trying hard to be acceptable and knowing I didn't make the grade.

For all my childhood and most of my adulthood, I hugged my mom, I kissed her—hello, goodbye, good night. Until the last years of her life, however, she never hugged or kissed me. She simply offered me her cheek.

I didn't understand why, but reliving that feeling of being unkissed made me very sad. I barely made it to the car before the tears started. I cried all the way home.

As I drove into our garage, I pulled myself together. Stevie was already here and I was ready for some hugs and some Steven and Nana bonding. Unfortunately, he and Ross were already deeply entrenched in Stevie's favorite activity with his Papa, a serious game of *Rise of Nations* on the computer. It's a consuming strategy game, requiring their full attention, so I got only a cursory greeting from my two guys. Normally I'd just smile, glad they were having such a great time together. Now, I had to make a quick exit to the kitchen before I started crying.

By the time I put supper on the table, I had my act together again. As Steven wolfed down his second hamburger, we joked about his seemingly perpetual growth spurts, which led to a round of comparing his hands to ours, and a discussion about who was taller, Stevie or Hannah. They were never more than a quarter inch apart any time they got together and both always claimed to be the tallest.

After supper we had the quality time I'd been so looking forward to. Steven and I snuggled on the couch as he read his assigned story. We talked and joked at the kitchen table as he completed his math worksheets. It felt normal and fun. Far too soon, it was eight o'clock and Lisa came to pick him up.

As soon as he left, I needed to lie down. I flung myself onto the couch and fell asleep, fully dressed, in a matter of minutes. I didn't wake up again until the next morning.

And then—dear God in heaven—it hit. Even before I opened my eyes I could feel it. The deadly hole I hadn't felt in more than 20 years had swallowed me. Suddenly I was at the bottom of a pit. I groaned when I recognized the coldness, the darkness. Every inch of my body was on high alert as the darkness intensified. I wasn't sad or lonely or in a funk—I was suicidal. I was depressed out of my mind.

I sat up. The birds were chirping through the open window. The sky was blue. The trees were the fresh green color of new growth.

"Oh, God, how I hate spring."

My thoughts began racing.

"No, I will not put up with another spring! Summer will soon be here. No, definitely, I will not be here to suffer through another fricken summer!! This is it! I'm done. I've fought too hard and too long. I will not go down this road again. I've tried my best. I promised myself I'd stay

alive to see my kids through school. Well, I've kept my damn promise. Hell, I've lived to see my kids have kids of their own. I've done my duty. I will not let another season come before I end this horrible life. Damn it. How did I stand it so long? I need this to be over. Now."

I wrapped my arms around my knees and rocked. All the light inside me was completely gone. The morning light mocked me. I frantically sought a way to stop the banshee wail that filled my head. But I couldn't. I had trouble breathing. Every breath felt like I was inhaling thick vapors of tar.

I tried to tell myself this was just a depressive episode. Given time, it would pass and life would be normal again. But the voice inside me knew better.

"This is the best it ever gets. The rest is just the illusion you've conjured up to hide reality, Sweetie. Life is garbage—layers and layers and layers of garbage with only the smallest amount of good sprinkled around to fool people into missing the garbage. But the garbage is what is real.

"You can fool yourself for a while, Connie, with all your damned positive thinking and spirituality. But it's all crap. You can stop looking for the light 'cause it just ain't here, Honey. It never has been. It never will be. That was the illusion. This, Baby Doll, is reality."

Then, as if 20 years hadn't intervened, as if I hadn't seen countless therapists, hadn't done Constellation work, hadn't experienced so much change through my work with Jonas and Carmen, as if November 18th hadn't happened, I again began to plan how I would end my life.

I knew how to do it. And, unlike the other times when depression had come on slowly and depleted me, I also had the energy to kill myself. I made some quick decisions. Hannah's dance recital was just five days away. I'd use that time to straighten my affairs—get rid of my journals, make sure the refrigerator wasn't harboring gross leftovers—and maybe say goodbye to some people.

"That's it. Ken and Les and the grandkids know we'll be there for the recital. They won't suspect it's my last visit. It will be perfect. I can hold out until then. Knowing the end is near, I can hold out five more days."

I unfolded my body from the couch and walked onto the deck. I started planning in earnest. For a few minutes I considered trying to make it look like an accident.

"Accidents are better than suicide. It would be less horrible for everyone if they thought this was unintentional. Can I risk it? What if I 'accidentally' drove off a bridge and then some jerk rescued me from the river? What if I plowed my car into a wall and somehow survived, crippled and maimed and unable to finish the job? No, damn it, I can't risk doing this badly. It has to be a sure death. No more games with this damn life. I'm sorry, there's no other way.

"The best I can do is kill myself somewhere away from home—maybe at a motel. I'll do it cleanly. No slit wrists or guns or blood. Nothing gross for people to clean up. I'll do it with pills. It might be sad, but it won't be gory. OK, another decision taken care of."

My brain spun into overdrive. As long as I could plan, as long as I could keep moving toward death, I could hold the worst of the flow of tar at bay. I continued to organize.

"How can I hold out until after Hannah's recital? How can I fill the days? Wait, wait, it's OK. It will be OK. I need to see Lisa and Steven one more time. And I need to write some notes. I can use the days I have left to have a good long visit with them and write the notes.

"I need to write to the people who will be most affected—apologizing for what I've done, for the pain I've caused. But not too many. Most people, even my friends, will only be affected for a little while. Hell, they have their own lives. It's not going to be a big deal.

263

"But I have to be realistic. I do owe a huge apology to Ross and the kids—and a couple of really good friends. I need to explain to them why, even loving them as much as I do, it isn't enough to keep me alive."

I made a list; it was pretty short. Just Ross, Lisa, Ken and three or four close friends who had walked with me through so much, they deserved a final goodbye. I'd have to count on Ross or one of the kids sharing their letters with other friends and my siblings. I couldn't do more than that.

I started to feel relieved.

"This is a job I can handle. Maybe I could even write each of the grandchildren a short note..."

I started to think of what I'd say. Ross, Lisa and Ken wouldn't be *that* hard. They'd seen me fight this demon so many times. I hadn't been this depressed in many years, but I knew they hadn't forgotten the really bad episodes. I remembered the panic in Ken's eyes the day he came home from school and found me curled in a ball in bed, sobbing. I recalled the day Lisa pounded frantically on the bathroom door because she could hear me crying uncontrollably above the sound of the shower. I remembered Ross pleading with me, "Con, tell me what I can do. I'll do anything to make this better." And there was nothing I could tell him.

"Surely they'll remember. Surely they'll understand how I couldn't go through that pain again. Hell, they'll probably be secretly glad I didn't drag them through this horror one more time. I'm probably doing them a favor."

I was on a roll. My pain beat back logic and reason at every turn. I made the same kind of ridiculously irrational decision about Hannah and Liam. *"Hey, they have another set of caring grandparents, ones who live right in their hometown. They'll be OK without me."*

I was in overdrive now. Nothing could stop my plunge toward freeing myself from life. I mentally whizzed down the list of people who might care.

"If I can make the letters just right, if I put some time and effort into these notes, I can do this in a way that won't hurt anyone. Hell, I'm a writer. I can make them understand just how horrific it would have been for me to continue living."

And then it happened. I got to Stevie's name. Just last night, after he'd hugged me goodbye, he'd said one of those quirky things only Steven could say. As he put on his shoes, he scrunched up his forehead in thought and said, "Nana, I know Mom's grandma, your mother, never played with her like you play with me." That's all. It was just a reflection of his. No follow-up. No rationale for saying it. Once his shoes were on, he scooted out the door.

Now his face, his eyes, his unpredictable little way of perceiving the world were right in front of me. I tried to imagine what I would write in a note that could possibly make him understand my choosing to end my life. I tried to picture Lisa sitting with him and explaining, in a way that would ease his pain, what I had done. I couldn't. I had no acceptable excuse for copping out, for not being his Nana as long as I possibly could. My façade shattered. I saw the pain I'd cause him by committing suicide.

And once I saw it for Stevie, I immediately saw it for Hannah and Liam, too. Image after image of them kept coming to me. I remembered how Hannah won every staring contest we had by just getting really close to my face and saying, very quietly, "Moo." Then we'd both giggle uncontrollably. I saw flashes of her and Liam visiting us, carefully unpacking pillowcases filled with all their stuffed animals because they wanted to be sure each animal got a turn to sleep at Nana and Papa's house. I saw Liam's courageous expression as he drew his plastic sword from his pajamas and explained how I'd never have to be afraid of monsters because he would always protect me. Damn! I couldn't pretend my intentional death would become magically acceptable if I just wrote the right words!

And then the realizations intensified. I didn't need mental pictures now. I knew how close Lisa and Ken and Ross were to me. I knew their love in the deepest part of my heart, in every pore of my skin. I felt our love for each other with every breath. Who the hell was I kidding? Of course they'd be hurt—deeply!

My tears turned into sobs of anger and frustration. I was stuck! I couldn't go on living, and I couldn't kill myself. Now what the hell was I supposed to do?

Although it felt as if I'd been awake for hours, the clock in the kitchen read only 8:00 when I came in from the deck. I didn't want to wake Ross. I knew there was nothing he could say to change things and I dreaded the look on his face when he realized the suicidal depression had returned after all these years.

As I paced the living room, I mentally ran down the list of people I could call for help. There had to be someone. But the insanity of severe depression was coursing through me. All I knew with complete certainty was that I was totally unlovable and alone. One by one, for different reasons, I rejected everyone. Some had real problems of their own and shouldn't be bothered by a foolish old woman who was too cowardly to live. Some were too busy, some wouldn't understand, some weren't smart enough to talk me out of it, and some, I was sure, had never really cared that much anyhow. I depleted the list in minutes.

I kept crying, looking for the next step. I couldn't find it. Not knowing what else to do, I walked upstairs to the computer, hoping I'd have some miraculous email to get me out of this spiral. Naturally, there wasn't one.

Then as I sat staring at the list of emails I didn't have the energy to open, I remembered the prayer Jonas taught me and what he'd said about his experience using it.

"Connie, after days of feeling so confused and alone I couldn't figure out why I should even bother taking another breath, I just surrendered. It was all I could do. I just said, 'Lord, I can't do this. I don't know what to do next. I surrender. I put everything in Your hands.'"

And, for him, it had worked. From that point on, he said, he began to regain his balance. Eventually, he said, he was graced with a sense of peace and love the likes of which he'd never felt before.

Well, I didn't give a damn about peace and love. I just wanted to be able to figure out how to get out of this state—how to find the strength to keep breathing.

"Would surrendering really make a difference now?" I started to weigh the options, but I was far too tired to debate anything. *"What the hell,"* I said as I pushed myself away from the computer, *"What have I got to lose?"*

I went into the back room where I often meditated. I did something as close to a meditation as I could. I said fragments of the prayers I often used. I tried to calm my breathing. But in the end I just continued to cry and say, over and over, "I don't know what to do. You do. I don't know the next step, but You do. If You're real, if any of this is real, I surrender. Please, please, please help me. I surrender completely. I don't know what to do next. Please."

When I finished, I didn't feel a lot better, but I did have the energy to take a shower. Then, barely acknowledging Ross, who had since gotten up and begun to work at his computer, I fell back on the couch and slept for several more hours.

When I woke up again, Ross came right into the living room. I saw the concern on his face. We talked a little but I was just too fragile to tell him what was really going on. I certainly didn't tell him how suicidal I was. I was neither forthcoming nor friendly. Finally, not knowing what to do with this weeping lump on the couch, he went for a walk. I continued to go between tears and sleep and desperate prayers.

When he came back an hour or so later, he simply offered to play cards with me. I said yes, grateful for a diversion from the pain. Playing cards would at least pass some time.

As we played, something happened. For some reason—an answer to prayer, perhaps, or Ross seeing something in my eyes that gave him a hint about how bad things were—Ross really talked to me. He talked about some of his own rough times. He talked about times before I knew him—when he was a fatherless teenager trying to find his role in the world. He told me stories about his life he'd never told me, or anyone, ever. Through this sharing, as we sat across the table from each other, cards in our hands, something shifted inside me. I felt his concern for me. I felt his pain as a young man. I felt him reaching out. Soon my heart opened a little. The desperation eased a bit.

Then, at exactly the same time, we both laid the cards down. Spontaneously, we got up, walked around the kitchen table and hugged each other hard. I cried in his arms. He let me hold him in my arms. I held him hard enough to crush him. I cried until there were no more tears left inside.

Then, after several minutes, we backed up and just looked into each other's eyes and smiled. After 41 years of marriage, we knew each other well enough to know this was enough. Wordlessly, we sat back down and finished our game. Now our only conversation was the light-hearted trash talk that usually accompanied gin games.

After that, we started doing some household chores. I sorted the laundry. Ross got a bucket of soapy water and went outside to give the cars a good spring cleaning. As I set the dials on the washer, I realized my desire to end my life was gone. I was still sad, still in a lot of pain, but the insanity of the suicidal thinking was gone.

I couldn't believe it. In the past this kind of depression usually lasted months. Only immense time, therapy, and some pretty heavy doses of anti-depressants were enough to cut through this level of despair and darkness. Now, in less than a day, the worst of it was over.

How could this change have happened so quickly? Almost immediately I thought, *"Hey, I hadn't known what to do next. I'd prayed. I'd surrendered. And now my suicidal thoughts have lifted. I've had my miracle. Maybe, just maybe, this spirituality stuff is real."* Then, from a place very deep within me, *"Thank you."*

Just as important, I slowly became aware of why and how this particular bout of depression happened. My work with Carmen had peeled away levels of protection and denial. Fran's offering me her cheek suddenly brought me back to the feelings I often felt as a child—to the desolation and confusion I'd often felt as a little girl. My childhood pain had been real. I had felt *that* alone and abandoned and unacceptable. I didn't have one huge traumatic event, but I did have long periods of sustained pain. What had happened this morning wasn't some inner-child, high drama mental rationalization. Hell, this had nothing to do with my thinking. This was my body's reaction—real, uncensored and undeniable.

These were the facts. No matter how normal I looked from the outside, no matter how I'd tried to disguise it as I grew up, I'd spent a good part of my life feeling unloved, alone and unworthy.

The tiny incident with Fran had been all I needed to put me fully in touch with the feelings of abandonment I'd worked so hard to hide, especially from myself. It brought me back to the depression that had almost killed me.

Even before I'd talked things through with Carmen the next day, I understood what this episode meant. No matter how it seemed from an adult vantage point (both my current one and my parents' so many years ago), on some level the little child I'd been had felt severely and profoundly unloved.

My clinical depressions, my need to always do better, my inability to ever be satisfied with even my best efforts, my perpetual need for approval and my food addiction had all been an effort to create a world in which I could keep that fact at bay.

No matter how hard I tried, I knew I could never be good enough. No matter how loved I was as an adult, it didn't count. Ross loved me with all his heart. I had incredible children and grandchildren who continually surprised me with expressions of their love. I had loyal, funny and generous friends who would do anything for me. It didn't make sense for me to still feel unlovable—so unaffected by the wondrous people in my life. Yet that was the truth. Now, finally, I was ready to accept reality.

It would take a lot more work. It would take some time to get a handle on things. But I was done denying the problem was real.

CHAPTER 28

AN END TO JOUSTING

When you have entered the world of the heart,
the question of who is right or wrong with regard to
belief or creed is pretty much irrelevant.
~ Wayne Teasdale

Although their approach to spirituality was quite different, both Jonas and Carmen agreed on one thing: My fear of God and my insistence on separating spirituality from real life were keeping me stuck. I didn't understand them. But if that was my problem, I was ready to solve it.

One morning in June I went to Jonas' office with my intention set for the craniosacral work. When he asked what I wanted to work on, I replied, "I want to be a person who has both a strong relationship with God and with the world."

"They're the same."

"They haven't been for me. Maybe that's been the difficulty."

As I explained, Jonas listened intently. I thought I was ready for his reply, but I wasn't. Jonas wanted to go back into the Bible for answers.

As he spoke, I immediately shifted into intellectual defense mode. I knew my arguments were just as logical, maybe more logical, than his. He went to John 3:16, a verse I'd been stumbling over for more than 40 years: "God so loved the world that he gave his only begotten Son..." Jonas knew how I felt about this verse. We'd talked about it. He'd read what I'd written about it in early drafts of this book.

I shifted on the table, leaned back a bit, ready to listen but also to disagree. He went into his interpretation of what he believed the passage meant. I began to form my responses, my counterarguments.

As he continued, however, I felt a different energy inside me. I noticed more than his words. I really saw Jonas. I saw the genuine caring and belief in his eyes, saw how much he wanted to share his truth with me. I knew I could listen with my head and immediately find the flaws in his argument—or I could listen with my heart. I'd done the head trip a thousand times and remained stuck. This time I opted to listen with my heart. To the best of my ability, I ignored the questions and doubts as they came into my mind.

When he finished, I realized I hadn't heard any dogmatism in his voice, no "my way or the highway." He'd simply shared his experience with me. There had been no challenge in his approach, no insistence I agree.

And that's what changed me. He'd shared his experience and left me with mine. I knew Jonas truly believed in a loving God. I knew my November 18th experience was of a loving God. Those facts were indisputable. I knew I could choose to argue and question the specifics of what he said or choose to accept the gift of his sharing. I understood the gravity of his gift. He gave from his very soul.

"Connie, I know it's hard to let go of the fear. But you have to understand, it's your fear that's making this so hard. As long as you hold on to the fear, you're going to be in pain."

Clang. These words were almost verbatim what Carmen had been saying to me about letting go and just allowing room for spirit in my daily life.

"Do I have to hear them a thousand more times before I do it? What if I just let go now?"

I didn't say anything to Jonas, but in my gut, I considered just letting go of the fear. Questions still flew through my brain but I ignored them. I'd already asked them a thousand times—of him, of Carm, of friends, of priests and nuns and psychologists—and had never received a satisfying answer. Maybe they weren't the right questions. Maybe I was just too tired, too beaten down to ask them again.

I heard the door to Jonas' outer office opening and shutting. He had other patients to see. I worried our discussion had thrown Jonas off schedule. We had to begin the cranial. I had to make a decision. From both my head, which was concerned with the time, and somewhere deep inside me, which wasn't, I took the next step. I really surrendered. It was no longer about getting the right answer. I didn't care about answers. I chose to do whatever it took to feel some inner peace. As I laid down on the table, I repeated in my head what was becoming my favorite prayer:

"Lord, I don't know what else to do. I surrender. Show me the way, I'll follow."

As I did, a picture of a medieval jousting tournament flashed before my eyes, accompanied by these words: "Intellectual jousting is a dilettante's sport."

I smiled as I understood them. *"It's fine to continue to argue and defend an intellectual view if your life doesn't depend on it. But my life does."* Responding to this image, I pictured myself putting down my intellectual sword. I chose to stand with my heart and my spirit defenseless before God.

Jonas began the adjustment working with my sacrum, the part of me that needed to be more grounded. I affirmed my intention to surrender. As he moved his hands, he said he felt a significant shift, a realignment. When he moved to a traditional cranial adjustment, with his hands cradling my skull, I felt just a glimmer of the love I felt on November 18th. It lasted a few seconds. It wasn't strong but it was there.

Later, as he finished the cranial, Jonas said, "Connie, you made a huge shift this morning. The pathway between your cranium and sacrum is clear. Now it's up to you to keep it that way. You'll be able to feel when it isn't. You'll feel a tension and you'll need to correct it."

"Sure. How do I do that?"

He smiled.

Immediately, I left my heart and was back in my head again—afraid he was unwilling to tell me. I must have winced or looked sad, because he instantly became serious.

"Honest, Connie, I don't know the answer for you. This will have to be your own process. It wouldn't do any good to tell you my process. My process won't work for you. You'll have to ask in prayer. You'll have to listen for answers."

I understood. In light of my new perception, I could accept his answer. I knew something important had happened during the session. I definitely felt different—lighter, more peaceful. The desperation that plagued me for the last few months had lifted perceptibly. I left the office feeling better than I can remember feeling in a long time.

But my mind was still my mind. On the way home I thought of the Bible verse Jonas had quoted. The holes in Jonas' interpretation popped back into my head. This time, however, there was also another thought. *"You don't have to have Jonas' beliefs to approach this sacred place within. This isn't a religion you're looking for, Con. You're looking* *for a relationship with God. You don't need to accept or reject a particular belief to be here. This isn't about a set belief. Your best attitude is to be open to the fact that **your** beliefs might not be The Ultimate Truth either."*

I laughed out loud. What wonderful news. Jonas didn't have to be right. I didn't have to be right. No one had to be right. No one on earth needed to have The Ultimate Truth to have a relationship with God. I could let it go. After all, being right was just a mind joust.

As I let go of the need to think it through, the solid feeling of peace continued to grow. When I got home and decided to write the morning's experience in my journal, I felt my heart opening—actually felt something physical—something happening in my fourth chakra. It felt like the work of the cranial was continuing. For the first time in months I felt solid again.

The rest of the day was good. The steady calm stayed with me. I accomplished a lot in the office and around the house. Work seemed effortless. I ate healthfully. But I had one more uprising in me—one more call to joust. Just before bed I decided to reread what I'd written earlier that day.

And as I did, I got scared again. I felt the adrenaline begin to flow and the panic kick in again. The fearful little Catholic girl in me rose up and shouted in my head.

"Heresy, heresy! You can't say beliefs are unimportant! We can't both be right. That's illogical! Jonas has the life I want—the relationship with God I'm seeking so desperately. I can't just blithely say what he believes doesn't matter! If he's right, I must be wrong! Can I really choose not to accept his beliefs without risking losing my way on the path he's been working so hard to show me? There must be some way for me to accept his way of thinking, to twist my brain, to...."

Just as I started to yield to the panic, my dad's favorite quote from St. Thomas Aquinas popped into my head. Aquinas, a 13th century theologian, wrote the ultimate text on Christian thought, the

Summa Theologica—a five-volume discourse on all the Church held true. Catholicism centered its theology around this treatise for centuries. However, after Aquinas completed it, as he neared the end of his life, this is what Dad said he uttered about his work: "It's all straw."

"See, Connie," a calm inner voice said, *"even Aquinas knew spirituality isn't about facts and ideas. You're finally feeling at peace; don't put yourself back on the never-ending intellectual merry-go-round again."*

But the merry-go-round rut in my brain was deep and well traveled. It took no effort for me to stumble right into it.

"Yeah, but what if it's not true? What if Aquinas never said that? What if Dad just made up the quote or got the quote wrong? What if, what if…." The fear had complete hold. I needed an answer—a definitive, *real*, intellectual answer.

So I looked it up. I found as many places as I could on the Internet—Catholic places, theology places, Aquinas places, whatever—to assure myself it actually was what he said.

(Yes, as I did it, I could also see the flaws in this logic too. *"Can I really trust the Internet? Good grief, no one gets theology from Google!"* However, as my desperation built, it didn't matter that my search had flaws too. I just knew I needed to find the quote.)

Then something wondrous happened. I not only found it, I found the *entire* quote—over and over again—on numerous websites:

*"What I have written is all straw **when compared to experiencing God**."*

November 18th flashed in front of my eyes. My heart was beating so hard I could hear the rush of blood in my ears. The truth I'd discovered in November was the same one Aquinas discovered after years of study and thought! My body relaxed completely. Tears of joy covered my smiling face.

*"I don't need to agree with someone else's beliefs, with the concepts they use to express their experience, with their **ideas** about God. Where we come together is not in our ideas. We come together in our **experience** of God and our willingness to share the experience of that love! That's it."*

Another part of me asked, *"Do you need more today?"*

"Nope."

No more words.

CHAPTER 29

A New Kind of Listening

We grownups like to think of childhood as a time of
total innocence. Kids know better.
~ *Linda Ellerbee*

I also experimented with eliminating the jousting from my work with Carmen. My new rule became, *"Once you agree with a premise, Connie, don't keep rethinking it. Give it time to grow."*

So rather than constantly trying to figure out how I got to be the way I was, I just accepted it—and chose to work from that point on. When I stayed true to my commitment, life became calmer and richer.

In early July, for example, it was time for my annual physical. The ride to my doctor's office took about 45 minutes—10 minutes to get to the Parkway, 30 minutes of parkway driving and then a short drive through town. I didn't especially relish it.

As I got into the car, I thought about how grateful I was that Jonas' office was much closer to home. This led to thoughts about how much I missed my weekly craniosacral adjustments and talks with Jonas since he'd amended his schedule. Those cranial sessions had been the touchstones in this new spiritual journey, both a grounding time and a time for new experiences. I began to feel pretty sad about this loss.

My condemning mind went, of course, for the jugular: "*Oh, you think you have it bad. Boo-hoo! Oh, poor Connie, she doesn't get her own private spiritual appointment whenever she wants it!*" But I caught myself pretty quickly and modified my self-talk to something more compassionate and curious: "*Yeah, this really does seem to be hurting a lot—more than I thought it would. I wonder what it means.*"

Within seconds I was in tears. And since I was in the car alone and didn't have to worry about being inappropriate in public, I just let them come. Almost immediately, by allowing the tears to flow, I got a mental picture of myself, five years old, crying because Grandma was dead. In the picture, I was alone, at night, in bed—trying not to cry. For just a brief second I felt I was right there, looking at the little girl I used to be, hiding her tears behind her silky dark green comforter because she knew she wasn't supposed to be sad.

Then came the thoughts little Connie was thinking: "*Grandma is in heaven with God. God missed her so much, He called her back home to be with Him. Grandma is happy. God is happy. It's bad for me to be so sad. I need to stop crying! Crying is bad!*"

The intensity of the image and the emotions that came to the surface surprised me—and made me curious. Instead of trying to escape the feelings, I allowed them.

Other images followed quickly. By allowing them, not frantically trying to find a way to make them go away, I began feeling things I hadn't felt in years. I had flashes of myself—alone and very sad—at other times in my life. I saw myself sitting on the wall in the back yard, looking at the old cherry tree, feeling no one really understood me or cared about me. I saw times when my mom would physically pull away from my hugs, untangle herself from my childish embraces. In another flash, I saw her so gentle with my brother and wondered why she was never like this with me. As they kept coming, I could sense the little girl reach a conclusion: "Something is wrong, very wrong, with me."

As I drove, remembering my decision not to joust, I let the flashes continue. I just acknowledged them.

What came next wasn't intellectual or profound. At first it wasn't even a thought. What came next was a feeling that jumped right over all the thoughts about blame and justification and accuracy I've so often had. It was just an acknowledgement, in my body, in my gut, that these feelings I'd just experienced were real and, for whatever reason, they existed inside me. All I sensed was their reality.

I took in a nice long breath. It felt good. As I took in another, I felt oddly calm.

This lasted less than a minute, however, before I started down my normal path of self doubt. *"Hey, this can't be right! I didn't have it bad! Lots of people had it worse! For God's sake, Connie, you weren't in a war, in a concentration camp, you weren't molested....you didn't have cancer! So your mother wasn't thrilled with you!! So your grandmother died. Everyone's grandmother dies! That's how life goes!!*

But I stopped the ranting again.

I simply acknowledged the images. No commentary, no judgment. I just saw the little girl I'd been. She didn't need my condemnation or a reminder of people who had it worse. She didn't need my adult perspective on how she *should* be! She was in pain—the biggest pain in her small life. It didn't matter how it compared to anyone else's pain. She couldn't, for whatever reason, express it then. And my cynicism and questioning were keeping her from expressing it now. Who was being served by my refusal to accept her pain as real?

So I took another deep breath and just accepted her pain as real. That's all. No ritual. No ceremony. Just acceptance.

And, much to my surprise, that was all I needed to do. The tears stopped. The pain stopped. The images stopped.

Then, as I took another deep breath, a thought bubbled up. *"All of us—whether we were raised in mansions or housing projects, in the midst of war and deprivation or in the midst of bounty—have been children in pain. At some time in each of our young lives we were alone in the dark with no one to talk to. All of us have cried ourselves to sleep. In the world of little-kid logic and understanding, a lot of things are scary. Being alone and sad at night is universal."*

I thought of my own grandchildren, who were deeply loved and protected, and knew each of them had experienced painful times, times when they were scared or confused or hurt. Whether or not the pain was from something we, as adults, would declare significant was not the issue. If it was real to them, it was real. Period.

I didn't need to hook into any specific theory about trauma. I didn't have to find out whether or not the level of pain was appropriate for the hurt. I just needed to acknowledge that the pain was real. And immediately (I've used this term so often, but it's accurate—each shift happened so quickly) my heart opened to every child, to every adult, because each of us has been a sad and lonely child. For just a second or so (Thankfully, this didn't last long. I don't think I could have handled more.) I could sense the generations and generations of sad and bewildered children who were my parents and grandparents and ancestors—who were all of our parents and grandparents and ancestors. I didn't need special credentials to belong to this group. We all belonged!

Buddha's saying that all life is suffering is true. Certainly it's true for children. None of us escapes the loneliness, confusion and pain of childhood. None of us escapes the fear of something creepy under the bed, in the eyes of a stranger or in the raised hand of an overwhelmed parent. Whether the tears came because of pain from a medical procedure that saved our life or a beating that threatened it, we've all been in pain. Whether the hurt was something as significant as the death of a parent, or as "insignificant" as the loss of a good friend, a puppy or a broken promise, we've all cried at night alone.

I'd spent my life telling myself I've had it so much better than most people and that I'd better just suck it up, grow up, shape up and get on with life. And I've been depressed most of my adult life. Maybe that wasn't the most healing way to think.

"What if," I said to myself, *"another way is more accurate? What if I acknowledge that every child, every person who has ever been born, has had pain? What if it's not about who has suffered enough to be allowed to have scars? What if it's about assuming that we all have scars and allowing each person—including myself—a respectful acknowledgement of the pain? That's all."*

The self-hater inside didn't want to give up just yet and countered with, *"So, you're saying, Chickie, everyone has a good reason to feel sorry for themselves, that we all have a built-in reason to act like victims?"*

But the loving part of me wasn't done yet. *"No. Of course not. But for a while, for right now, it feels good to just put down the yard stick by which I've always measured myself against everyone else—and which always found someone lacking. For this moment, I choose to be kind to all of us. Each of us has had the experience of untended tears. Each of us needs to be acknowledged as the wounded healers we all are—because we are both, we are wounded and we are healers."*

For the first time in my life I understood that being mature was not about disparaging my pain by comparing it to someone else's. Maturity—real maturity—was about standing in the space that acknowledges the pain with compassion and love.

And then I came to the entrance to the Parkway. It had all happened that quickly.

CHAPTER 30

AN ILLOGICAL CHOICE

Even if you're lost, you can't lose the love because it's in your heart.
~ Avatar: the Last Airbender, Cave of Two Lovers

Had you told me a cartoon character was going to play a part in my spiritual journey, I would have recoiled in embarrassment. For a very long time, I've resisted putting this section into the book.

When Hannah was four and Liam was three, they introduced Ross and me to a cartoon series on Nickelodeon called *Avatar: The Last Airbender*. It's the story of several young people who must rally the forces of their land and lead them against the evil Lord of the Fire Nation who is threatening to control or destroy the planet. It's a classic heroes' adventure of courage, love, friendship and honor, told with heart, humor and integrity. I liked it from the first episode.

General Iroh is one of the best developed characters in the series. He had once been first in line to become the next Fire Lord, known as The Dragon of the West because of his fierce fighting skills. But after the death of his son in battle, he lost his taste for war and became, in the eyes of many contemporaries, a doddering old fool.

In reality, of course, Iroh was anything but. Behind his tea-drinking, nap-loving façade, he was a skilled warrior, diplomat and philosopher. I adored Iroh. He was a true hero: smart, self-deprecating, strong yet gentle, with a wicked sense of humor. Eventually we bought DVDs of the series and watched all 60 episodes with the grandchildren. Surprisingly, Iroh had a role to play in my story as well.

~

In the rarefied atmosphere of my combined work with Carmen and Jonas, one of my deepest fears came to light: I didn't think I was worthy of anyone's love.

Fortunately, after working with Carmen on my childhood issues, I was able to see the flaw in that belief concerning people. Once I got my unlovability out in the open, once I understood my childhood ideas weren't necessarily facts, I began to believe I was worthy of love. I eventually accepted, realized and finally felt the love of my family and friends. Once I also stopped seeing myself as a cringing, whiny wimp who was depressed for no reason and saw myself as a strong woman who fought through some serious childhood pain, I was able to begin to love and accept myself too.

God's love, however, was a very different matter.

Jonas stressed that I needed to create a quiet place inside me where my realization of God could grow. "Connie, this isn't about your earning God's love. You already have it. Instead of trying to make yourself worthy, do less. Quit trying to find the *right* words or do the *right* things that will make this relationship happen—just allow it to happen."

I tried, but it felt awful. I was too lonely in the place where I had nothing to do but wait and allow.

One Monday, the day before I had an appointment for some craniosacral work, I sent Jonas the following excerpt from my journal with a note saying, "Here's where I am. I don't know what to do next. Can we work on this tomorrow?"

The quiet times—now that I'm not filling them with food or helping people or anticipating or remembering—are horrifically lonely. Then the lack of love I feel comes into focus all the more. Then the loneliness takes over, and the hope of ever feeling really loved disappears.

It seems I can't ask for it. It seems I can't wait for it. It seems I can't work to make myself worthy of it. I can't **do** anything. Then what do I need to **be**?

What I want desperately is to feel really, really loved, cherished—the way I love and cherish Hanni and Stevie and Liam.

Right now, today, at 62, when I think these particular thoughts, when I stop censoring and really feel this need, I'm in tears. . . . This is different from before. Before [November 18th] I didn't know this kind of love existed. I didn't expect it because I hadn't experienced it. . .

It seems Jonas is saying he gets this feeling of being loved and cared for from God. I think he's saying—the books [on spirituality] are saying—it's something we can have. If we trust, if we're open, we can allow the feelings of that real love into our lives.

Despite all the miracles in my life right now—and I **know** I'm surrounded by them—I still don't know how to stay firm in my belief, in my trust. Am I shooting too high? Am I asking for the impossible? Are my very questions making it impossible for me to get where I need to go?

This is a strangely hard time. I feel I've gotten to a good place. Yet, even here, I feel so empty, so alone. Is this just part of the process? Is this vacuum the holding area for the next change or is the vacuum really what most of life is all about?

Am I causing my own pain? If I am, how do I stop? If I'm not, how do I handle this?

I know I'm at a stage where going back is impossible. I'm willing to sit in the aloneness if that's what has to be. But, if there's a way to work with the aloneness, if there's a possibility I can someday feel loved, or worthy, or just OK, for more than just a few minutes. . . .

There must be a better way than yelling at myself to shut up and wait. There must be a gentler way of waiting. . . . There must be a way of strengthening the trust. But right now, I don't know how.

Jonas could have focused on any of the questions I asked, on any of the myriad ideas in those paragraphs. He came into the treatment room with this sentence circled:

What I want desperately is to feel really, really loved, cherished—the way I love and cherish Hanni and Stevie and Liam.

He started, "You know, I can't tell you what you need to…." and then stopped. After a moment, he began again, "Connie, I honestly believe you can't want anything else! This is *your job*. Your job is to want this, to get this, to have this.

"You can't give what you don't have. It's your job to give your best to the world! And to give it, you have to possess it. You *have to* know and feel God's love.

"You're a wonderful grandma. That's one of your best gifts. But even at your best grandmothering, you only give such a small part of what is possible to give. However, when you connect to Source, to God, then you can give infinite love every time you love. So, yes, you're right in seeking this connection. You *have* to find this connection. You *have* to feel God's love. It's not just your *right* to experience God's love, it's your *job*.

"There's a difference between someone who gives or heals from within themselves and someone who is a conduit of God's love. I've felt it in my practice. When, in the past, I gave out of my own energy, the more I gave, the more depleted I became. If I had continued that way, in a few years I would have been exhausted—burned out.

"But when I'm a conduit for God's healing energy, I give from a boundless source. Now, the more I give, the more I have to give because my supply is unlimited—infinite. Now I remain energized. I remain eager for the new day, the new challenges.

"Connie, you can be a conduit too. You can give through the book you're writing. You can give through the way you interact with people. I see how you are with people, how easily you connect. Use it. It's your job to lift the world. Don't be a slacker who keeps saying 'I'm not worthy.' Don't let false humility keep you from what is yours. You can know God's love. Just claim it.

"Do you know how I've been facing life lately? Like a puppy. Every morning in prayer I say to God, 'OK, Lord, I'm ready. Throw the ball. I'll catch it. I'll run for it. Thanks for playing with me, over and over again. This is great. I'm delighted to have this day playing catch with You. I'm ready!'

"It's a great way to live, Connie. Every day is an adventure. I know where my allegiance is. I know where the love comes from. I can just relax and trust. I know the day God creates with me will be an adventure. I know I'm loved. I can trust Him with my wife and kids and house and office. So I'm free to follow His lead, to chase the ball with abandon. You might want to give this a try."

I was following along, caught up in his enthusiasm, trying to imagine what it would feel like to live this way, when Jonas added:

"Have you ever thought of *demanding* what is promised in the Bible?"

"No!!"

Immediately the energy shifted. Now Jonas stepped back onto the path that sent my heart into fear and trembling. Now he was being as outrageous as Carmen had been when she suggested I was too formal in my approach to God. I tried to imagine my seeing God as someone I could make a demand of. Maybe I could see God as loving as well as regal. Maybe I could see God as a father, not just as a deity. But, no, I could not demand!

"No. Jonas. I can't."

But Jonas was relentless, smiling and egging me on.

"C'mon. Take the risk, Connie. Go out on the limb and demand what the Bible promised. Ask for the presence of God's love in your life. You've been on this fence so long. Are you worried about being struck by lightning? You're going to die someday anyway. Why not today?"

His smile broadened.

"I'll tell you what. I'll do it with you. If I'm wrong, I'll take the lightning bolt too. But I know I'm not wrong."

Then, as he began the cranial adjustment, Jonas prayed with me and for me. "Lord, this is what Connie is demanding. She is demanding to know Your love, to feel Your love in her life."

To me he said, "You can do it, Connie. Take the risk. Trust a little more. Let your heart open a little more."

I tried relaxing into accepting this idea. I tried to allow Jonas' thoughts to be my own, to make my trust in God match his. I couldn't.

After he'd completed the cranial adjustment, before he left the room Jonas gently said, "Connie, just stay here. Don't leave this room until you ask for the knowledge of God's love, in your own words."

After he left, I sat on the table, as open as I could be—and asked.

An image came immediately. It was of Iroh. Oddly, unexpectedly, my heart opened. My body relaxed instinctively with this image. I could trust the love I received from Iroh. I could be open to asking for, even demanding, a relationship with him. I could sit at his feet with my head in his lap and feel protected and loved. I could accept this love—and a cup of tea—gladly, without fear.

A second later, however, my mind protested vehemently. *"An image of Iroh as God? Come on! Give me a break! That's not just blasphemous, it's stupid! Now, let's do it right!"*

I started to fight the Iroh image, to find the bigger answer—The Correct Answer—when the second image came—of Joseph Campbell's book, *The Masks of God.* I took a deep breath. I calmed down a bit.

"Isn't this all we can really have?" I heard the calm part of me say. *"As humans, we can never fully comprehend the essence of God, the immensity of God. It's impossible. The best we can have is an image—a mask—that points us toward God. Right now, maybe this is all I can handle. Maybe the Iroh image is a Connie-sized answer."*

When I stopped fighting, stopped looking for The One True Image, tears came. Tears of relief and gratitude. A peace came into my heart that hadn't been there for months.

At home, still stunned by what happened, I made the decision to live with the concept for a while—to experiment with it, because something in that visualization felt so right. Just as I'd done in the first weeks after my Constellation, I decided to go with my experience rather than cold reason.

One of the most gentle, growth-producing parts of my journey began with what I thought was one of the least logical decisions I ever made. Each morning, when I began my prayers, instead of shipping them off to a cold, indifferent Universe or a vision of what I *hoped* God might be, I spoke them to Iroh—and found both myself and my prayers acceptable.

Naturally, my inner cynic had a field day. *"Well, Chickie, you've made it official. You are now definitely certifiable."*

But soon my inner wise woman had something to say too.

"There is a precedent for this, you know. This is similar to Catholics praying to St. Francis or the Blessed Mother. Maybe it's not so different from Hindus praying to the one god among their hundreds who seems best suited to handle a particular prayer, a particular situation. Maybe this is just the way people instinctively take a step toward All That Is without being frozen in fear or unworthiness. It allows us to come to a place where we're comfortable with the Omnipotent.

"Right now I can't even consider a relationship with The Creator and Lord of the Universe. It's impossible. But I can make this small step. Let's just leave it alone for a while and see what happens."

When I measured this way of relating to God against my One Big Rule for testing intuition, it got a great score. When I asked:

Am I staying with my commitments to meditation, exercise, eating healthfully?

Are my actions based in love?

Am I working at my other jobs more efficiently?

Am I bouncing back from setbacks more quickly?

Am I more peaceful?

The answer to all the questions was Yes.

Several days into the Iroh experiment I wrote the following in my journal:

> I'm so grateful [for this new image]. What I thought was impossible, is now my reality. I feel comfortable with God. I couldn't imagine how I would get from where I was to where I am. But You could, Lord. And as I followed, I got here. I asked. I received. Thank You!!

John Denver's song, *Sweet Surrender,* keeps coming to my mind. I went from *lost and alone on some forgotten highway* to feeling like *a fish in the water, like a bird in the air.*

The serendipitous aspects of life returned. One day, as I was indexing a Milton Erickson manuscript, I wrote in my journal:

[I'm] thinking of Erickson's Utilization Principle: Use whatever the patient brings to the session—his problem, his breathing, his quirkiness etc.

Maybe that's how spirituality works too. God just uses whatever we are, wherever we are [to communicate with us].

"Here, little one, are you playing in mud today? Well, let Me show you what you can learn from this mud. Are you reading poetry today? Let Me show you My reflection in this poem. Are you depressed? I'm here too. Stay open.

"Here, My love, can I show you the secret of this shell, this leaf, this rash, this heartbreak? They all hold secrets, you know. Everything holds My secrets. Here, let Me show you. Hush. Just breathe. It's OK. Yes, you can cry. (Sometimes, I'll cry with you.)

"And then, when you're ready for something more, come back. I'll show you another secret."

This belief—this image of Iroh as a Mask of God I could relate to—lasted for months. After a while I gave up my need to prove it was true, because doing it this way *felt* so right.

But you can't keep the cynicism from a life-long cynic forever. Despite the peacefulness and growth in this way of doing things, eventually my old need for objective, unintuitive, left-brain proof surfaced and brought me into the pits one more time.

CHAPTER 31

THE PATH OF MOST RESISTANCE

Why do you stay in prison when the door is so wide open?
Move outside the tangle of fear-thinking.
~ Rumi

By fall 2009, I had everything I needed to build a satisfying spiritual life. I just didn't know it. I had:

The experience of the love of God,
The wisdom and healing tools of Constellation work,
An understanding of my childhood pain and the knowledge of how to deal with it,
Tangible support from the generations behind me,
A wise and generous mentor,
A supportive and understanding husband,
Amazing, wise friends who were willing to talk with me about spirituality,
A wondrous family who generously shared the path with me, and
Time to study, reflect and work with what I'd learned.

I imagine my life would have been different if I had relaxed and simply accepted these gifts. Life would definitely have been simpler if I had followed my inner guidance and relied on its inspiration. If

I'd remained centered and allowed myself to go through the emotional ups and downs of integrating new experiences, I may have continued to slowly assimilate the insights they produced. I wish I had considered these possibilities.

I did just the opposite. I questioned each realization. I doubted every forward step. I kept doing the work, kept leaping off higher and higher cliffs—then immediately judging my efforts inadequate and wondering what was wrong with me.

Of all the choices I could have made after my November 18th experience, I chose to become fixated on my need to find enlightenment as quickly as possible—and to define enlightenment solely as the ability to feel that connection with God as often as possible.

There's a Zen parable:

The young student approached the Zen Master with a deep bow.

"Master, I really want to be enlightened. Please, tell me how long it will take."

"My son, it takes a long time. Perhaps as much as ten years."

"But what if I work really hard, then how long?"

"Really hard....?"

"Yes, really hard. What if I'm willing to fast and pray and meditate and help the poor and get up in the middle of the night and chant?"

"Ah, in that case—it takes 20 years."

Damn, I hated that story! I also hated this saying: *It's a Process.*

Although both were true, I couldn't seem to refrain from trying to make everything happen magically and quickly. I thought I should be able to plant the seeds of newfound wisdom on Monday and reap the harvest on Tuesday. And when it didn't happen, I questioned the seeds, the soil, my planting ability and the theory that seeds really turned into plants.

I fussed and fumed even when things went relatively well. If one of my spiritual seeds didn't seem to be growing fast enough, I felt I had no choice but to doubt them all. I left no room for experimentation or normal errors. One mistake made everything I was doing invalid. One doubt opened the door to all of them. I was often confused, with a visceral need to hide under the couch with a warm bowl of chocolate pudding.

During this period each doubt and concern seemed to repeat in an infinite recycle mode. Each one recurred, sometimes alone, sometimes in varying combinations with other concerns—frequently *ad nauseam*. The following is a list of the most prevalent beliefs and a synopsis of my thinking at the time.

Spirituality might be an illusion. My life is so good right now. I feel like such a jerk to be down and sad, but the truth is I am. Oddly, I think this search for spirituality, for a relationship with God is what has me down. I'm back to questioning—for the thousandth time—the validity of this search. So many people seem to lead happy and fulfilling lives without spirituality. Maybe we're here to just *live* and leave the spiritual things for the afterlife, whatever that is.

A personal spirituality is dangerous. I'm still having problems with this whole concept of a personal spirituality. I can't even imagine how this would work. What's to say the messages—the intuitions— I get are of any value at all? I often think of Stephen Colbert's brilliantly crafted word: *truthiness—the quality of preferring concepts or facts one wishes or believes to be true, rather than concepts or facts known to be true.* How can I really tell what's from God and what's just wishful thinking?

A personal spirituality may be worse than organized religion.
We can't all go around willy-nilly saying my vision of God is the
real one. That's as dangerous as saying my religion has the truth and
yours doesn't. At least most religions and wisdom traditions have
some history behind them. They've been around long enough to pick
up some credibility. But personal spirituality! It feels like a hippie
free-for-all with no boundaries, no framework for truth.

I have two memories of the kind of personal spirituality that has
always driven me away from the personal path. In the first, an old
woman in our parish—a grandmother and daily communicant—
used to put her statue of the Blessed Mother on the windowsill in
her kitchen, facing out, on school picnic or parish festival days. She
believed that the Blessed Mother, knowing the *special-windowsill
code*, would realize it was *our* event, and make sure God didn't allow
it to rain. Even as a kid, this felt wrong to me. Not only did it feel
manipulative of God, it felt unfair. What about the public school
kids' picnics? What about other parish fairs? Even though many
people regarded her as one of the holiest people in our neighborhood, I didn't like or trust her.

The other memory involves a woman at one of the first Overeaters
Anonymous meetings I attended. She said something like this: "I've
been struggling with my food plan for a while because I'm putting in
so much overtime at work. I was just so tired of coming home and
making a salad every night! I've been really praying about this! Then,
just this past week, my Higher Power put a salad bar in my neighborhood supermarket. Now it's no longer a problem. I'm so happy!"

Damn, she made me angry!! *"Yeah,"* I thought *"a third of the
world goes to bed hungry every night, children are dying of starvation
every second, and the Lord and Creator of the Universe took time out of
His busy schedule to put a salad bar in your Shop 'N Save! Yep, that's a
Higher Power we can all believe in!"*

298

I thought I'd moved so far from the judgmental person I was then. Yet, recalling that incident, knowing how wrong and arrogant I was, I still felt angry towards that woman. Is it any wonder I was no good at all in a Twelve Step program? Why had I been so surprised the others in the program didn't feel comfortable with me either?

Spirituality might just be a form of mental illness. If I'm being honest, I know some folks whose spirituality isn't all that far removed from some sort of—OK, let's be really frank—mental illness.

We've all seen them. Some people's spiritual beliefs are blatantly "out there." There are some folks who, on a manic high, know they are agents for the Second Coming and have no choice but to quit their jobs and begin stockpiling canned food for the perilous End Days ahead. More frightening are the relatively functional people who use their special relationship with God to anchor their own mistrust and fear of people who are different. These people really scare me—the ones who feel God is whispering in their ears, telling them truths that other folks aren't spiritual enough to hear.

After a discussion with a really normal-looking young man named Jed (a pseudonym), who told me about his secret missions for the Lord, I wrote in my journal:

> Damn, now that I've finally admitted there is something beyond the limited reaches of my cynicism and agnosticism, now that I've begun to take some small steps into that possibility [of spirituality], I'm really starting to fear it may not be healthy! Is this my resistance to the next step or a real concern? Where is the line between trusting your intuition and self-delusion? Jed surely crossed it. Who's to say I won't too?

Spirituality could be a handy way to whitewash reality. Do I want to become one of those people who use their spirituality to avoid life, to protect themselves from life? It feels like whistling in the dark or avoiding black cats. Life is not safe. Guardian angels do not protect little children from harm. As tempting as it is to believe that faith in God will keep me and everyone I love from harm, it isn't true. I don't want my peace of mind built on this kind of illusion. No thinking adult can afford to. But it sure is tempting.

I was better off mistrusting the whole concept of a caring God. Once I hit the issue of safety, I went again into my old fears about God. What price will I pay for a relationship with God? Who will I lose to His jealous power? How can I dare approach God without the right words and the right attitude? This led, as always, to the questions: How can I find my way through this spiritual world? I'm too new. I'm too scared. I'm too caught up in my mind instead of my heart. From here I was back to the Bible conundrum: If Jonas is my mentor, how can I ask for his advice and then not follow it? And if I'm going to follow it, I've got to make myself read the Bible, respect it and believe in the Bible as the unadulterated, unerring Word of God.

But I couldn't.

CHAPTER 32

THE BIBLE CLASS

The voyage of discovery is not in seeking new landscapes,
but in having new eyes.
~ Marcel Proust

March 23, 2010 was a Monday, but not one of Jonas' regularly scheduled Monday Wellness Classes. When Jonas' office manager called and invited me to an impromptu new class that evening, I accepted without hesitation. In hindsight, I wonder if extending the invitation to me had been a miscommunication between them.

I went expecting a class on health and wholeness. I walked into a Bible study—a very structured one.

Initially, just three of us sat around a table—Jonas, Gary (a pseudonym), a guy about my age and I. Jonas gave a short description of how the meeting would proceed. The ground rules, which Gary seemed to already know and accept, were simple: Only the Bible would be discussed, and it would be discussed only in positive sharing. There would be no questioning of the Bible and no discussion of other religious beliefs.

When he finished Jonas looked at me and smiled, "This is probably not what you bargained for, Connie. If you want to leave, I understand completely."

I considered leaving, but just for a second. In three years of his classes, I'd never attended one that didn't yield something important, even when the proposed topic didn't appear interesting. Also, this would give me a chance to better understand Jonas' Biblical spirituality.

"Thanks, but I think I'll stay. And I'll respect your ground rules."

I opened my notebook and uncapped my pen. I fully expected to simply sit and listen for the evening.

Jonas and Gary chose to work with two Bible verses—one from the Old Testament and one from the New Testament. I jotted them down and listened. They not only compared the verses to each other, they took out their concordances—Jonas had a book, Gary's concordance was on his laptop—and compared different versions of the verses. It went something like this: "Well, here's how this verse is stated in the King James' version and here's how it reads in the New American Standard version. The nuances of the phrasings would seem to suggest...."

This approach felt very head-based. The tone reminded me of the prayer groups Ross and I attended when we were dating. But I worked to keep an open mind. *"Hey,"* I told myself, *"This is Jonas. I trust him. I'm sure I'll find my place here."*

About a half hour later Debbie, a fellow classmate from the *Health and Wholeness* Monday night classes, joined us. I became hopeful. Debbie was a former Catholic with 12 years of nun-based education behind her. I sensed the presence of a kindred spirit. She was also one of the most down-to-earth and honest spiritual seekers I knew. She immediately brought some heart into the discussion. It gradually moved from, "This is more correct" to "This is my experience." I began to relax a bit.

As the discussion continued, however, the emphasis eventually returned to the ultimate, unwavering truth of the Bible. Actually,

Gary soon began to argue that all discussions should center around a specific version of the King James Bible he said was totally error free.

I smiled as I gently reminded them that no source of the Bible was totally uncorrupted.

"We have to be realistic. We know from historical facts that there was tampering by early Church councils, translation errors from the Greek and Latin, and the high probability of simple copying errors as monks transcribed hundreds of pages by hand."

Gary responded immediately and adamantly, "This particular version of the Bible is 100% error free, passed down perfectly through the ages. That's it!"

I waited for Jonas or Deb to disagree with him, to affirm the obvious historical reality. Neither did. Actually, at this point, Jonas reiterated his belief that there was only one true source of knowledge. "If I were God," he said, "I would want to make one sure way to guarantee my message got through to mankind. I think He did—and it's the Bible."

I could feel pressure pushing against my skull trying to make room for these ideas. I couldn't imagine those words coming from Jonas. More important, I couldn't imagine what would have to happen inside my brain for these words to be believable to me.

Jonas continued, "This doesn't mean that I think the Buddhists and Muslims are bad or wrong—I've never found a place in the Book where this is said...."

Gary interrupted with, "Well, I have and I'll be glad to share the verses with you...."

I reacted instinctively. I interrupted Gary with, "That's my cue." I didn't argue. I didn't question them. I just stood up, packed up my pen and notebook and walked out the door.

My hands shook as I unlocked the car. My head pounded. Once in the car, I sat for a few minutes taking really deep breaths. I knew I should start the car and drive home, but I was too stunned to move.

My thoughts kept spinning until they came to the following conclusion:

"If this is where Jonas is, if he is comfortable with these beliefs, I have no choice. I have to face the truth. I am unable—no matter how much I stretch my brain—to believe as Jonas believes."

Still, I couldn't move; I couldn't start the car. I just sat.

Then, after a few more minutes, from underneath the pain and confusion, another thought—a surprisingly good thought—bubbled up:

"Hey, this time was different. This was so different from the other times I've walked out on a group of true believers. This time, I didn't leave because I was angry with Gary and Jonas. I didn't leave because I was angry with God. I didn't leave because I'd once again discovered that true believers are jerks! I didn't leave because I'd come hoping to find the truth and was disappointed! I didn't leave because there was something wrong with me.

*"This time I left—without tears, without anger, without judgment of myself or them—because I knew **their vision of God** simply didn't match **my experience of God**. The God portrayed in that room was too small, too mean-spirited for me to accept. This time, unlike all the other times, I didn't reject God. I rejected their beliefs, but I didn't reject God."*

My next breath really filled my lungs. The fog in my brain lifted. I started the car and drove home.

That night I wrote in my journal:

I'd come to the meeting to learn, to share. It was not the place where I could do either. **No, that's not true.** I couldn't share but I did learn—a lot. I KNEW that Gary's God was not the God I'd experienced on November 18th. It was just that simple. The God of my experience doesn't exclude Muslims or Buddhists from his embrace. He doesn't limit access to Himself to one book or belief or religion. I didn't leave because God let me down or because my road to God was blocked one more fricken' time. **I left because the God in my heart transcended the God in that discussion.** I had no place there. I didn't belong. And oddly enough, I left feeling OK.

I slept peacefully. The next morning I wrote Jonas a lighthearted email stating we'd have a lot to talk about next time we got together. He wrote back thanking me for being willing to move out of my comfort zone and give the class a try.

What I didn't realize until several days later was that the class heralded more than my walk on a path separate from Jonas. It marked the beginning of many months of confusion, pain and frustration.

Until that Monday evening—until I understood we were not able to walk the same path—I hadn't realized how much of my spiritual journey revolved around my assumption that my spirituality would simply evolve under Jonas' mentorship. Without consciously acknowledging it, I had imagined limitless years of his gradually teaching me all he knew.

Now I was rudderless. Again.

CHAPTER 33

MAKING THE BREAK

A guru gives us himself and then his system;
a teacher gives us his subject and then ourselves.
~ Adam Gopnick

The decision to leave or stay on Jonas' path was mine alone. Jonas stood firmly in his truth—and in his offer of guidance—whether I agreed with him or not. He offered to be of service in any way I needed and found helpful. I created the rules for myself and for our interactions. I think he was often mystified by the pain I brought to the process.

He couldn't have been clearer: "Connie, if you think I'm trying to lead you to the God of *my* experience, you're misunderstanding me. I'm trying to point you to the God of *your* experience. But when you keep asking me how I do it, how I open myself to God, I can only give you *my* answer. In the past I've tried to put it in terms you found comfortable—in terms of energy work, for example. But our discussions have moved beyond that. Now when we're talking about how I relate to God, I have no other words, no other advice. I'm not telling you we can't work together if you can't accept it. I'm just saying I don't have anything else to give you when you ask me how I do it. For me the Bible is the way, the only way."

After that Monday class, my decisions should have been easy. Now that I understood why I was having so much trouble with the Bible-only path, I should have just walked away from Jonas and his path. It would have been logical.

But I wasn't working from logic. I still worked from a strong foundation of fear and longing. I was afraid I would be totally lost without a mentor. Forty years of wandering aimlessly on my own convinced me I didn't have the best instincts for spiritual searches. I still doubted the worth of a personal spirituality. I wanted some sort of accountability, some sort of checks and balances outside my highly untrustworthy self. When I measured my uncertainty against Jonas' certainty—and the peace of mind and personal power it gave him—I wanted to go with the power.

Also, truth be told, despite my numerous surrenders, I still feared God. I didn't feel confident about how to approach God without Jonas' guidance. His path had led me to my first experience of God's love—one of the most important experiences of my new spiritual life. I wanted to stay under the protection of his wisdom, his familiarity with proper spiritual behavior. I was in a double bind. I couldn't stay on his path but I was afraid to move too far from it.

So even after the Bible class realizations, I felt I had too much to lose by giving up work with Jonas. I kept trying to find a way to make his path mine. Several months after that evening, I wrote in my journal:

> Boy, [Jonas] was adamant about my reading the Bible with new eyes today. . . . It's obvious he wants me to understand things from his perspective because he believes what has worked so well for him will work for me. . . . That's the truth. I can like it or lump it. But I can't deny he's so adamant because he believes it

and because he cares about me. I know he takes his job as a mentor very seriously.

That's part of the reason I keep coming back to his way. I love that he cares. I love the sincerity and surety in his eyes as we talk. I want the kind of relationship with God he has—and I want to continue having the kind of relationship I have with Jonas. It makes me feel loved and hopeful. . . . I don't want to give it up!

The Church taught me to love God. Jonas is teaching me to be loved by God—to accept God's love as real and tangible and knowable.

So, while I do not—cannot—accept his belief that the Bible is the *only* way, I can accept it as *one* of the ways and, through studying it with an open heart, I can come closer to God.

Here's my commitment for the week: To read one chapter every day and find one line in each chapter to carry with me through the day—to think about and pray about. I'll begin by asking God's guidance before I read it. I can do this for a week.

But I never could make it even a week. My body, not just my mind, hurt when I tried.

I experimented with other spiritual reading. For days I would choose Rumi, Bert Hellinger, Jack Kornfield or Joseph Campbell for my spiritual reading—and I loved them. Then the fearful little rule-keeping girl inside me who knew I was "doing it all wrong" would get scared. I would pick up the Bible or some Christian book again. Interestingly, the emotional dance I did moving away from Jonas' path felt a lot like what I went through two years earlier as I'd moved onto it: Take three steps forward, four steps back, turn, spin, make myself a little crazy, fall down, get up, and start all over again.

I was once again living in a state of painful confusion. For example, after a really long week of internal stress, the name of a book I'd been given by an acquaintance popped into my head. I wondered if this stray thought was some sort of spiritual direction or just a fluke. Naturally, I couldn't tell. I just remembered it was hailed as a classic in Christian literature and had helped my buddy through some hard times. So I dug through my bookshelves until I found it. I sat down one Sunday morning and read C. S. Lewis' *Mere Christianity* cover to cover. I prayed before I began. I prayed in the middle to find the parts within it applicable to me. By the time I finished, however, I was in a deeper storm of confusion than when I'd started. I found myself alternating between hating the book because it wasn't helpful and hating myself for not understanding it.

The only-the-Bible stance became harder and harder each time I went back to it. Things were shifting. I began to allow for the possibility of following my own road, even if I couldn't imagine how it would be possible.

To make my new path more tangible, I created a different prayer for myself.

Lord, I stand with You, in deep reverence and gratitude, calling upon Your name, here with my family, asking that, every day, every moment, You give me the strength, the courage and the guidance to open my heart to Your love, and to my life.

I felt the immensity of this step. I needed to stand on my own two feet to say it. In it, I asked for the ability to find my own road and the guidance to walk down it. And while it included support from the generations that came before me—I still wasn't willing to stand before God alone—it no longer relied solely on Jonas and Biblical prayer.

A few days later, thumbing through Coleman Barks' wondrously accessible translation of Rumi's poetry, *The Essential Rumi*, I came across the poem, *Moving Waters*. It begins:

> When you do things from your soul, you feel a river moving in you, a joy.
> When actions come from another section, the feeling disappears.

Then, near the end:

> We are born and live inside black water in a well.
> How could we know what an open field of sunlight is?
> Don't insist on going where you think you want to go.
> Ask the way to the spring.
> Your living pieces will form a harmony.

I felt such relief when I read it. It felt like an answer to my new prayer. Maybe this was my next step. My experimenting self fairly danced with excitement.

"See, Con, this poem isn't just telling you there is another path, it's telling you how to find it—and it's giving you criteria to determine when you're doing it right.

"Let's try this out. Before you pick up a book for spiritual reading, or when you get scared and don't know what to do, ask for the way to the spring. Then listen with your whole self—with your body as well as your brain. Does this book bring you peace? Do you feel inspired or at least balanced as you read it? Then trust yourself. Continue to read it; allow yourself to experience its sunlight.

"If you feel the river of joy moving through you, assume you're on the right path. If you feel some inner harmony, trust your instincts. What can it hurt? Can it really make things worse than they are right now?"

311

More often than not, this decision held me in good stead. When I allowed myself to relax and assume I could discern what was true and helpful, I began to enjoy spiritual reading. My meditations became less stressful.

But my commitment to this course of action wasn't solid. Even as I went along enjoying the freedom of experimentation and choice, I fully expected I'd soon have to go back to Jonas' path. I felt like a kid who had permission to eat anything she wanted. I knew eventually the grownups would realize I was eating too much chocolate and withdraw my privileges. I still needed outside validation for my choices. My belief in The One Ultimate Truth, which I knew I couldn't find without outside guidance, was still alive and wreaking havoc—just with a little less bravado.

Surprisingly, a craniosacral adjustment session with Jonas finally broke the hold of that magical belief. If November 18, 2008 had been my rebirth, June 8, 2010 was my Independence Day.

It had been several months since I'd had a cranial and I prepared for it seriously. A week before my appointment, I decided to use the cranial time to determine which path I would continue to follow. I no longer had the energy to keep one foot on each.

One last time I examined my options. If I chose Jonas' path as my way to God, I needed to commit to following his advice no matter what. I couldn't continue to ask for his advice if I wasn't willing to follow it. I might be uncomfortable, but I would have a mentor I trusted.

On the other hand, if I chose to strike out on my own path, I would probably feel better but I'd be set adrift in a spiritual world where I probably wouldn't find God on my own.

Both decisions felt wrong. I saw myself in a lose-lose situation, but was too exhausted to continue the debate.

For days I felt the weight of this choice. Despite all I'd learned in the last few years, I still saw my decision as a test. I still saw God as the taskmaster with the list of hoops I had to jump through.

That morning, as I got ready to leave for Jonas' office, I made my decision.

"OK, if I've got to prove myself by giving up Jonas, I'll do it. If that's the price I have to pay for moving to the next level, I'll pay. It seems cruel for God to take away my mentor before I fully understand how to live a good spiritual life, but I'm willing to do it.

"If that's what it costs, I'm willing to pay. Lord, I don't understand the next step, but You do. No matter what it is, You lead and I'll follow."

I tried to approach this decision with humility but I was also pretty angry I had to make the choice. I was on the verge of tears for the whole ride to Jonas' office. When I got into the treatment room, I let go of all pretense of composure. I just sat and cried. When Jonas came in, I preempted any small talk by simply lying down on the table. As he began the cranial adjustment, we were both silent.

After a few moments Jonas said, "Connie, I've been praying a lot about our work together. I know you've really been struggling with this too. I've asked God what I should be doing differently."

"Did you get an answer?"

"Yes, but I don't think you're going to like it."

"I doubt it can be worse than what I've been thinking. What was it?"

"God told me I should stop talking to you about your spirituality. The actual words I heard were: 'Stop talking to her about that. She has to find her own way.'"

Immediately an image flashed before me. I saw a little girl, standing outside the door of a powerful king's throne room. She'd always been too scared to go in, so her friend, the king's advisor, had brought messages to and from the king. Now she heard the king say to the advisor, "You can stop talking to her about me, Courtier. Stop telling her who I am. She's old enough now. She has to find her own way—and I know she can."

I stopped crying.

"Jonas, are you kidding? Did you really think I wouldn't like that message? It's the best news I've ever heard.

"Before I came here this morning I surrendered our relationship to God. I fully expected to lose it, to lose the privilege of our working together, to lose your mentoring. Now I don't have to. Now there's an alternative. With this new way of looking at things, we can continue to work together. We can continue the healing work, the chiropractic and the energy work. We just need to understand that I need to do one part of the journey on my own. I need to be on my own spiritual path. This is great."

As we continued the cranial, my heart overflowed with love and gratitude—and surprise. There had been a *win* built into what I thought was my lose-lose proposition! What had never occurred to me—as I fussed for weeks with the decision about whether or not to choose God—was that God might choose me.

When Jonas finished, he started to leave and then came back. "There's one more part." His voice seemed an octave lower. I sat up and turned to face him. His eyes locked mine.

"From now on, you can come here for any reason on earth—except to find God. You can come here for healing, for chiropractic work, to discuss anything you want. But you can't come here to find God."

"No, Jonas, that's not what the message meant. You just need to stop talking to me about God. I can still come here to find Him. That's *why* I come here. It's why I came here today. And I found God's answer *here* today."

"I know, Connie. But, as of today, you need to understand that you're beyond that kind of thinking. You can't find God outside of yourself. You have to find God on your own, within yourself."

Clang. A huge bell of recognition tolled inside me. I recognized the truth. I no longer needed an intermediary, an intercessor. I needed to begin to trust my own *experience* with God. I didn't just have to leave Jonas' Bible-centered path, I needed to let go of my dependence on Jonas to interpret everything I discovered on my *own* path.

We could still work together. We could still discuss different aspects of healing. But I now had the responsibility to keep myself open and responsive to the spirit of God that dwelled within me—to come home to my own relationship with God.

CHAPTER 34

MY OWN PATH

Where there is a way or path, it is someone else's path.
You are not on your own path.
~ Joseph Campbell

As usual, I handled this new phase in my life with a myriad of reactions. Part of me enjoyed being on my own. Part of me was scared to death. Another part was simply lonely. The June craniosacral experience left me less fearful of God, but I still doubted myself—doubted I'd have the discipline to wait patiently for God to speak or the discernment to recognize a message. And I hated the idea of walking the road alone.

For a week or so I just ran on emotions, bouncing between fearfulness and hopeful anticipation. I didn't know where to begin without Jonas' guidance. The Monday after my cranial I wrote in my journal:

> It's been almost a week since the [craniosacral] experience. In some ways it feels like a day ago. In other ways it seems like forever. Right after, it seemed good. . . . But being in Jonas' office Friday and today and *not* talking about spirituality, felt really awful and lonely. I cried both days when I got into the car. Suddenly,

we're acquaintances. I swear, the first time he says to me something like, "Hey, how about those Steelers," I'll quit going there.

OK, here's my plan. Tonight, I'll meditate and ask for guidance. I'll ask it the way Jonas taught me—to claim it. [I'll] ask believing that I'll get an answer. Tonight I'll sleep on it and get up
early tomorrow and start to work right away!!

I had some editing deadlines, so I had work to keep me busy.
Fortunately, in large part because of Jonas' consistent counsel, I'd
established enough of a spiritual discipline to keep me going until I got my bearings. I continued to meditate and pray, relying on
a variation of my Swiss Army Knife prayer, "Lord, I don't know
what to do in this void, but You do. I'll just keep on moving,
knowing the path is there." I continued to read books that gave
me hope.

But this was my part-time stance. At other times I still feared
God and the new spiritual lessons on the horizon. Even when I
felt emotionally fine on any given day, I had to work hard to stop
imagining the bleak void of mentor-less wandering that was surely
ahead of me. When things got rough, I surfed the Internet, played
computer games or browsed *Amazon.com*.

And on Amazon I got the first answer to that prayer. One day, as
I bounced from topic to topic, I decided to see if Joe Dispenza, one
of my favorite authors, had a new book. I typed his name into the
Search box. Several books into the search, I saw a Dispenza book I'd
never seen before.

The title, *God on Your Own: Finding A Spiritual Path Outside
Religion*, naturally pulled me in. I clicked on the *Look Inside* box
and began reading. No, this wasn't a new book by the Joe Dispenza
I knew. This was by Joseph Dispenza—an ex-Catholic and an ex-
monk.

I ordered it immediately and devoured it as soon as it arrived. Wow, his writing seemed hand-tailored to my needs.

Some of Dispenza's experiences when leaving the monastery were similar to mine when I left the convent. However, instead of chucking everything and leaving in anger, he'd kept what he felt had value and added to it. His balanced approach was in stark contrast to my all-or-nothing, door-slamming departure from Catholicism and God. I also recognized that, since leaving Jonas' path was a lot like leaving the convent, I had the chance to make some reasonable choices here too. This time, instead of dumping the baby with the bathwater, I could be a little more selective. I could hold tight to the baby—the wisdom I'd learned from Jonas these last two years—and let go of the parts that didn't serve me.

Buoyed by Dispenza's approach to finding God outside the structures of a traditional belief system, I relaxed a little. I appreciated his insights. His story gave me hope. He wasn't lost forever because he took the less-traveled road. Maybe I wouldn't be either.

God on Your Own contained solid, gentle advice. It suggested ways to learn to trust my own spirit. Dispenza hadn't just found a new life outside the framework of religion; he'd created a good, spiritually-based, rewarding life. Eventually he also found kindred spirits, others who could share it. Maybe I could do the same. It would be difficult to continue without a mentor, but it could be done. Although my spiritual legs were still a little wobbly, I moved forward.

A second answer to my prayers came soon after. For several days, as I meditated, I could feel my dad's presence very strongly. This surprised me a little. I still began my meditations with, *"Lord, I stand with you . . . here with my family..."* so I often had a sense of the generations of my family around me. But this was different. Now I sensed just my dad. It felt a lot like the early days after my Constellation in 2005. I felt a request from him:

Feeling Dad's presence strongly. . . . This morning in meditation, felt Dad urge me to put my hands face up [on my lap] so that he could hold them . . . . Felt a cool and strong presence, almost a pressure of Dad's hands on mine.

Felt Dad asking me to put my hands over my heart chakra to verify my commitment to making this next part of the journey without Jonas' help. As I did, it felt very real, but I—as I always have done—began to question it. Felt Dad's insistence that this was real and that I had to begin to trust my own spiritual experiences. [He suggested I remember that] The Green Words came to me outside Jonas' office.

[Then] as I pressed my hands over my heart, I felt a very real opening—a shift and opening as deep as I've felt during a cranial.

The next part of Dad's message was one I didn't like. He said it was important for me to cancel the next two cranials I'd scheduled—that I needed time to establish my relationship with God without them. I fought the idea, but not long. I made the commitment to Dad to cancel them. With that came [Dad's] assurance that this didn't have to be forever, just for now. It felt very right.

Now, several hours after it happened, as I'm putting it into this journal, the good feelings are again surfacing. For now, this seems to be the correct decision. Thank you. Thanks Dad. This feels both strange and right, frightening and the answer to my prayers.

And just now, as I thanked Dad again, and waited to see if there was more . . . I got the old message, "Work with the work in front of you. Get your indexing job done. What we have just done together will work on its own, without the need for your attention."

I cancelled the cranials and dove into indexing Ernest Rossi's chapters on Epigenetics in the seventh volume of *The Collected Works of Milton H. Erickson.*

A day later what I read stopped me cold. It was so surprising I kept rereading the text to make sure I hadn't misread it. Rossi stated the newest research showed that, contrary to what we'd always believed, our genetic makeup is not set at birth. It can be changed—our genes can be altered—by occurrences in our lives!

This was a big deal. One of the *absolute truths* of the science I'd grown up with stated that our genetic makeup was set at birth. Once the egg and sperm made their initial contributions, each of us was set for life—brown hair, blue eyes, a propensity toward breast cancer, etc. Things were written in stone. The *new absolute truth* was that circumstances in our lives, both positive and negative, could affect our DNA.

The first work in the field of Epigenetics focused on how trauma—through war or molestation or accidents—altered the genes. A lot of work was done in war-torn countries and with women pregnant during 9/11 that substantiated these claims. It offered evidence that post-traumatic stress affected us on a level folks hadn't even imagined.

But now there was more! The work Ernest Rossi chronicled suggested another fact. Profound positive experiences, what Rossi called *numinosum*, could also alter our genes. Immensely positive experiences—a vision, a near-death incident, a mystical experience, falling in love, even a profound experience of wonder—sometimes caused a change so deep it altered a person's genes. Unfathomable. Unbelievable. And yet true.

Immediately my mind went to November 18th and my first Constellation. Somehow the scientific verification of the changes I'd felt on those two occasions validated both of them in a way nothing else had. Now there was *scientific* evidence that the changes I'd experienced were not just in my imagination. They had altered my physiology, possibly my genetics. Now the skeptical part of me harboring the secret fear that change, healing and spirituality were just wishful thinking had evidence they were real.

This was a life changer. Just as tapping one domino in a line of dominos sets every other one in motion, this one fact set up a chain reaction in my brain that went back almost 60 years.

For as much as I'd loved them, I always thought of psychology and spirituality as *soft* studies. They were theoretical and fuzzy around the edges. Their truths weren't immutable like *hard* science—like gravity and centrifugal force. But now the *science* of Epigenetics affirmed, with hard data and reproducible tests, that one of the basic tenets of psychology and spirituality was true. We really can change! We can change the very essence of who we are. And change is not something supernatural! It's built into us. This information meant that what I'd considered exceptions to the rules of nature might actually be natural. Miraculous changes—cripples walking, drug addicts kicking the habit after a conversion experience and tumors shrinking—were not outside the realm of humanity—they are a part of our humanity. Wow, if genes could change, anything could change!

More than once I had to stop reading and just catch my breath. These statements were the death knell of one of my most persistent fears, that people really didn't change, that all of my changes weren't real. Now I could dump that fear forever. People did change. People healed. Changes—miraculous changes—weren't just a big pile of self-delusion. They were scientifically provable facts.

It meant that things like November 18th, a Constellation, unconditional love or a mystical experience all fell into the category of natural changes. Miracles weren't beyond our humanity; they were built into our humanity. A profound positive experience could affect not just our thoughts and feelings, not just our blood pressure and parasympathetic nervous system. It could reach down into the minutest part of us, into our cells, into the intimacy of our DNA, and change us.

I thought back to the questions about healing and change that had plagued me since childhood. I'd spent so much time trying to figure out which healer was The True One. Now I had a new answer. Neither the healer, nor the belief system nor the ritual created the healing. People did not heal because a particular healer had The Ultimate Truth. It wasn't because someone finally got the ritual right or the planets were in the proper alignment. It was because there exists in everyone, in each and every human being, the capacity to be changed—unquestionably altered—by a positive experience in their lives.

I stopped indexing and went to my journal:

> This is it!! This is the answer. Oral Roberts works just as well as Fatima and cranials and voodoo and psychoanalysis and hypnosis—and, and, and all other forms of healing because the healing power is BUILT INTO US!!! If the change—inside or outside—is powerful enough, it changes us!!!! That's it!! We are built to accept and use the chemical, psychological and spiritual stimuli of our lives!
>
> This doesn't deny the validity of spiritual experiences or near-death experiences or miracles. It embraces all of them!!! We can use all of them!
>
> Does it deny God? No! Rather it paints the picture of a most loving and benign Creator who built into us a thousand ways to

heal, a thousand ways to change—and a thousand ways to be of service to each other, facilitating those changes!!!

The only thing it negates, at least for me, is the right way/ wrong way question. There is no right or wrong way! All roads can lead to healing and change because the power to change is INSIDE US!!! . . .

What an amazing and blessed world we live in!!!! What potential we have within us to change everything, now that we know this.

Now, Jonas' words on November 18th make sense. "Connie, I didn't give you anything. It was all inside you."

Now the cynical part of me, the part that never allowed me to relax into the world of spirit and healing, had some new facts to ponder.

Before I went back to work, I thought of the meditation message I'd gotten from my dad just the day before—his insistence that I cancel my next cranials and throw myself into indexing Rossi. Somehow Dad knew the tectonic plates were about to shift again—this time on my own path, on my own watch.

Chapter 35

Reflecting and Opening

When you follow your bliss, doors will open where you would
not have thought there would be doors;
and where there wouldn't be a door for anyone else.
~ Joseph Campbell

It's hard to express how much the Epigenetics discovery meant to me. It really did change everything. Miracles—which I'd thought lived only in the rarefied atmosphere of high-level spirituality—were not supernatural. They were natural, built into us. And access to miracles—which I thought was limited to those who had found The Ultimate Truth—was open to all of us, no matter what we believed. The essential part of the miracle equation was the act of opening up to the possibility of change and healing. All of the rituals and sacred places and blessed relics were simply the keys each of us needed to open the door to our hearts to the Transcendent and to the possibility of a miracle.

I could, once and for all, let go of the need to follow Jonas' path. It was the perfect one for him, and the part we'd shared had led me out of years of darkness. But now, as our paths diverged, I realized I needed to examine and understand my own.

So one summer day I sat down and wrote all the things I believed:

I know there is a Loving Force within the universe.

I know my openness to this Force determines, at least in part, how I am able to experience this Force.

I know that, despite how it sometimes looks and feels, we are all loved by the One who created us.

I know this Loving Force, which I choose to call God, is approachable, because the Force lives in the very essence of Its creation.

I know we live beyond our lifetimes here on earth. I know our families live beyond death and can reach past the barrier of death to lovingly support us.

I know that God, the creator of the universe, is beyond the comprehension of our tiny minds, but can be experienced in our minds and hearts.

I know our labels for God are determined by our own inability to understand the unfathomable.

I know that, although we cannot understand or define God, we can experience God.

The experience of God's love is a gift, but it's a gift offered to everyone. We just need to reach beyond our fears and misperceptions to receive it.

There is help to reach beyond our fears and misperceptions.

Our insistence that the God of our experience is the REAL God, and that others experience a false god, is brought about by our fear—and misunderstanding of the unfathomable essence of God.

Our experience of God is just that, *our experience.* It's not Ultimate Truth. It's just the amount of truth and love we are capable of experiencing.

Our experience of God as humans, contained in these bodies, minds and souls, can be enhanced by fully participating in this life of body, mind and spirit. How we live this life determines how open we are to experience this Essence.

Becoming more healthy and open to life allows for a greater and more joyful experience of life.

The gift of knowing God's love is always present. AND we sometimes have to work to get out of the way so that we can experience it.

When we shut down—often unknowingly, often because of fears or trauma or misunderstanding—we cannot see the truth that's all around us.

When we have trouble opening our eyes, help is available to us if we ask.

AND all of these words are totally inadequate; they're just the best I have right now.

When I reread these thoughts a few days later, I was taken aback. It's odd to say but, until I saw them in black and white, I hadn't realized how concrete my beliefs had become. I was surprised to see how many times I wrote "I know" instead of "I hope" or "I believe." I also realized, as illogical as it sounds, that I didn't *always* believe them. My cynicism seemed to be wounded, but it wasn't demolished. The experience of rereading what I had written reminded me of my reaction to The Green Words. Maybe I needed to slowly grow into these new ideas just as I'd needed to grow into The Green Words.

~

Moving from Jonas' path also gave me the opportunity to look at the past year or so with new eyes. Once I took out the argument about the Bible, once I stopped focusing on that one point of contention between Jonas and me, I could see all the positive things we'd done.

I reread a year's worth of journal entries and saw the immeasurable good our work together produced. For instance, Jonas had helped me plant the seed of self-acceptance by unswervingly challenging my negativity. He often stopped me when I began our discussions with my standard self-deprecating remarks.

"Listen to what you're saying, Connie: 'I'm such a jerk. I'm so messed up.' Do you really want to be filling your mind and spirit with those thoughts? If you don't choose to stop, at least be aware of the messages you're sending yourself."

He also challenged my frustration with humor and common sense. "How long have you been working on this shift in your perspective? A whole week? And you still haven't found enlightenment? Perhaps a major life change like this might take a week and a half." Or, "Connie, look inside you. Your new attitude brought you all the building blocks you need. That's a big deal. It just may take some more time to build the new edifice you want. Stay the course."

Perhaps most important, he'd convinced me to be constant and consistent in my new spiritual practices.

"Connie, your passion for God cannot replace your consistency in opening to God. Bold gestures need to be balanced with day-to-day discipline. Meditating on bad days and meditating when it feels boring and senseless are part of the path to growth. We need to let our bodies and minds know who's in charge. We make room for spirit by consistently making it first."

When I overlooked the Biblical language I found disconcerting, I realized the solidity of his message. If I looked beyond the references to salvation and the quotes from Deuteronomy and Psalms that pushed my buttons, I appreciated the truth in what he said.

Bottom line—we still agreed on the very basics: There is a loving God whose love for His creation is limitless. It's our duty and privilege to return this love and to, in turn, love everyone as God loves us. That was a lot.

In this reflective space, I also returned to the Hellinger work with new eyes. I had been facilitating occasional Constellation workshops and attending those of another facilitator in the area. Now with a mind uncluttered by the constant question "Is this The Ultimate Truth?" I went back to Hellinger's writings and discovered a new layer of beauty. This time around, when I no longer needed to keep testing the validity of the spiritual aspects of Constellations, I sank deeper into the amazing truths they revealed. I felt their sacred foundation.

For example, as I reread Hellinger's *Love's Hidden Symmetry*, I came across a quote about taking our parents into our hearts that I'd read a dozen times.

> Often the search for self-realization and enlightenment is, in reality, a search for the not-yet-taken father and the not-yet-taken mother. The search for God often stops or becomes different when the father and mother are taken.

This time, I saw something I'd never seen before. The words I'd missed the other dozen times I'd read it were "or becomes different." I caught my breath as I realized the truth of those words. This part of my journey, my finding God after so many years of searching, had begun—*had become something different*—the day I took my mother into my heart during my first Constellation!

Still, I really missed someone to talk with as I'd talked with Jonas over the last several years. The discussion group I'd started a few years earlier had petered out. I'd looked into several local churches and found they weren't a good fit. I thought finding a spiritual community I could relate to was highly improbable.

I was proven wrong within days. In late August, as we finally celebrated the 80th birthday of my friend Flo over a long-anticipated lunch, she invited me to join her at a workshop given by the Science of Mind church on the other side of the city.

"Let's make it a day, Connie. Let's go to the service as well as the workshop. They have a lunch scheduled. It'll be fun."

I couldn't refuse Flo. She was one of the most spiritually alive people I knew—and one of the most fun. I rearranged my schedule to go with her the first Sunday in September. We even enjoyed our drive to the Center, although we got lost twice. The speaker was informative and engaging. I learned something new about prayer. Lunch was good. The people and the service were welcoming and comfortable. When Linda, a woman who lived on my side of town, gave me her phone number and offered to carpool with me if I wanted to return, I gratefully agreed to give her a call.

During the week I read the information in the first-timers packet they'd given me and talked a little more with Flo. A lot of Science of Mind beliefs felt familiar and nourishing. I found myself eagerly anticipating the next service.

When Sunday arrived, Linda and I talked easily on the ride to the center. I expected another pleasant experience at the service. I was surprised to feel tears of joy on my cheeks as the first hymn began. The music, the prayers, the sermon, the special way the children were included in the service and the friendliness of the members of this small congregation touched a very deep place inside me. When I returned the next week, I signed up for the *Foundations of Science of Mind* class. I wanted to know more about these people and their beliefs.

CHAPTER 36

A PATH EVOLVING

Believe in yourself. Have confidence in the high
impulsions that come to you.
Listen deeply to the Divine Nature which
forevermore imparts Itself to you.
Spirit is right where you are.
~ Ernest Holmes

The Foundations Class started at the end of September. For eleven weeks, a small group of us met at Reverend Nancy Kandel's home on Friday mornings and studied Ernest Holmes' book, *The Science of Mind: A Philosophy, A Faith, A Way of Life.* We used experiential exercises and reflections on Holmes' writings to develop a basic understanding of his beliefs.

Holmes' message gave me a lot to think about. He spoke of God's presence in a way unfamiliar to me. He saw no way to separate ourselves from God because we are all created from the energy that is God. A simple cliché expressed this Science of Mind belief: "There is no spot where God is not."

On first reading, this idea didn't seem much different from the concept of "God is everywhere" I'd learned as a child. But as I got deeper into Holmes' writings, the tone felt very different. As a kid,

"God is everywhere" meant we should always be good. It meant God was watching, taking notes in His record book and making sure we behaved. In the way Holmes stated it, "God is everywhere" meant God was in the very fabric of His creation, intimately a part of everything. We were created of God's essence. God's presence wasn't as watcher or judge. God didn't just create us and turn us loose. There was no separation between Creator and creation. God became one with us by the act of creation.

The first couple times I read this, I couldn't even imagine it. Then, as I began to understand it a bit, my little-Catholic-girl brain rejected it. *"This can't be right! This is putting us too close to God! There's something too prideful, too arrogant in this!"*

But as I allowed a space for this possibility, I realized the belief was an answer to some of the dichotomies I'd encountered in the last few years. If God is eternal and omnipresent and infinite—and I had no trouble imagining God as all those things—what else could we be made of but that eternal, omnipresent essence? What else is there? And if we are made of God's essence, aren't we all part of God? Maybe these principles weren't heresy; maybe they were simply a reiteration of the oneness all mystics experienced. Maybe, instead of being blasphemy, they expressed what Jesus meant when he said, "I and the Father are one"?

As I read Holmes, I felt myself in a brain-stretching period similar to what I felt when I began working with Mark, Jonas and Carmen. The concepts were, at first, so foreign I'd understand them for only a fleeting second before they would disappear. But this time, familiar with the pattern, I didn't panic when it happened. I was willing to allow for the lag time between seeing and understanding.

This didn't mean I accepted everything without protests or questions. None of us in the Foundations class did. We were open to new perceptions but we didn't simply accept them without challenge. We needed to understand them with our hearts *and* our heads.

For most of us, examining the new concepts also meant uncovering, once again, painful questions. From the start, each person in the class took the risk of being vulnerable and honest—and angry. Several classes were filled with tears, questions and stories of unfairness, abuse, and pain. Each of us asked deep-felt questions that Holmes' principles brought to light: "If God is within all of His creation, how is there room for evil? Why was I molested? Why was my brother killed? If God is within us all, why aren't my prayers answered? Why aren't everyone's prayers answered?"

Nancy didn't demean our questions and stories with trite answers and assurances. She listened respectfully and empathetically. She understood our pain and gave us a safe space to express it. She often added her own stories of early confusion and heartbreak. Then, very gently, fully acknowledging our frustrations, she nudged us into testing Holmes' precepts for ourselves. She stood in her own truth and demonstrated, by her attitude and actions, how it was possible to find answers that satisfied us on many levels. I made a conscious decision not to demand the perfect answer, or even the most logical one, as I began these studies. Instead I allowed for the possibility there could simply be a satisfactory answer for me—right there, right then, at a level I could handle.

Perhaps because I didn't fight so hard, I began to understand things I hadn't before. For example, the "*choice* argument" that Holmes used made more sense to me than it had when I'd run into similar explanations. In the past I'd understood that, by giving us choice, God naturally gave us the ability to choose well or poorly—to make either hurtful or beneficial selections. Thus, after thousands of years and billions of bad choices, mankind had created a world in which evil and selfishness often dominated. But I never knew what to do with this knowledge.

This time around I saw it as analogous to my food problem. After years of harming my body with junk food and little exercise, one day of eating correctly wasn't enough to instantly make me healthy and trim. Now I understood that one or two or a hundred days of positively affirming new beliefs and making good choices wouldn't completely change my world. They were a good beginning. But the process would take time.

With this new perspective, I saw spirituality differently. I became willing to work with my spiritual practices even when I didn't see immediate results. My personal beliefs had created my inner world for the last 60 years. Changes might take some time to manifest.

I began to understand, on an emotional level—not just an intellectual one—that spiritual growth was just like any other growth. The rules were the same for spirituality as for everything else, from riding a bike to playing the piano. We all start out a little clumsy. Accidents or wrong notes are the norm, not reasons for self-condemnation and self-doubts. We don't become accomplished by wishing we were better. We improve with practice as we integrate new ideas and skills into our everyday lives. I also realized—finally—that I practice better when I don't stop and doubt myself with every other step. These were important shifts.

Other beliefs also changed during the months of class. Listening to my fellow students' stories helped me to realize how much of my spiritual search still involved my pursuit of safety and security. In spite of everything, I still clung to the possibility I could find an Ultimate Belief that, once I held it perfectly, would lift me above the fray of humanity.

This time, on perhaps the thousandth go-round, I decided this conviction no longer served me. The truth was simpler. Life—everyone's life—was messy. It was filled with unfairness, sadness and discord as well as beauty, love and connection. That is, was and will be the reality on this planet. Period. Perhaps the solution didn't come in continuing to search for a way to eliminate life's messiness. Rather, happiness came in learning to live in the disorder and unfairness without giving in to despair. Maybe I needed to find a way to keep my heart open within the chaos. Maybe the real challenge was not to reason or breathe or meditate my way *out* of life but rather to open myself to life—with all its disarray—and find a space of peace, goodness and love. These weren't new concepts, but they were now ones I understood a lot better.

I also came to respect Holmes' approach to spirituality. On the one hand, he demonstrated a desire to put his spiritual beliefs under a microscope and show them to be provable and scientifically accurate. That's why he called his concepts *Science of Mind*. He encouraged his readers to test his hypotheses; he urged his followers to research and document their experiences of healings and answered prayers. But he also had a very personal, non-scientific relationship with God that emerged throughout his writings.

In his chapter, *Finding the Christ*, after more than 350 pages describing, examining and explaining the principles behind his belief, it seemed he couldn't go on another moment without allowing his personal relationship with God to burst forth. After stating, in capital letters, GOD IS MORE THAN LAW OR PRINCIPLE, his next words were a poem ending with the lines:

> Inner Voice, that speaks supremely,
> Inner Good, that binds me to Thee,
> HOLY, HOLY, HOLY—
> Lord God within me.

This was a man who knew God, who understood the experience of going within and finding an intimacy with a Transcendent Spirit he could not begin to comprehend. He understood what he called the "Personalness" of God.

In the company of other like-minded people, in a space where I defined my beliefs instead of fighting for them, I grew into them.

After years of searching alone, after more than a year of disagreeing with Jonas about some basic principles, it was comforting to be among people who thought some of the things I thought. When I compared my August list of beliefs to those of the Science of Mind folks, I found enough similarities between them to relax a bit with mine. People who had devoted their lives to this search had come to similar conclusions. Certainly Science of Mind went far beyond my thoughts and experiences, into depths it would probably take years to fully understand. But I was heartened to see my inner experiences were not unique.

~

Oddly, a month or so after the Foundations class ended, I found myself drifting from this church. This genuinely surprised me. I'd assumed I'd stay with them for years. I liked these people and their message. Being part of the church filled such a social and intellectual need for me. It also gave me some relief from that tricky trap of personal spirituality.

Every Saturday I'd plan to attend the services. I'd even make arrangements to carpool. But on Sunday morning I couldn't make myself go. My reaction was the same to the newly formed Science of Mind weekly discussion group that met on Saturdays. I went a few times and really enjoyed it, but couldn't seem to get into the flow of regularly attending.

It took a few months to realize what was happening. Some part of me—definitely not the part that was usually in charge—required time to continue the journey on my own for a while. I'd spent years opening up to spirituality with Mark, Suzi and Family Constellation work. I'd spent the next years working with Jonas and Carmen as my spirituality began to bud. For several months I'd solidified my new beliefs with the people in the church. Now, like it or not, I needed to spend time alone, in relationship with God. I had to recognize and incorporate the internal changes I made without checking with someone else to ensure their validity. I'd gone through the spring, summer and fall of spiritual rebirth surrounded by teachers and mentors. Now I needed to face it in the solitude of winter.

CHAPTER 37

IN SOLITUDE

Life isn't about waiting for the storm to pass.
It's about learning to dance in the rain.
~ Martha Graham

Working alone, taking responsibility for my spirituality, I came to understand that spirituality is essentially natural, not supernatural. For me, a human on this planet, it had to be earthly in order to be functional. As long as spirituality was outside me, on that high, slippery sidewalk I kept falling from, I didn't have the ability to maintain and foster it, and I lived in fear of losing it. Once I saw it as part of real life, many of my problems faded.

This was tricky at first because sometimes spirituality seemed to be expressed in things that felt *otherworldly*. However, once I realized that inspiration, just like intuition, was natural—something that has been happening to people since the beginning of our appearance on the planet—I became more comfortable in the natural spiritual realm. In my reading, as I revisited other cultures and beliefs, I saw that my long-held cynic's stance of only believing what I could experience with my five senses or what people could replicate in a science lab was the exception in human history. Perhaps I needed to see My

17ᵗʰ-century Western prejudices for just what they were—one opinion—with their own built-in magic.

Mystics have always looked within and found transcendence. Every culture has sought—and found—spirit within nature, in honoring predecessors and in adherence to sacred words and rituals. Every mythology and religion has been a combination of man's reaching toward Spirit and Spirit's reaching toward mankind. That's what my spirituality needed to become.

During 2011, in that year of reflection, some changes began with a simple thought or experience. One evening, for instance, as I balked at meditating because I was again experiencing doubts about the reality of God, I stopped. I looked at what I was doing and saw the built-in futility of my stance of alternately believing and not believing.

"OK, Donaldson," I said to myself, *"either you believe in God or you don't. No more of this maybe yes, maybe no stuff. It's just too exhausting to continue this way every damn day! Jonas is right. Being on the fence is the worst place to be. If you don't believe, then choose to stay on the side of disbelief. Stop bouncing around and go back to who you used to be! If you don't believe in God, stop meditating. Period. Can you do that? Can you choose not to meditate, ever again?*

"No? OK, then if you can't choose to never meditate, what does that mean? It means you believe in God and you believe in meditation as a way to open yourself to God. These are now facts, your facts. You believe in God. Where you go from here, whether you choose to skip meditation one night or meditate 30 times a day, this is the truth: You believe in God."

That decision not only felt right, it further changed how I felt. That simple acknowledgement became my reality. From then on, whether I meditated or not, I knew I believed in God. It was a fact, not a possibility. I had moved out of the realm of theory, and life became more peaceful.

Sometime later I also realized I needed to change how I prayed. I loved my *"Lord, I stand with You"* prayer. Saying it centered and calmed me. Just like lighting a candle or taking slow deep breaths, it helped me to slip into the place where I could be open to Spirit. Now I realized I needed to adapt it to another truth. Now the words "...*asking* that every day You give me the strength, courage and guidance..." needed to be changed to "*grateful* that every day You give me the strength, courage and guidance...." I had to acknowledge I was receiving the strength and guidance I'd been praying for. As that prayer became my habitual approach to God, my heart continued to open to God and to my life.

This brought me to another big shift. One day, probably a month or so after I'd revised the prayer, I had another revelation. *"This prayer is working. I'm changing enough to allow the space within me to be open to guidance. Not every day, not in all circumstances, but I am becoming more open. If this is true, what else is true about prayer?"*

Immediately the memory of what Jonas had said years before popped into my head.

"Connie, some day you're going to see that all of your prayers are answered. And the answer is always yes. You don't have to keep asking. You just have to be willing to accept the yes."

He'd said it to me a hundred times, in as many different ways as he could. But I'd never understood what he meant. Now I decided to examine the concept a little closer, play with it a bit.

"OK," I thought, *"what if this is true? What if this prayer is always answered with a yes? What would that mean?"*

I went to my computer journal and pulled up the words:

Lord, I stand with You, in deep reverence and deep gratitude,
calling upon Your name, here with my family, grateful that every

day, every moment, You give me the strength, the courage, and
the guidance, to open my heart to Your love and to my life.

If I truly believed this prayer, it meant that everything in my
life—not just the cool miracles and serendipitous coincidences I
loved—was there to give me the strength, courage and guidance I
sought. And everything had to mean *everything*! It had to include
the depression that still sometimes crept up on me and threatened to
pull me under. It had to include the times I felt hurt and confused.
It had to mean the misunderstandings I had with people I loved.
Everything meant the current horrible state of the world that made
me frightened for my children and grandchildren. It meant careless
drivers and unfairness and achy joints and the blight on my tomato
plants. Somehow, in a way that I couldn't completely understand,
everything was—had to be—part of that yes.

*"So what would that mean? How would I live if I truly believed that
every moment of my life was a yes to my desire to be more open to God's
love and my life?"*

As I tried to sit with it, my old cynical thinking kicked into gear.
After a few minutes I began to reject the premise.

*"That's Pollyanna crap, Chickie! Do you really believe all of life's
garbage is 'God's yes'? That doesn't make life better—for you or for anyone! That just creates a stupid passivity that helps no one! You've got to
fight your depression. You've got to fight things that are unfair or wrong!
You have to fight against greed and evil, against the political corruption
that's threatening to harm children by decimating the educational system. You need to fight against companies that are threatening to destroy
the environment for the sake of short-term profits. If you believe everything is just a la-di-da Yes, why don't you just sit on the couch and stop
caring about anything—stop trying to love more, stop sending checks
to groups looking for a cure for disease or protecting abused children? If*

everything is God's yes, you might as well accept cruelty and greed as God's will."

But then I calmed down and allowed the new thoughts to just have a place in my mind—unchallenged by my judgmental ego. I moved away from my old all-or-nothing stance to a place where subtle distinctions and multiple views, and perhaps some dichotomies, reside. I chose to allow the initial premise to grow, to take root without digging it up and rejecting it out of hand.

When I did, in the course of several days, a middle ground emerged. Very slowly, in bits and pieces, new thoughts formed.

*"What if the concept of answered prayer is true, not in the One Ultimate Truth way, but in a subtle personal way? What if answered prayer is true, for me, in a way that calls only for a different attitude? What if, instead of reacting to changes and pain and suffering—mine and those around me—as a sign that God isn't real or has abandoned the world and we're completely lost and will be lost forever, I saw them as signs that I was being led into a new way of opening my heart a little more? What if the yes I accepted was real **and** I had to play with it, inspect it and help to bring it into fruition?*

"What if my attitude is all that changes? What if, knowing that what shows up in my life answers my prayer, I still act—I still try to relieve the pain or right the wrong—but the difference would be in my approach. In my old approach, I was anxious, frantic and desperate—trying to figure out what was wrong with me or life or God. But in the new way, I'd be open and expectant—trusting that God is real and works through us. What if I stood in faith instead of doubt? What if I saw the problems as puzzles, as ways to get me to think and act differently—with compassion instead of fear, with curiosity instead of blame?

"I could still take risks. I could still try to make life better, but I would do so with a different stance. Instead of taking action with my normal fearful attitude and an overdose of adrenalin or cortisol coursing through

my veins, I could do the same things with hope and compassion—and a big old dose of serotonin and dopamine rippling through me.

*"Hey, given the choice, might it be better to believe in the power of God's love and prayer **and** my ability to work with them rather than to constantly doubt them? After all, what would happen if I were wrong?"*

I again took some deep breaths and allowed the thoughts to bubble on the back burner of my brain. After a while, the argument continued.

My inner cynic was, as usual, loaded for bear, *"This is too stupid to even consider! Just about everyone prays! Do you think people pray FOR droughts and famines and disease and war!!?? This world is a sea of unanswered prayers! How do you explain that?"*

But the feisty old woman inside me held her ground. *"I don't explain that! We've been down this road a hundred times before. I don't understand how life works for everyone—even for me. I don't have the ability to know how God interacts with anyone—even with me. And I certainly don't have the capacity to judge the Creator of the Universe. That's not the issue anymore. Let's look at the real issue, right now, right here, just for me."*

"OK! Then the issue is simple," barked the cynic. *"Your premise is totally unproven—and unprovable! What if you're choosing to believe something absolutely wrong? What if you're just making all this up? What if there is no such thing as answered prayer? What then?"*

The old woman smiled. *"Yep. What if, someday, I discover, beyond the shadow of a doubt, that this answered-prayer stuff was all just a load of crap, a total falsehood? What if, someday, what I've come to experience as God's love and peace are just horrific illusions—and I had all of these calming, nurturing, health-producing feelings and experiences for no good reason at all? Could I live with that?"*

The cynic replied with gusto, *"Get off it, Chickie. Are you saying your belief is true because it feels good? That's crazy. That's what*

Stephen Colbert so rightly satirized when he created the word 'truthiness.' That's the feel-good, illogical religiosity you've been fighting against all your life."

"No," replied the old woman calmly. *"I'm saying let's look at the evidence. The person I am now, who believes in God's love, the one who prays and meditates and listens for the still, small voice within, is far happier, better, more functional, more generous, and more loving than the person I was when I didn't believe. It's not just my opinion. Ask Ross. Ask my kids and my friends. My life, my relationships and my health are all better now. What do I gain by going back to cynicism? How do I dare risk everything I now have by choosing to pit my limited logical reasoning against the evidence in my new life? It really is that simple."*

And it was. That particular argument became my decision point. The cynic in me knew that I'd never have the answers to the spiritual questions and wanted me to give up the quest until I had intellectual certainty. The frantic child in me wanted to stop arguing and just surrender to any beliefs that felt safe. Finally, the adult in me made the logical decision. The evidence was in. I was a better person, truer to myself, when I opened myself up to a relationship with God. Living from only a childish emotional base wasn't the answer. Living from only an intellectual base wasn't the answer. Living from a balanced base of heart and mind and soul, from experience of the God I could no longer deny, was the answer.

Did it mean I had the answer to all my questions? Definitely not. Did it mean I understood why violence and illness and disasters existed? No. Did it mean all my prayers would be answered just the way I wanted them to be answered? No. It simply meant that I was willing to allow that my mind—my limited understanding—wasn't the final word.

But that decision wasn't enough. As time passed, I realized I also needed to reevaluate my magical belief in The Ultimate Truth. This understanding came in bits and pieces over several months. Then one day I wrote in my journal:

> How easy it is to confuse a personal experience of God with the definition of God.
>
> When we have an experience of God, it feels so right, so good, so all-encompassing for us, I think we each fall into the temptation of assuming that we have The One True Connection to God and that our experience defines what God is. And if we find that connection in conjunction with others—at a retreat, at a prayer meeting, in a sweat lodge—and have experiences similar to those of the others with us, we are sure that ours is The Ultimate Truth.
>
> This may be where we get lost in our beliefs instead of our experience—in our egos instead of our hearts. What if, instead, our experience of the Transcendent is simply that—our experience? What if it's a very real, very profound, very life-changing and life-enhancing experience, and simply true *for us*—at our level of ability to perceive and receive the experience of the Almighty?

I remembered the old story of the three blind men who tried to describe an elephant after each had touched a part of it through the slats in a fence. In the story, the one who touched only the trunk said an elephant was a large snake, perhaps like a boa constrictor, which could crush a man in its grasp. The next one, who touched only the tail, argued vehemently that an elephant was a tiny snake incapable of doing much harm to a man at all. And the third, who had touched the huge body of the elephant and couldn't even reach the top of it, stated that the other two were totally crazed, and condemned them for their very stupid and wrong descriptions. "What are you two thinking? This giant animal is *nothing* like a snake! It's more like a walking boulder!"

All three perceptions were accurate for that individual's limited experience of the elephant—but none could encompass the truth of what the elephant was. If this were true for something as small and simple as an elephant, how much more true would it be when we try to categorize our experience of the Creator of Everything?

I liked this idea. It said that I could disagree with some of Jonas' perceptions and still be OK with my own. It explained how devout Christians and devout Jews could both feel that they were right when their interpretations of a verse in scripture differed significantly.

I liked this answer a lot less when I realized that it also meant that people whose views were diametrically opposed to mine also experienced God's presence in their lives. This understanding meant that Phil, the guy who hurt Ross so badly with his self-righteous prattle about not being with him in heaven, could have, in his own way, encountered God. It meant that those people I *knew* were wrong—rigid fundamentalists who viewed gays as abominations and inflexible clergymen who demanded that women become pregnant with children they couldn't feed or care for—might have experienced the presence of God in their lives too. Their filters—their inner stained glass—may not have been the same as mine. Their perceptions of the world may have been totally at odds with mine. But, like it or not, their experience of the Transcendent may have been just as true and real for them as mine was for me. This view required me to accept something I couldn't understand intellectually *and* had a hard time coming to grips with emotionally. Not only was my understanding of the Unlimited Transcendence I call God inadequate, my understanding of God's relationships with everyone else was totally inadequate too. That was much harder to accept!

Some changes were triggered by something I saw or heard. I remember how I felt after watching the documentary, *For the Bible Tells Me So*, the story of five deeply religious couples who each gave

347

birth to a gay child, and their reactions to their children and their faith. In it I found the answer to my "Bible as the only source of truth" question once and for all. In those stories, in the interaction of parents and children and theology, I found my truth: Any theology of exclusion, no matter what the pedigree of sacred books or holy lineage, was not in line with the God of my experience. Any theology that excluded anyone—gays, Muslims, women, blacks, Satanists, fundamentalists, *anyone*—from God's love was not a theology I could accept. The God of my experience loves every one of us and is incapable of doing otherwise. I could never again entertain the idea of aligning my mind or heart with a dogma that excluded anyone. It was that simple. I was that certain. The debate in my mind was over.

Eventually—certainly not on that day—this led to some thoughts I didn't especially relish. With time I realized I needed to understand that God—the God who transcended my thoughts and beliefs and my emotional certainty—could also be present in the lives of people who believed in a theology of exclusion. If God made no exceptions, then these people I disagreed with—passionately disagreed with—were included in God's loving interaction too.

That took me a bit more time—and humility—to accept!

～

In seeing spirituality as natural, I also began to understand the *process* of creating a spiritual life. I recognized that while a point of view could change in an instant, integration of a new view took time, practice and commitment—like any process. When I continued to be steady in meditation and prayer, I managed the rough times better. When I practiced the principles I'd learned, I could face life on life's terms. So I stopped making grand gestures and started taking small consistent steps.

This didn't mean, as I once feared it would, that I'd lose touch with the serendipitous and surprising facets of spirituality. They still appeared.

One afternoon, for instance, when I couldn't write another word, I decided to clear at least one layer of clutter from my office. As I shifted piles of books and stacks of papers, I stumbled across Susan Seddon-Boulet's books and was again in awe of the power and transcendent loveliness of her artwork. When I came to a piece called *Dream Basket*, a painting of a young girl safely ensconced in the embrace of a bear, the moon and the stars, I remembered how much I'd ached to feel that kind of love in my spiritual life. Now I sometimes did.

It was a small moment, but it helped me get in touch with just how much my emotional life had changed.

I had large serendipitous moments too. Occasionally, as I meditated, I'd still feel my grandmother's presence, her hand on my heart. Sometimes I just felt her love. At other times I'd feel her support, her urging me to finish this book. Once, while making supper, I was in tears because I didn't want to be as honest as I knew I needed to be to write it well. For the hundredth time I wanted to quit. On that day Grandma's presence was so strong, I felt compelled to go to the computer and just write down what I felt were her thoughts. I turned off the burners on the stove and went upstairs to the computer. Within seconds of sitting down, this is what I typed:

Honey,

Don't cry—or cry if you must. It's OK to cry.

But realize that these are the tears of fear—of fearing to live your life, of fearing to dance your dance. Remember the Martha Graham quote. Learn to dance in the rain, my Connie. You are such a beautiful dancer—you have such a dance inside you. Love it. Dance it! *Coraggio*! [Courage!] Five years later, my message to you is still the same—*Coraggio*!

Be open to life. The bad stuff may get you—or NOT—in your hiding place. But it's a guarantee that, if you stay in hiding, you'll wither and shrivel and die sadly! The bad stuff may get you—or NOT—if you dance right in the middle of the storm. But I promise you this, no matter what comes, you'll be more alive and joyful and healthy and limber and peaceful and beautiful if you dance rather than cower in the corner! . . . Raise your arms to the heavens and say:

Life, I love your dance!

Life, I open myself to your dance!

Life, come dance the Connie Dance.

I'll teach you. You teach me. Let's expand and create together.

Life, I love your dance!

I'm so grateful to be dancing with you!

One more time, swing me around the floor.

Hold me close, make me catch my breath.

Show me more, teach me more, create with me.

Rock with me, tango with me, polka with me, waltz with me, do-si-do with me, chicken dance with me, Mexican hat dance with me!

Pull me close, swing me out, pull me close again.

Whisper a song in my ear.

Listen to the songs in my heart.

Rest with me.

Kneel with me.

Pray with me, weep with me, laugh with me, play with me.

Life, hold me, hold me, hold me in your dance.

I finished typing with very different tears. I knew these were not my thoughts. This was not my approach to life by any stretch of the imagination. This overweight body hadn't danced for years—and I'd probably never danced with abandon. I seldom did anything with abandon; I was still trying to get through life without making horrific mistakes. These words were Grandma's—reaching out to me in love, inviting me to see life differently, to open up, let loose and appreciate its gifts. She, who had died at 51, was pushing this 64-year old to give life a chance.

A couple days later my friend Les brought me a gift. She was hesitant, almost apologetic as she handed it to me. "Con, I know you'll never wear this but today, when I saw this shawl, I knew I had to get it for you. I loved what you told me about your grandma's message and this feels connected with her. This is your *Coraggio* shawl. Keep it close. Maybe wrap it around you when you feel scared."

The shawl was a leopard print, with pink, purple and orange flowers and foot-long purple fringe. I agreed with Les. I'd never wear it. But it hangs at the entrance to my loft office, its fringe fluttering with the slightest change in the air. It's the first thing I see as I come upstairs to work. And every time I see it, I think of Grandma, her love and her message—*Coraggio*.

During that year, as my beliefs became my reality, as I grew into them, I grew up spiritually. There's no other way to put it. One day I noticed I saw life through the eyes of an adult who had a relationship with God instead of a scared little child frantically grasping at every new idea or possibility. I was still often unsure, still questioning, still tentative, but it was the hesitance of an adult, not the panic of a frightened little girl.

On that day I wrote in my journal:

A little child drowning, or fighting for her survival, feels she never has enough anything—enough safety, enough love, enough food, enough proof that she's loved. She needs to keep grasping.

A grown woman who is rooted in her own center can be satisfied with *just enough.*

I printed it out and taped it to my computer tower—one of the few spaces left in my office without a quote stuck to it. I looked at it often. Now that I understood the process of change, I knew that the idea would need time and attention to take root, to become part of my everyday life. I knew that, if I kept bringing this concept to the forefront of my mind, it would become part of my new mindset. I also suspected that just the act of being aware of the grasping—and choosing to relax and not always frantically clutch at everything—would be the source of more changes.

Over time that proved to be true. Not grasping, not frenetically searching, had benefits I hadn't imagined. I noticed deeper feelings of love in interactions with my children, grandchildren, friends and Ross. When I was open and relaxed, I could hear the voice of love surrounding me at every turn, often in little ways I'd never noticed before.

When I stopped looking for signs under every rock, in every sunset, in every encounter and conversation, I began to appreciate the rocks, sunsets and conversations for themselves. The separation between my spiritual and regular life began to blur. A magnificent fall day could be just that—a beautiful, crisp enjoyable day that filled my lungs with the kind of air that can only be inhaled as leaves begin to turn. Spending an evening with friends wasn't just something I did before I got back to the real job of finding my spiritual path.

Now it became important in its own right. It had a beauty and richness that didn't need to produce insights or answer questions.

Conversations about jobs or vacations or a friend's plans to redecorate a spare bedroom weren't just fillers until we could get back to talking about the important things. Now they were important, fun and meaningful. I began to move into the Middle Garden Carmen had introduced me to—and that I couldn't even imagine when she suggested it—and I enjoyed it. A good example of this was my friendship with Flo. When the two of us got together, we always talked about God and spirit and writing—and little else. But when we decided to expand our relationship by including our husbands in an occasional evening playing cards, we added so much to our friendship. All four of us loved our card nights. John and I teased and trash-talked each other unmercifully. Flo and I playfully stretched the rules of bidding far beyond reason—and the guys let us get away with it. Ross and John had some great conversations—about politics, gardening and the challenges of being married to women on a spiritual journey. I began relaxing a bit more into everyday life and loving it a lot more.

As usual, I made the shift in fits and starts, but I stayed open to the possibility of making the shift. Once after a deep conversation over lunch, my friend Carol smiled and said, "Wow, Connie, I'm exhausted listening to what goes on in your mind for just an hour. I'm going home to take a nap! I wonder if you wouldn't sometimes be better off taking things more lightly, holding the questions looser, not demanding so much of yourself and of life every moment."

And I heard her. On that day another piece of the process that had begun years before—with insights from Ross, Carmen and Jonas—blossomed. I finally understood that I'd rarely lived a non-intense minute. I was either searching or feeling guilty for not searching, trying to be better or feeling ashamed I wasn't working harder to improve—or collapsing in a heap from the effort. Beginning that day, I began to hold things a bit more lightly—especially the doubts and fears.

When confusion blurred my thinking, I reminded myself that I'd been confused before and I'd survived. I also remembered that sometimes confusion was part of the learning process. Instead of my old pattern of panic and self-condemnation, I began to choose patience and kindness. It didn't work every time, but when it did, I savored the moments—and noticed that I came out of a mental fog a lot faster with patience than with pushing.

My relationship with Jonas changed appreciably. As I stopped needing him to be the repository for all of my spiritual answers, I stepped back and appreciated the immense wisdom and practical knowledge he had to share. He'd been walking the road far longer than I. He habitually lived as I was just beginning to live. I was deeply grateful—to God and to Jonas—for his presence in my life.

Jonas and I worked through the hard times together and he continued to be my mentor. But now he mentored an adult. We discussed. We differed. Sometimes his insights were razor sharp and cut through tons of intellectual debris. At other times they were simply his opinions—to be pondered and appreciated as they were offered, with love.

Interestingly, without the drama of frantic questioning, I eventually made my peace with the Bible. As I put aside my arguments with fundamentalists and my history with the Catholic Church, I softened. I stopped making the decision to read the Bible an either/ or decision—either the Bible or Rumi, either the Bible or Hellinger. Looking at the Bible as Joseph Campbell did, as the magnificent poetry of generations of my ancestors seeking and finding a relationship with God, I was able to read it with new eyes—and with respect. I read it as one source of inspiration among many, as something that had the possibility of feeding my soul just as it fed the souls of those who came before me.

I also realized that one of the greatest gifts of my relationship with Jonas was our disagreement on the path to follow. If I had been able to accept all of his beliefs, I would have never left the safety of his wisdom and dared to look within to find God. I would have been quite happy with an intercessor for the rest of my life. And I would have missed so much.

I would have missed the experience of learning from sources that truly fit my needs in my new spiritual life. For instance, the antidote to my fear of a judgmental God was the soothing—and totally unfamiliar—Buddhist philosophy I learned from books and CDs by Cheri Huber, Pema Chodron and Jack Kornfield. I needed to step deeply into that non-judgmental viewpoint for a while. Kornfield's *After the Ecstasy, the Laundry,* a book about what happens after profound spiritual experiences, gave me such peace of mind. It was wonderful to know that people far more learned and committed to their spiritual practices than I also faced confusion, doubts and the need for counseling. And it was good to know they eventually regained their footing and continued to deepen their practice.

Finding Chodron's explanation of the concept of *maitre*—unconditional friendship with ourselves—as the root of true compassion, felt like the discovery of a new color or new musical instrument. I joyfully played with it for weeks, in awe of the possibility of growing spiritually through kindness to myself.

Following Huber's suggestions to see my fears as passports to deeper knowledge rather than sins and failures allowed me to work with them rather than simply condemn myself for being afraid. Seeing in writing, over and over again, that I was already fine and lovable allowed me to exhale and give myself permission to examine various wisdom traditions with beginner's eyes, because I was, truly, a beginner.

Equally important, in following my own path instead of Jonas' I opened to God in a way I hadn't known was possible. If I had stayed on Jonas' path, I would have missed the experience of a relationship with God that required no outside interpretation, no translation, no kind hand opening a door that I feared opening. I would have missed the indescribable feeling of God's presence in my life that can come only in solitude and listening.

~

Was it all sunshine and roses after these discoveries? Of course not. I still had rough times. I still had days when I didn't feel at home in my own skin. I still had times when I was far more fearful than loving. I had times when I got stuck and had to go back into therapy to get me through a rough patch. I still had problems with food and overeating. I had days when I could not pray and days when I was too stubborn, immature or scared to take what I knew were the next steps.

But here's the exciting part. I also had days when I could. And in the process, I noticed something important. I learned my life was much better when I remained consistent and disciplined. I noticed that when I continued to be steady in meditation and prayer I managed the rough times better. Life didn't become easier; I became more able to face life on life's terms.

Sometime in that year, I discarded my most limiting thought. I dumped the belief that God was The Ultimate Magic. I finally understood that a relationship with God doesn't guarantee us some special problem-free status in life. Life happens. Pain and grief and loss are part of life. Belief in God doesn't make us safe. Instead, a relationship with God creates within us a loving center from which to face life's pain.

I learned that being spiritual didn't mean being perfect—or even really good. I was still crabby when I was hungry and tired. My first response when someone hurt me was often a vindictive thought. And I was still spiritual. I didn't have to wait until I had no unkind thoughts and whiny moments to qualify as spiritual. Perhaps some of my most spiritual acts on a given day were showing some compassion for the cranky woman I was—and remembering that others deserved compassion too.

I also began to see that I needed to rely on myself to be a part of my own healing process. I needed to trust in God. I needed to stay open to God. But I also needed to flex my muscles, roll up my sleeves and do the work. My path had to include both.

I was again at a point of dichotomy. Surrendering to God was the way to inner peace *and* taking responsibility for my life and thoughts was the way to inner peace. This time I chose to face that old conundrum differently. Instead of freezing in my tracks until I could figure it out, I chose to live with it, experiment with it and play with it.

CHAPTER 38

NO MIND CAN CONCEIVE

The best things can't be told because they transcend thought.
The second best are misunderstood, because those are the thoughts that
are supposed to refer to that which can't be thought about.
The third best are what we talk about.
~ Joseph Campbell

I'm aware of the pitfalls of writing this chapter. The best things cannot be told. That's the truth.

When they are told, they fall painfully short of the experience they aim to describe. Just as no words can ever come close to adequately expressing a mother's feeling of love for her baby or a father's feeling of protectiveness when his child is threatened, no words can do justice to the feelings of love experienced in a relationship with God.

It's easy to do a poor job here—to make the description syrupy sweet and filled with only superlatives. Several of my first drafts were so filled with saccharine hyperbole my teeth ached as I reread them. Yet I've got to try because what I've written until now doesn't tell the whole story—and that's been my commitment from the beginning—to tell my story. This is as close as I can come after countless rewrites.

Somewhere in the midst of all these changes I realized I needed to go a bit further in my understanding of my beliefs. This was different from what I'd done in the summer of 2010. This time, I needed to concretize what I believed about my *relationship* with God.

I printed all 300 single-spaced pages of my journal and read them from beginning to end. Amazed, I saw how much had changed in my life—how much I had changed—in the past six years. As I read, I realized that I'd traveled miles from my old intellectual spirituality. Somehow, in the mix of the emotional experiences of Constellations, craniosacral adjustments, visualizations with my parents and ancestors and my November 18th experience, I had given up my tidy intellectual definition of spirituality.

Over the course of several days I gathered my thoughts—*and my feelings*. I wrote them down so I could think about them often and make sure of what was now true for me. I wrote them in my journal:

> This is what I've come to believe from my own experience.
>
> We do not own God. We cannot define God. We cannot begin to comprehend the Transcendent. When we try, we are like tiny thimbles trying to hold an entire galaxy.
>
> We don't know, *can't know*, God beyond our tiny (albeit sometimes overwhelming) relationship with Him. We are hampered by our own stained-glass filters—by our personalities, perceptions, background beliefs, and wishes for how we hope the Creator of the Universe may be. The best we can say is what is true for us—and admit we probably do not have the entire picture.
>
> But we can experience God. When we make the connection—no, that's not right—when we are open enough to allow the connection that is always here to take place, the best we can do is translate our experiences into a metaphor that allows Transcendence to be understood.

I can see now that this has been said by all wisdom traditions. The sacred writings have all given us a hint of this. "I am that I am" has no translation into human logic. "Do not theorize about essence" also says it.

Things I've ignored in my own religious background as I struggled to prove it wrong state it wonderfully: "God is Love and he who abides in Love abides in God, and God in him." This is what Augustine meant when he said, "It is all straw." It's what Merton meant when he said, "There is 'no such thing' as God because God is neither a 'what' nor a 'thing' but pure '*Who*'. He is the 'Thou' before whom our inmost 'I' springs into awareness."

As Joseph Campbell stated so beautifully, "All religions are true in this sense . . . they all point us to the Transcendent."

My quest is no longer to understand God. My goal is not to figure out the meaning of life or learn the rules that guarantee success or safety or happiness. This can't be done on this journey, on this planet, in this time—at least not by me. I'll always be faced with things I don't understand—earthquakes that destroy entire cities, wars that decimate countries, famines and rapists and child molesters and unspeakable cruelty. The way to peace is not in trying to understand them. The way, for me, is to give up trying to know all the answers for anyone—including myself.

Poets and mystics know this. Rumi always gives me a taste of that special letting go.

> Beyond our ideas of right-doing and wrong-doing,
> there is a field. I'll meet you there.
> When the soul lies down in that grass,
> the world is too full to talk about.

This beautiful line in e.e. cummings' poem, *somewhere i have never traveled,* comes as close to my experience of God as any words I've ever found:

> (i do not know what it is about you that closes
> and opens; only something in me understands
> the voice of your eyes is deeper than all roses)

The answer, for me—today—is in asking to be opened up more, and trusting that the astonishing God of love will answer my prayer. And then allowing it to happen.

I realized a relationship with God—an emotional, intellectually indefensible relationship—was far more important to me than an intellectual understanding of God. My new spirituality didn't simply allow emotional input, it demanded it. That's why November 18th was so important. That's why I never tired of being a part of Constellations—even after more than 400 of them. That's why the visualizations with the generations of women and the craniosacral adjustment in which God told Jonas to stop talking to me about spirituality had been so pivotal. That's why I was so touched by communications from Dad and Grandma. They weren't simply intellectual understandings. They were profoundly, overwhelmingly emotional occurrences.

I realized that a relationship with God had been what I'd been seeking all along. The part of spirituality I'd pushed away for so many years as undependable and illogical was the *essential* part—the part that brought me home. I looked back over nearly 60 years and saw that the thing that kept me from my deepest desire had been my insistence on an intellectual definition of spirituality.

One Wednesday in November of 2011, almost three years after the experience that changed my life, when I was once again struggling with my worthiness and the reality of God's presence in my everyday life, I got this message in meditation.

> Con, I'm always here. I'm never angry or disgusted or unwilling to be with you. *You* create that scenario. I'm always ready. You are my baby, my child, my friend. I always want to be near you, with you, working together, dancing together.
>
> The dark night comes when you leave Me, not when I leave you. Stay. I'll stay too. Hold out your hand. I'll take it and walk with you. Always. Always. Always. You're never unworthy. You're never too stubborn or bratty or scared or tired for Me to be with you. Always. Always. Always.
>
> This is a new time for us. Don't waste it by going through all of the cynicism again. Accept My gift and allow Me to continue to give to you. Allow Me this dance, Connie. Trust our ability to move closer. Trust your ability to change and My ability to be eternally faithful. Always. Always. Always.
>
> You have the gift of My love. Nothing can take it from you. Choose NOT to walk away from its embrace.

Was this experience real? Were the words real? Perhaps not in The Ultimate Truth way. They weren't God breaking through the clouds and giving me The One True Way for all the world to see. But yes, these words were real. They were real because they reflected the feeling that was in my heart. They represented my best understanding of the Love I know is real. They were what my heart could hold that day. That's what I believe we get in a relationship with God—the most we can hold.

Are they enough?

My dear, please trust a bruised, weary, stubborn old ex-cynic when she says it—they're enough. On days when I can stop the brain chatter and live with that experience and others like it, when I can get out of the way enough to gratefully accept the presence of God in my heart, I walk on sacred ground. I am loved. I feel at home in my body and in this world.

I breathe better. I love better. I'm more compassionate and less demanding. I'm less afraid. I'm more alive. Sometimes, I'm joyful.

When I believe them, do I transcend my humanity and go into a spiritual place where I'm free from doubts and fears, where I finally understand life's mysteries? No. Actually, when I try that, when I try to get into some perfect spiritual place, I always fall short. I always make myself unhappy. When, instead, I simply allow that I'm a creature who is loved by her Creator, living in a world that is profoundly and deeply loved by this Creator, I feel loved—cherished. And it's far more than enough.

And might I be wrong? You bet. Might this message be totally wrong for you as you read this, or wrong for my children, grandchildren, husband or for my dearest friends? Yes, it might be. Might this be wrong for me 20 years from now—or 20 minutes from now? Sure. And it doesn't matter. Right and wrong are not the questions here. The questions are only these: Is this my experience, as clean as I can make it? And does it bring me closer to, or farther from, Love? If the answer is closer, then it's sufficient.

It's not The Magical Answer. It's not The Ultimate Answer. It's simply all I can hold today. It opens someone like me—who has questioned life and struggled to control, to avoid, to protect myself from life—a way to begin to live.

CHAPTER 39

THIS AND NOTHING MORE

The entire heavenly realm is within us,
but to find it we have to relate to what's outside.
~ Joseph Campbell

At least a hundred times in writing this book I worried because I couldn't figure out how it would end. At first I set arbitrary ending points—the first anniversary of November 18th or the second anniversary of the day I started the book. But these came and went without an end in sight. I tried to set practical ends. "I'm speaking at a conference next October. I'll have it ready to bring to the conference." That didn't work either.

Finally, the end came, just as most of the book had, in its own time. For the last several weeks, as I've tried to write more, I found I was simply repeating myself.

Just recently I remembered what Carmen had suggested when I began writing. "Con, the Native Americans I studied with had an interesting way to imagine distant goals. They thought of them as having an energy of their own. As they worked toward their goal, they imagined the completed goal moving closer to them. You might want to try that with the book. Think of it as having its own energy.

See it, as you begin, far in the distance. Then, as you write, imagine the book meeting you half way."

When she'd made the suggestion, I liked it. I pictured the book as a man in vibrantly colorful clothes, on a distant hill, walking slowly toward me. But in the three-year struggle to write this book I seldom thought of that image. Now, as I recalled it, I decided to play with the concept, to see if I could get some insight into what still needed to be written.

One evening, I sat at my desk and brought the image back to mind. I imagined my friend in the radiantly colored attire right here in the room with me, smiling.

"So, Book, what do you think?"

"I'm ready, my dear. The story is done."

"It doesn't feel done. Shouldn't I write a synopsis of what I've learned? Shouldn't I wrap up the loose ends or……"

"No, you've told your story. That's what you set out to do. Your job is done. "

"But I've already written four different endings! Some of those pages are the best ones I wrote!"

"They were for you. They answered *your* questions. The story doesn't need them."

"But what if the readers need more….?"

"The readers need the story. They don't need you to wrap it in pink paper and tie a ribbon around it."

"What if I need to write more—for me?"

"What you need now, my dear, is to *live* the rest of your story. You've spent so many years trying to find a way to live safely above the chaos of life. You've spent so much of the last three years in introspection. Now you need the opposite. Now it's time to live life fully—hip-deep in the chaos, arms open wide, heart fully rooted in the Love you know is real. Now is the time to leave this office, live your abundance and joyfully share it.

"Now, my dear, it's time to dance."

Suggested Reading

Babcock, M. (2000). *The Power of the Bear: Paintings by Susan Sedon Boulet.* Petaluma, CA: Pomegranate Communications.

Barks, C. (2002). *The Soul of Rumi.* New York: Harper Collins.

Barks, C. (1995). *The Essential Rumi.* New York: Harper Collins.

Beck, M. (2005). *Leaving the Saints: How I Lost the Mormons and Found My Faith.* New York: Three Rivers Press.

Booth, L. (1994). *The God Game: It's Your Move.* Walpole, NH: Stillpoint Publishing.

Boring, F. M. (2012). *Connecting to Our Ancestral Past: Healing Through Constellation, Ceremony and Ritual.* Berkley, CA: North Atlantic Books.

Boring, F.M. (2004). *Feather Medicine: Walking in Shoshone Dreamtime.* Tamarac, FL: Llumina Press.

Boyd, M. (2006). *Are You Running With Me, Jesus?* Lanham, MD: Cowley Publications.

Boulet, S.S. (1994). *The Goddess Paintings.* Petaluma, CA: Pomegranate Communications

Boulet, S.S. (1989). *Shaman.* Petaluma, CA: Pomegranate Communications

Campbell, J. (2002). *The Inner Reaches of Outer Space: Metaphor as Myth and as Religion.* Novato, CA: New World Library.

Campbell, J. (2001). *Thou Art That: Transforming Religious Metaphor.* Novato, CA: New World Library.

Campbell, J. (1999). *Transformation of Myth Through Time*. New York: Harper Perennial.

Campbell, J. (1993). *Myths to Live By*. New York: Penguin.

Campbell, J. (1991). *The Masks of God, Vol. 1: Primitive Mythology*. New York: Penguin Arkana.

Campbell, J. (1991). *The Masks of God, Vol. 3: Occidental Mythology*. New York: Penguin Arkana.

Campbell, J. and Moyers, B. (1988). *The Power of Myth*. New York: Doubleday.

Carnabucci, K. & Anderson, R. (2012). *Integrating Psychodrama and Systemic Constellation Work*. Philadelphia, PA: Jessica Kingsley.

Chodron, P. (2005). *The Places That Scare You: A Guide to Fearlessness in Difficult Times*. Boston: Shambhala Publications.

Chodron, P. (2001). *The Wisdom of No Escape and the Path of Loving Kindness*. Boston: Shambhala Publications.

Cohen, D. B. (2009). *I Carry Your Heart in My Heart: Family Constellations in Prison*. Heidelberg: Carl-Auer.

Cummings, e.e. (1994). *100 Selected Poems*. (Evergreen Ed.) New York: Grove Press.

Dispenza J. (2008). *Evolve Your Brain: The Science of Changing Your Mind*. Deerfield Beach, FL: Health Communications.

Dispenza J. (2006). *God on Your Own: Finding a Spiritual Path Outside Religion*. San Francisco: Jossey-Bass.

Guareschi, G. (1958). *My Secret Diary*. New York: Farrar, Straus and Cudahy

Harvey, A. (2000). *The Direct Path: Creating a Personal Journey to the Divine Using the World's Spiritual Traditions*. New York: Random House.

Hellinger, B. (2007). *With God in Mind*. Bischofwiesen, Germany: Hellinger Publications.

Hellinger, B. (2001). *Love's Own Truth: Bonding and Balancing in Close Relationships.* Phoenix, AZ: Zeig, Tucker & Theisen.

Hellinger, B. and ten Hovel, G. (1999). *Acknowledging What Is: Conversations with Bert Hellinger.* Phoenix, AZ: Zeig, Tucker & Theisen.

Hellinger, B., Weber, G. & Beaumont, H. (1998). *Love's Hidden Symmetry: What Makes Love Work in Relationships.* Phoenix, AZ: Zeig, Tucker & Theisen.

Holmes, E. (1938). *The Science of Mind: A Philosophy, A Faith, A Way of Life.* New York: Penguin Putnam.

Huber, C. (2010). *There Is Nothing Wrong with You: Going Beyond Self-hate.* Chicago, IL: Keep It Simple Books.

Huber, C. (1995). *The Fear Book: Facing Fear Once and For All.* Chicago, IL: Keep It Simple Books.

Hunt, H. (2004). *Faith and Feminism: A Holy Alliance.* New York: Atria.

Lesser, E. (2005). *Broken Open: How Difficult Times Can Help Us Grow.* New York: Vallard Press.

Levine, S. (1998). *A Year to Live: How to Live This Year as If It Were Your Last.* New York: Bell Tower.

Levine, S. (1991). *Guided Meditations, Explorations and Healings.* New York: Anchor Books.

Lewis, C. S. (1952). *Mere Christianity.* San Francisco: Harper Collins

Lipton, B. (2005). *The Biology of Belief: Unleashing the Power of Conscious Matter and Miracles.* Santa Rosa, CA: Mountain of Love.

Lynch, J. E. & Tucker, S. (Eds.) (2005). *Messengers of Healing: The Family Constellations of Bert Hellinger Through the Eyes of a new Generation of Practitioners.* Phoenix, AZ: Zeig, Tucker & Theisen.

Kornfield, J. (2008). *The Wise Heart: A Guide to the Universal Teachings of Buddhist Psychology.* New York: Bantam.

Kornfield, J. (2000). *After the Ecstasy, the Laundry*. New York: Bantam.

McTaggart, L. (2008). *The Field: The Quest for the Secret Force of the Universe*. (Updated ed.) New York: Harper Collins.

McTaggart, L. (2007). *The Intention Experiment*. New York: Simon & Schuster.

Merton, T. (2008). *Choosing to Love the World*. Boulder, CO: Sounds True, Inc.

Merton, T. (2007). *Seeds of Contemplation*. New York: New Directions.

Milne, H. (1995). *The Heart of Listening: A Visionary Approach to Craniosacral Work (Volume 1)*. Berkeley, CA: North Atlantic Books.

Myss, C. (2011). *Defy Gravity: Healing Beyond the Bounds of Reason*. Carlsbad, CA: Hay House.

Myss, C. (1997). *Why People Don't Heal and How They Can*. New York: Three Rivers Press.

Occhiogrosso, P. (2000). *The Joy of Sects: A Spirited Guide to the World's Religious Traditions*. New York: Bantam Books.

Pert, C. (1997). *Molecules of Emotion: The Science Behind Mind–Body Medicine*. New York: Touchstone.

Pert, C. (2006). *Everything You Need to Know to Feel Go(o)d*. Carlsbad, CA: Hay House, Inc.

Phillips, J. B. (1952). *Your God is Too Small: A Guide for Believers and Skeptics Alike*. (Touchstone edition) New York: Simon & Schuster.

Roberts, J. (1972). *Seth Speaks: The Eternal Validity of the Soul*. San Rafael, CA: Amber-Allen Publishing.

Rossi, E.L., Erickson-Klein, R. & Rossi, K. L. (Eds.) (2010). *The Collected Works of Milton H. Erickson, Volume 7*. Phoenix, AZ: The Milton H. Erickson Foundation Press.

Rossi, E. L. and Rossi, K. L. (2008). *The New Neuroscience of Psychotherapy, Therapeutic Hypnosis and Rehabilitation: A Creative*

Dialogue with Our Genes. [This book may be downloaded from *www.ernestrossi.com*]

Stark, H. (2005). *Systemic Constellation Work is an Art: About Deep Dimensions of Family Therapy*, Hulett, WY: Many Kites Press.

Upledger, J. E. and Vredevoogd, J. D. (1983). *Craniosacral Therapy.* Seattle, WA: Eastland Press.

Wilkerson, D. (1963). *The Cross and the Switchblade.* New York: Jove Books

Zeig, J. K. (2006). *Confluence: The Selected Papers of Jeffrey K. Zeig.* Phoenix, AZ: Zeig, Tucker & Theisen.

Zeig, J. K. (Ed.) (1980). *A Teaching Seminar with Milton H. Erickson.* Phoenix, AZ: Zeig, Tucker & Theisen.

About the Author

Connie Donaldson, MA, lives near Pittsburgh, Pennsylvania with her husband Ross. She continues to study and investigate the relationship between modern science and ancient wisdom in the fields of healing and spirituality.

For updates on this work, check out the following sites:

www.hearthstonerose.com

www.facebook.com/DumpingtheMagic

13497807R00211

Made in the USA
Charleston, SC
14 July 2012